YOUNG MEN
GO WEST

YOUNG MEN GO WEST

The Hungarian Revolution of 1956 and
One Teenager's Risky Escape

Dawn-Eve Mertz

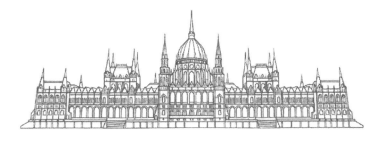

KLEO PRESS

Kleo Press

First paperback edition June 2024

ISBN 978-1-964781-03-7

Nonfiction/Narrative Nonfiction — Hungarian History

In memory of my grandfather

"The revolution has always been in the hands of the young."

— Huey Newton

CONTENTS

MAPS

The Districts of Budapest

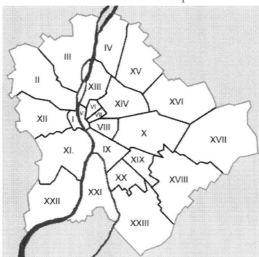

District I, "The Buda Castle District:" where a few dozen freedom fighters
  held out against the Soviet tanks and ruthless shelling for several days
  after the invasion of Budapest.

District II: Where the protesters first marched to the statue of József Bem,
  close to the riverside. The Széna Square stronghold was located a few
  blocks west of the river, where one of the main groups of freedom
  fighters congregated.

District V, "The Inner City/Leopold Town:" where many major attractions are located, including the Parliament and Ministry buildings, the site of the Bloody Thursday massacre.

District VIII, "Joseph Town:" where the Battle for Budapest Radio took place on the first night of the revolution at the radio building on the western side, near district 5. Also where the Corvin Cinema and Kilian Barracks were located, a major stronghold for the freedom fighters; where the former Communist Party headquarters was located; and the site of the Republic Square Massacre.

District XI, "New Buda:" where the Budapest University of Technology and Economics is located.

District XIV, "Zugló:" Memento Park lies on the western edge of the district, next to districts 6 and 7, that was where the statue of Stalin was torn down.

District XXI, "Red Csepel:" the northernmost part of an island in the Danube River, the industrial district where factory workers bravely fought against the Soviets until November 11.[1]

---

[1] Maps from the CIA World Factbook 1998

DEFINITIONS AND PEOPLE

Államvédelmi Hatóság [Al-um-ve-del-mi Ha-toe-shag]: the AVH, or State Protection Authority, was the secret police of Hungary from 1945 to 1956. They were created as an extension of the Soviet Union's KGB and were responsible for supporting the Hungarian Working People's Party (loyal to the Soviets) and persecuting political opponents. The AVH performed brutal purges and gained a reputation for being one of the worst, if not the worst, secret police force in the Eastern Bloc. In 1956 the AVH dissolved and was replaced with the Ministry of Internal Affairs.

Budapest [Buda-pesht]: The capital of Hungary is in northern and central Hungary. It was, and is, the most populated city in Hungary and the center of the Hungarian Revolution.

Csepel [Che-pel]: The 21st district of Budapest, officially incorporated in 1950. The district is located on the northern tip of Csepel Island in the Danube River and was known as "Red Csepel" because of the industrial factories which were supposed to be the backbone of communism.

Ernő Gerő [Er-no Jerr-oh] 1889-1980: a communist who spent two decades in the USSR after the Hungarian Revolution of 1919, where he became a KGB agent. He returned to Hungary and became a communist leader after WWII and was the most powerful man in Hungary while he briefly acted as the First Secretary of the Hungarian Workers' Party from July 18 to October 25 of 1956, he was ousted by the Russians on the second day of the revolution.

János Kádár [Yan-osh Kar-dar] 1912-1989: the communist Interior Minister under **Rákosi,** 1948-51. Jailed from 1951-54, joined **Nagy**'s revolutionary government in October 1956 but betrayed it on November 1. Following the revolution, he was installed as one of the primary leaders in Hungary until 1988, serving in positions such as the First Secretary of the Hungarian Socialist Workers' Party and the Prime Minister. The "Kádár years" are from 1956 to 1988.

Nikita Khrushchev [Ne-key-ta Krus-shuv] 1894-1971: First Secretary of the Communist Party of the Soviet Union from 1953-64 and was one of the most powerful people in the USSR. After Stalin' death in 1953, Khrushchev engaged in a power struggle with Georgy Malenkov who had taken over as Premier of the USSR, subsequently ousted by Khrushchev who became the Premier of the USSR in 1958 until 1964. He denounced his predecessor Joseph Stalin and launched a series of political reforms referred to as de-Stalinization.

Béla Király [Bay-la Keer-a-ye] 1912-2009: the former Major-General of the Hungarian Army who served in WWII and in 1952 was sentenced to life in prison, and later released in September of 1956. He became the commander-in-chief of the Hungarian Revolutionary Armed Forces during the revolution. He escaped to Austria after the revolution and was given a death sentence *in absentia*.

Sándor Kopácsi [Shan-door Kop-ah-chi] 1922-2001: The chief of the Budapest Police from 1952-1956 and later a member of the Parliament, and on November 3, 1956, he became the deputy commander of the new National Guard. He was arrested on November 5 and tried with Nagy and other revolutionary leaders as a conspirator of the revolution. He was sentenced to life in prison but was released in 1963.

Edit Kutnyak [Eh-dit Koot-nyuk] 1952-1990: József's little sister.

Ilona Kutnyak [E-lo-na] -1989: József's mother.

József Kutnyak [Yo-zhef] 1940-2023: my grandfather, who escaped Hungary in November 1956.

Károly Kutnyak [Kah-roi] 1937-2023: József's elder brother, also the name of their father, -2001.

László Kutnyak [Laz-low] 1943-2016: József's youngest brother. **Laci** [Lot-zi] - László's nickname. Sometimes the spelling of this name has accents, sometimes it doesn't. Hungarian names vary with accents.

Pál Maléter [Pall Mal-eh-ter] 1917-1958: the Colonel-General of the

Hungarian Army who joined the revolution and led the defense of the main strongholds the freedom fighters used in Budapest. He was promoted to Major-General and to the Minister of Defense by Imre Nagy during the revolution. He was arrested by the Soviets and sentenced to death; he was executed on the same day as Nagy, June 16, 1958.

Anastas Mikoyan [An-a-staz Me-ko-yawn] 1895-1978: The Deputy Chairman of the Council of Ministers of the Soviet Union from 1955-1964, and the only "old Bolshevik Soviet" who retained his power in the Party for his entire career until a peaceful retirement. Mikoyan was sent to Hungary when the revolution began to act as liaison and oversee the transfer of power from Gerő to Nagy.

Imre Nagy [Im-reh Nodge] 1896-1958: the Hungarian Prime Minister from 1953-55 and from October 24 to November 4, 1956, when he served as the unelected political leader of the Hungarian Revolution. Deported to Romania after the revolution, later returned to Budapest to be tried in secret and sentenced to death on June 16, 1956.

Pécs [Paych]: the city József and Károly lived in before their escape.

Gábor Péter 1906-1993: a Hungarian communist and the leader of the State Protection Authority, the AVH, which was responsible the arrest, torture, and imprisonment of Hungarian citizens. Péter personally tortured at least 25,000 people in his career with the AVH between 1945 and 1952.

Mátyás Rákosi [Mat-yash Ra-koh-she] 1892-1971: the *de facto* leader of Hungary from 1947 to 1956; leader of the Hungarian emigres in the Soviet Union 1940-44; First Secretary of the Hungarian Working Peoples' Party (the Communist Party in the one-party system) 1945 to July 1956; and Prime Minister from 1952 to 1953. He was removed from the latter position by the Soviets after Stalin's death, Imre Nagy took his place. He was the "boss" during the harshest of the political purges and hated among the population; the "Rákosi years" were 1945 or 1947, depending on who you ask, until 1956.

Soviet Union: officially known as the Union of Soviet Socialist Republics, or USSR, lasted from 1922 to 1991. It was the successor state to the Russian Empire, but it was not just Russia, the USSR became the federal union of 15 republics (Russia, Ukraine, Belarus,

Uzbekistan, Kazakhstan, Georgia, Azerbaijan, Lithuania, Moldavia, Latvia, Kyrgyzstan, Tajikistan, Armenia, Turkmenistan, and Estonia). After WWII, the Soviets remained in several countries and created a Stalinist system in which they installed a communist government and gained control of the education, press, radio, and police in 9 satellite states (Albania, Poland, Bulgaria, Romania, Czechoslovakia, Germany,[2] Hungary, Yugoslavia, and Mongolia).

Joseph Stalin 1878-1953: the communist dictator of the Soviet Union from 1929 to 1953. He was a revolutionary in his youth and adhered to the Marxist-Leninist ideology of communism, but his ruthless policies led to the term "Stalinist communism" or "Stalinism."

Tamás [Ta-mash]: the young given to the man József escaped Hungary with.

---

[2] After WWII Germany was split into four zones of Allied occupation to rebuild the country and government as a result of the Potsdam Agreement of August 1, 1945, the northeastern zone was occupied by the Soviet Union and thereafter called East Germany. The German Democratic Republic was established in East Germany on October 7, 1949, and not disestablished until October 3, 1990, when East Germany was reunified with West Germany. The Soviet Union dissolved in December 1991.

Timeline of Events Leading up to and of the Hungarian Revolution

1944

March 15: The Nazi Wehrmacht and SS occupied Hungary. Nazi troops boarded with families across Hungary.

October 29: The Soviet Union tried, but failed, to capture Budapest.

December 26: Red Army and Romanian Army troops encircled Budapest and waged a 50-day battle in which around 38,000 civilians died due to starvation, mass executions, and military actions.

1945

February 13: German troops in Hungary surrendered unconditionally to the Soviets, ending the Siege of Budapest.

November 4: In the aftermath of WWII, the Hungarian government tried rebuilding itself and the Independent Smallholders Party won the Parliamentary election.

1946

March 5: The Left Bloc was formed in Hungary, a political alliance between left wing politicians and parties, a main purpose of forming the Left Bloc was to counteract the Independent Smallholders Party which had the majority vote the previous year. The Bloc was supported by the Soviets, its objectives were to exclude "reactionaries," create a political deadlock with the Smallholders Party, and nationalize banks, mines, and heavy industries.

1947

August 31: The Left Bloc was dissolved after successfully eliminating opposition to the communists through "salami tactics."[3]

1948

Political opponents to the Communist Party were imprisoned or exiled to Siberia. In December, the head of the Catholic Church, Prince Primate József Mindszenty, was charged with treason and sentenced to life in prison after being brutally tortured and forced to confess.

1949

June 12: The Communist Party and Social Democratic Parties (left parties) merged into the Hungarian Working Peoples' Party, which was loyal to the Soviet Union.

Throughout 1949: Mátyás Rákosi purged the government to get rid of opponents. The secret police, the AVO (later the AVH), sought out people who criticized Rákosi, the Soviet Union, and Communism. Industry was nationalized and collectivization was introduced. Russian was taught in schools and religious beliefs were discouraged.

1953

March 5: Joseph Stalin, the Premier and First Secretary of the Communist Party of the Soviet Union, the most powerful man in the USSR, died at 73 years old. Georgy Malenkov took over as the leader.

July 4: Imre Nagy took over as the Prime Minister of the Hungarian Republic upon Rákosi's resignation. Nagy promised a "New Course" and pledged to release political prisoners, close the internment camps, allow the "class enemies" who'd been deported to return home, end discrimination against kulaks, allow farmers to leave the collective farming system, and allow private businesses to operate again. His speech was broadcasted live, his promises were

---

[3] The Soviets used "salami tactics" in the Eastern Bloc in order to gain control. Also called "salami slicing" or "salami attacks," it is a series of small actions that will result in a larger effect that would typically be illegal to perform all at once.

significant; none of it would have happened during Stalin's lifetime, and Nagy was known as a man of his word. Even though Nagy was still a communist, he was the hope that the Hungarian populace needed.

September 8: Nikita Khrushchev became the First Secretary of the Communist Party and the leader of the USSR after a power struggle with Georgy Malenkov, who briefly replaced Stalin.

1955

May 14: The Warsaw Pact was formed: it was the response to the formation of NATO in the west and it bound Hungary to the Soviet Union and the Eastern Bloc.

1956

February 25: Khrushchev delivered a Secret Speech to a few delegates in which he denounced Stalin as a criminal and exposed the severe political repression such as the "Great Purges" in the 1930s which killed millions of people. He criticized those who still admired and supported Stalin's policies. The speech marked a turning point in Soviet history and spurred internal debate and worldwide attention, revealing the cracks within Soviet Communism. Afterwards, news of the Secret Speech spread and people in the Eastern Bloc hoped that Khrushchev's condemnation of Stalin's policies would mean positive changes and freedom would follow.

June 28: Industrial workers in Poznań, Poland, started a spontaneous demonstration which spurred a popular uprising against the communist government. Poles were suffering from economic hardships, low wages, worsening working conditions, rising cost of living, and a lack of freedom under the political oppression. Military troops were sent in to crush the demonstrations which resulted in violence, at least 57 people died and 600 were wounded. Many moderate communists recognized the need for reform which happened due to the protests in the following months.

July 18: Rákosi was forced to resign from his position as the First Secretary of the Hungarian Working Peoples' Party due to his continued loyalty to Stalinism and was replaced by his deputy, Ernő Gerő, a former KGB agent.

October 6: László Rajk, 1909-1949, a Hungarian communist and the former Minister of Interior and Minister of Foreign Affairs, was reburied in a cemetery for Hungarian heroes. The ceremony, which roughly 100,000 people attended, strengthened Hungarian nationalism and the opposition to the communists; the people of Hungary saw him as a victim of the communist regime after his execution.

October 22: Thinking they could gain more autonomy and political reform like Poland did after the June protests, students at the Technical University in Budapest created a list of sixteen demands for reform.[4] They included the withdrawal of Soviet troops, free elections, a livable wage, readjustment of production quotas, and freedom of speech.

October 23: Tens of thousands of people rallied near a statue of Józef Bem, a Polish General who helped the Hungarians in the revolution of 1848. Peter Veres read the Sixteen Points.

Ernő Gerő made a broadcast condemning the students' Sixteen Points. Imre Nagy addressed the crowd and promised reforms.

An 18-meter statue of Stalin in the city was knocked over by protesters, they ripped down the communist flags and cut out the sickle and hammer symbol from flags and uniforms.

After nightfall, protesters gathered outside of Budapest Radio and a group of students was detained by the AVH while trying to gain access to the radio to broadcast their demands as they'd been promised. The AVH began firing into the crowd of protesters.

The protesters became freedom fighters; they left to gather weapons and returned for the fight with the AVH.

Hungarian soldiers who were ordered to support the AVH instead ripped the red stars from their clothing and joined the revolution.

Ernő Gerő requested Soviet military intervention.

October 24: Soviet tanks entered Budapest after midnight, less than twelve hours after the protest began.

Hungarian freedom fighters armed themselves and set up barricades in Budapest while Soviet tanks stationed themselves throughout the city.

Imre Nagy was appointed the Prime Minister of Hungary by the Soviets to appease the protesters. He called for an end to the violence, he

---

[4] The complete list of the Sixteen Points can be found in the back of the book.

promised that change would come.

Freedom fighters took control of the Budapest Radio building and were able to broadcast the news about the revolution which quickly motivated other cities to protest as well.

October 25 (Bloody Thursday): Thousands of protesters gathered outside of the Parliament and the Ministry of Agriculture in Budapest. Secret police and Soviet troops surrounded thousands of people and began firing from the outside and inside of the Ministry of Agriculture building. Eyewitnesses say 800-1,000 people were killed that day, their bodies were buried in unmarked graves and evidence was hidden about one of the largest public massacres in Europe after the end of WWII.

The Soviets forced Ernő Gerő to resign from his position as First Secretary of the Communist Party and exiled him to the Soviet Union.

October 28: Nagy called for a ceasefire and made grand promises including democracy, freedom of speech and freedom of religion.

October 30: Nagy released political prisoners, legalized other political parties, and openly supported the revolutionary councils (the demonstrators, including the students from the University).

The freedom fighters executed dozens of AVH officers at the Communist Party headquarters while the ceasefire order was in place.

Soviet tanks began leaving Budapest.

Soviet leaders decided not to remove Nagy and stated that they were prepared to negotiate for a resolution.

October 31: Nagy announced reforms and that Hungary would withdraw from the Warsaw Pact and asked the United Nations for help.

November 1: Nagy declared that Hungary withdrew from the Warsaw Pact and became a "neutral" country. Later, he learned that Soviet tanks and troops were on their way to Budapest again after already withdrawing—that was a ploy.

November 3: Nagy announced the new members of the government. Several Hungarian delegates discussed Soviet withdrawal, and later were arrested after the full-scale invasion.

November 4: Soviet forces attacked Budapest in the early hours and the Hungarian army and freedom fighters tried to resist.

Nagy announced to the world that Hungary was under attack and asked for western nations to help end the Soviet occupation. The United States and United Nations were hesitant to intervene, they feared a global confrontation with the Soviet Union. Britain and France already had their forces within Egypt to regain control after the Suez Canal Crisis in October, so their resources and attention were divided.

János Kádár declared Nagy's government illegal and installed the Hungarian Revolutionary Worker-Peasant Government, which was created with Soviet support in order to replace Nagy's government.

The Parliamentary Guard laid down their weapons. The Hungarian Free Radio stopped broadcasting. Nagy retreated to the Yugoslav embassy for protection.

November 11: By then, most freedom fighters were caught or gave themselves up to the Soviets who brutally crushed the resistance, bringing the revolution to an end after several days of fighting. Thousands of people were arrested, imprisoned, deported, or hanged for their part in the revolution over the next several weeks.

PREFACE

I started this book in 2017, but I wrote it from a first-person present point of view, and it was odd because I am not a sixteen-year-old boy from 1956. So, I rewrote it in 2018 from a third-person past point of view, like a *normal* person, but I became busy with life and stopped writing for several years. In 2023, my grandpa's health began declining and I knew I had to finish this book.

He died on September 29, 2023, I watched as his body was taken away, and I didn't even cry. I felt sad, of course, but I didn't cry. I don't feel the normal range of human emotions (thank you, mom and dad), but I'm not repressing his death or in denial. It's not like he was "too young," it wasn't completely unexpected, and he's no longer in pain. He had Alzheimer's and three types of cancer when he died: blood, bone, and liver. He had prostate cancer in his 60s, then stomach and esophageal cancers in his 70s. Apparently, if you get prostate cancer, you're more likely to get other types of cancers later on, even if the disease is eradicated from your body, you'll probably get more—but don't quote me on that, I'm not a doctor, that's just what they told us. Stomach cancer is also something that seems to run in the family, probably due to a mutated gene, so I have that to look forward to.

Even though his death wasn't completely unexpected, his Alzheimer's progressed quicker than they anticipated. My grandma even said he seemed fine 90% of the time up until the week before his death. He had a hospice nurse for about two weeks as his body failed him.

Six days before his death, he began rapidly losing control of his gross motor skills, but he was conscious. Five days before, he had laid down on the couch to sleep and fallen into a coma-like state. Four days before, the hospice nurse told my grandmother to call everyone in the family. He wasn't getting any fluids or nutrition, he was about 110 pounds to begin with, and the hospice nurse told her that all he needed until the end was morphine to keep him comfortable. He weighed so little due to a poor appetite after the surgeries to remove the stomach and esophageal cancers not long before the COVID19 pandemic. Three days before, my grandmother told me of his sudden decline; she said something like, "We just need to get through this," but hadn't come to terms with it being the end. One day before, I flew to Oregon to see my grandpa for the last time.

I feel guilty that I barely spoke to him while I was there. I knew he could hear me; they say that hearing is the last thing to go, but I didn't know what to say, and I forgot to promise to finish this book for him.

On the day of his death, I went back to spend time with my grandparents, figuring it would be the last day. I took my time getting ready at the hotel, I went through a long coffee shop drive-thru, and when I walked into the motorhome around 9 a.m. my grandmother was on the phone saying, "He died around an hour ago." He was still warm when she woke up, but he had died in his sleep.

I didn't cry, I didn't even flinch or feel the need to look away as I sat across from his body for several hours until they took him away. My grandma was smiling and joking around until they wrapped his body in a white sheet and lifted him out. She even offered to make me breakfast when I arrived, and then offered to make sandwiches for my uncle and aunt when they arrived.

She literally said, "Are you hungry? I'm not hungry but I can make you all some sandwiches," while we waited for the coroner to collect grandpa's body. My uncle kept telling her to stop offering people food, and she kept saying, "It's no problem!" I suppose that strange coping skills run in the family.

This book felt incomplete without a fuller picture of the Hungarian Revolution and the effects of communism, so I began my research in earnest last year. At first, it was just the story of my grandpa's escape, with a mixture of his memories in his own words. At least a third of this book is now a historical nonfiction about the revolution, communism, the Soviet Union, the AVH, and the refugee crisis, but this is still not a complete history; it's about my grandpa first and foremost. If you'd like a complete history of the revolution, I highly recommend Victor Sebestyen's *Twelve Days*, which was paramount to my research, and the other resources in the bibliography.

I'd never really been proud of my family or felt a great connection with my heritage, but while researching for this book I developed a new sense of pride in my heritage. When I read about the teenage freedom fighters who armed themselves and faced off against Russian tanks in the name of freedom, I can't help but feel proud. Revolutions begin with the youth, and the resistance is always the correct side of history.

Introduction

Before reading this book, you must recognize a few things: first, that nothing happens in a vacuum, second, every action has a reaction, third, two things can be true at the same time, and finally, when the oppressed stand up to their oppressor it's usually violent in nature. The freedom fighters of the Hungarian Revolution were in an armed struggle against their occupier, and their resistance became violent when the secret police began arresting and killing the student protesters.

Russian propaganda still distorts history for their benefit, and some people in the west have fallen for it as well. Students in Russia still learn from Russian history textbooks which paint the Hungarian freedom fighters as violent, fascist, counter-revolutionary, reactionaries who, for no reason, revolted against the Soviets who "liberated them from the evils of capitalism."

The freedom fighters were violent, that is true, but not nearly as violent as the Soviets had been, or even than they were during the revolution. They were not fascist, the myth that anybody who opposes the communists must therefore be fascist has continued to spread since its inception. They were not "counter-revolutionary," that was Soviet propaganda to fuel the Soviet's need for control over their satellite states and of the narrative. They were not "reactionaries" either, because by definition a reactionary is somebody who wishes for the political system to return to, or stay with, the status quo, somebody who opposed political reform or liberalization—e.g. a man who does not want women to have rights because he does not want the status quo to change. The freedom fighters wanted changes within the economic and political systems, they were rightfully unhappy with the communist government, but they didn't wish to return to the capitalist and fascist government from before the Soviet invasion, they wanted real reform.

The Soviets knew that by assigning words with specific meanings to the freedom fighters they were creating the narrative that they wanted, it was propaganda. The definition of a counter-revolutionary is a person who opposes and wants to reverse the progress made by the previous revolution, in other words, a reactionary who wants the system to return to the status quo. By calling the freedom fighters counter-revolutionaries it implies that the previous revolution was the Soviet takeover in 1945. The previous revolution shouldn't refer to the Russian Revolution that began in 1917 in this context because that was in Russia, not Hungary, so the freedom fighters wouldn't have been counter-revolutionary to the Russian Revolution.

Nikita Khrushchev, premier of the USSR, once admitted that "the press is [their] chief ideological weapon." If you can't get people to support you, trick them or force them.

One could make the argument that the Soviet takeover of Hungary was technically a revolution, since the definition of a revolution is a sudden radical change or a forcible overthrow of a government to install a new one, but that would be a bastardization. We don't call the Nazi invasion of Poland a revolution, nor the Imperial Japanese invasion of China, nor any other instance in which a violent and oppressive regime conquered another country. Revolutions aren't always beneficial, nor do they always work, but the implication is that they're a good thing, and that they happen *within* one's own country, not through the colonization of other countries.

I'd also like you to recognize that there is a difference between communism and the Soviet Union. The Soviet Union never achieved true communism, but that point will be argued by the diehard devotees who woke up to the evils of capitalism (of which there are many), read *The Communist Manifesto* by Marx and Engels, and then chose to ignore—or never learned about—the atrocities and genocides the Soviet Union committed. Political ideology isn't an either-or situation; it's not, "Either you're a communist or you're a capitalist!" and it's definitely not, "Either you're a communist or you're a fascist!" That ignores an entire political spectrum in between the theoretical opposites of fascism and communism. There's also the horseshoe theory; the further to the extreme left you go, eventually you'll end up on the extreme right. Fascism and communism have historically shared more in common than they differed in—but that will also be fiercely argued by both sides, they *hate* being compared to each other. Chapter 27, The

Reputation, expands on the similarities between the two and the propaganda used by the Soviets to smear the freedom fighters.

The extreme socialist political manifesto first published in 1848 during the Russian Empire makes some good points about class structure, equality, and the downfall of capitalism, and even I think that Marxism looks appealing on paper, but it has not been seen in history. The USSR didn't practice what Marx and Engels preached, nor did the 50 countries which adopted communism, largely due to Soviet influence. Communism works in small groups, such as the idealized notion of a commune, but when a large group of people all become "equal," issues arise as a person, or persons, struggle to concentrate power. While everybody is busy working for the greater good, a dictator rises.

Vladimir Lenin, the first de facto Soviet leader from 1917 until his death in 1924, was considerably more moderate than his successor, Joseph Stalin, who consolidated power and ruled with an iron fist, and wall, until his death in 1953. Soviet communism under Stalin's tyranny is referred to as Stalinism and was marked by considerable evil and mass murder. After his death the USSR went through a process of "de-Stalinization" to reverse some of the policies that helped his dictatorship reign power for nearly thirty years, but unfortunately went back to some of the same practices when the next premier of the USSR was ousted in 1964.

Under Stalin, a minimum of 14 million people were sent to a gulag[5] and another 7 to 8 million people were exiled or deported. The best estimates that historians can come up with based on the minimal and unreliable records are that at least 1 million people but up to 1.7 million died in the gulags.

From 1937 to 1938, during the Great Purge, about 1.5 million political opponents, religious leaders, kulaks,[6] and Red Army leadership were arrested, and roughly half, at least 700,000 people, were

---

[5] The Soviets had a penchant for acronyms. "Gulag" stands for Glavnoye Uprevleniya Ispravitelno-Trudovyak Lagerey, "Chief Administration of Corrective Labour Camps." You'll sometimes see GULAG in capitals the way acronyms usually are, or in italics the way foreign words usually are, or simply as "gulag" because it has become a noun much like "concentration camp."
[6] Kulaks were peasants who owned over 8 acres of property, at least two large animals, and could afford to hire a farmhand; they were called "class enemies." They were still peasants, but they were slightly less poor than other peasants.

sentenced to death after their arrest. Not to mention numerous operations of ethnic cleansing against minorities carried out by the NKVD (the People's Commissariat for Internal Affairs; the predecessor to the KGB) which included one of the largest operations of executing over 111,000 Poles, the Polish Operation. Those who weren't executed for a political crime, whether imagined or exaggerated, were sent to a gulag. Families were torn apart and those who weren't imprisoned or executed lived in constant fear that they would be, it didn't matter if they hadn't broken any laws.[7]

The Soviet famine of 1930-1933, called the Holodomor genocide, was an intentional famine that starved at least 5.7 million, but up to 7 million people, to death, primarily in Ukraine. Then, from 1946 to 1947, there was another great famine in which 1 to 1.5 million people died. Causes of that famine include collectivization, the loss of manpower and equipment from WWII, a drought in the summer of 1946, and a *tremendous* amount of grain being exported in spite of the obvious famine. Historians sometimes differ on whether or not these famines can be classified as genocides, but the fact is that they were consequences of forced collectivization of farming, and most damningly, the USSR was aware of the starvation and intentionally let people die.

Up to 15 million kulaks were deported to Siberia (the region that makes up the majority of Eastern Russia) and central Asian countries between 1917 and 1937. 1.8 million of them were deported between 1930 and 1931. Kulaks were often denounced by their neighbors, their land confiscated, their children barred from a university education, and they were deported. Kulaks were deported from the USSR and countries they occupied, such as Hungary. Rákosi, one of Hungary's most hated leaders, believed that beating up kulaks was revolutionary.

In the (non-USSR) countries the Soviets occupied, at least 5.8 million ethnic minorities were forcibly displaced from their homes and deported to forced settlements within the USSR. They weren't allowed to return until after Stalin's deaths, but most couldn't or didn't want to return because they'd rebuilt their life tens of thousands of miles away, many years or even decades had passed, they weren't given transportation back to their home country, and they didn't have a home or farm

---

[7] Suggested reading: *The Unquiet Ghost* by Adam Hochschild, and *The Whisperers: Private Life in Stalin's Russia* by Orlando Figes.

to return to anyways. It was not uncommon for those who were deported out of the USSR or displaced within to suffer from illness or starvation during transit and die before arrival.

And one more example, but not the last one by a long shot: the Katyn massacre. The execution of about 22,000 captured members of the Polish officer corps on March 5, 1940, a single day of slaughter.

The exact figures will never be known due to unreliable, incomplete, and in some cases nonexistent records. Researchers began studying archival data that was finally declassified after the Soviet Union's dissolution in 1991 which included census data that marked net losses on the censuses by up to 10 million people in some cases. There are mass graves around hundreds of former gulags that are still being discovered, but the minimum estimate of people who died at a labor camp is about 1 million. What historians have come up with is that a bare minimum of 5.5 million people's deaths can be *directly* attributed to Stalin's regime, but the argument can be made that up to 20 million deaths should be attributed to Stalin. Additionally, due to the Soviet Union's colonialism, communism was adopted in many countries such as China, Vietnam, Cambodia, and North Korea, which all have many millions of deaths attributed to their own oppressive regimes and genocides.

The death toll doesn't even include the deaths of civilians the Soviets killed during World War II, which hasn't been estimated accurately due to the overwhelming focus on the atrocities the Nazis committed and lack of reliable data. It will never be known how many women and girls the Soviets raped throughout the entire history of the Soviet Union, but the number likely rivals or exceeds the number of people they ever murdered.[8]

Estimates of how many German women were raped by Soviets at the end of the war soar up to 2 million. Military historian and acclaimed author Antony Beevor estimated that at least 1.4 million women were raped in the areas of Silesia, Pomerania, and East Prussia alone, which does not include any other country the Soviets invaded or passed through. In Berlin, in the final few months of war, at least 100,000 German women and girls were raped; this estimate was reached based

---

[8]All statistics regarding the victims of the Soviet Union can be found in these suggested readings: *Stalin and His Hangmen* by Donald Rayfield, and *Stalin's Genocides* by Norman Naimark.

on the spike in abortions and in the births some 9 months later by those who chose not to abort, but the rapes often went unreported and almost always went unpunished.

The full extent of the horrors of the Soviet Union went unpublished as historical atrocities often do when the victor suppresses its population with secret police, writes the history books, and records the data, but the victims remember.

I've spelled my grandfather's name as József throughout the book because that was his birth name, he only changed it to Joseph in 1966 when he became a naturalized American citizen. Similarly, I spelled my great-uncle's name as Károly throughout the book because that was his birth name, but after becoming Americanized he went by Charles but he never changed his legal name.

I had to take liberties to elaborate on certain events that he didn't remember, or didn't want to talk about, in order to complete the narrative. I manufactured the conversations, inner thoughts and emotions, and "filler" scenes based on my interviews with my grandpa while he was still alive. He hadn't remembered exact conversations or any names after all that time, so except for members of my family, I created the names as well. Some of his memories are preserved in his own words, imperfect English and all, to emphasize his perspective.

For complete transparency, I created the torture scene based on common torture techniques the Soviets and secret police used because he wouldn't divulge what happened to him. I also added the scenes at the abandoned house in Austria to develop the relationship between the characters and tell Tamás' backstory in a low-stress environment; from my grandfather's recollections they'd been picked up by the Austrian police shortly after crossing the border. Several minor characters in the narrative were created with the sole purpose of explaining historical events through a first-person lens, and to display an array of different backgrounds, cultures, and emotions. For instance, a gay couple, a student whose father died in the revolution, a Judas who betrays his compatriots to the Soviets at the border, and even a character whose tongue was cut out by the Soviets as a punishment because they used that method to silence people. You'll find that the truth is often stranger than fiction.

PART ONE:
THE CHOICE

"When governments fear the people, there is liberty.
When the people fear the government, there is tyranny."

Attributed to Thomas Jefferson

CHAPTER 1
THE LAST MORNING
NOVEMBER 1956, PÉCS, HUNGARY

"Dodi. *Dodi.* . . Dodi!" Károly hissed in the darkness, "Wake up, it's time to go!" When he saw József's eyes open, he left.

József couldn't shake the dreadful feeling in his stomach, but he had no other choice but to get up and face it. He stretched his legs, reached for the nightstand, and fumbled blindly in the dark until he found the watch his grandfather had given him. The handsome watch was one of his few prized possessions, and the only one of real value. The style of watch had almost completely vanished from civilian life during the occupation, having been stolen by and sold among the Soviet soldiers.

He checked the time, it wasn't even 4 a.m., but despite the time, everyone in the house was awake except for his little sister. He rolled out of bed and quickly dressed in the layers of the thickest clothing he had. The goal was to wear enough to keep warm but not too much so that they couldn't move freely, and to save space in their bags they'd wear most of the clothing they took.

József and Károly packed their modest messenger-style bags with a few pieces of clothes, their identification, and a few inessential personal items they couldn't live without, like his pocket-sized Bible and his favorite photo. He'd packed it the night before to ensure he wouldn't forget it, so he double checked his bag to make sure it was still there.

The photo had been taken around Christmas when József was 14. Ilona, their mother, had the weary smile of a woman who'd seen it all; their father a tall and serious man in the middle of his life, stood behind his wife; all three boys were well dressed and sported the Elvis-style haircut; and baby Edit sat happily on their mother's lap. Most of them stared without expression at the camera, but József instead smiled down at his baby sister, whom he loved dearly. He tucked the photo back inside his identification booklet for safe keeping and put it inside his bag inside an interior pocket.

They'd only made the decision to leave the night before, but deep down they'd always know it might come to this one day; they were ready. Truth be told, if they would've had more time to think about the gravity of the situation, they all would have had more doubts and worries.

József quickly used the bathroom, slicked his hair back and brushed his teeth, then he tip-toed down the hall to the last bedroom on the right. He knew his parents were already waiting for them both downstairs, but he needed to see his sister one last time.

He hoped that Edit would be awake so he could give her a proper hug, but she was still peacefully asleep, completely unaware of how her life would change forever. József was too afraid to wake her up, he wouldn't have known what to say or if he'd have the stomach to actually leave her. She was too little to understand why her brothers would never come home, but József trusted that their parents would explain it to her later. He knew that she might blame him, or even hate him for it, and that was the worst part of it all.

He bent his knees and bowed his head beside her pillow to say a silent prayer for her; he asked forgiveness, prayed that she would one day understand, that she would be safe and happy, and most importantly, that she would grow old.

When he opened his eyes, he leaned over and placed a soft kiss on her forehead. Her little chest heaved with a sweet sigh; he whispered his final goodbye with a lump in his throat.

His brother and parents waited for him in the kitchen downstairs. He dipped into his room for the last time to retrieve his knapsack, he flicked the small lamp off and left without even a second glance.

Ilona met József at the bottom of the stairs, she hugged him softly then held him at an arm's length to look him in the eye. She moved her mouth as if to say something but couldn't find the right words to describe her pain. He wanted her to say that they didn't have to leave, or even to beg him to stay, but instead she said, "You should eat."

Their father, Károly senior, sat at the dining table next to his eldest son and namesake, stoically as always, József joined them. They sat around the dining table where their mother had laid out two bowls of hot cereal: her mix of oatmeal, wheat bran and sugar. It had been a special treat to add sugar to it; the ration for sugar wasn't enough for them to have it whenever they pleased.

"Do you remember what we talked about?" she asked. He did. "You have to look after each other," she pressed as the worry lines on her forehead sank in further. She was terrified, and she never stopped worrying. "Stay together and always walk quietly. Don't talk to strangers, don't tell them where you're going. You know you can't trust anybody."

"Yes, Mama," they said in unison, "We know what to do."

Father began to lecture them again, "If you get caught, they *will* kill you. You understand me? If you stay hidden, you stay alive. Don't do anything stupid! Whatever you do, just keep going. . ." he stopped mid-sentence because at the bottom of the stairs, a small brown-haired boy stood clinging to the wall.

László wasn't supposed to be awake but he'd snuck down the stairs to say goodbye one more time. He was very aware that the more he knew, the more danger he could be in if the secret police ever found out, he was given that lecture the night before. Károly and József had to leave immediately, it was too dangerous to stay, and the fewer people who knew, the better.

"I—I just—I only wanted to say goodbye," he murmured softly.

Károly looked at him sternly, he'd told László not to get involved the night before. On any regular day, Ilona wouldn't have challenged her husband, and he would not have given in, but they weren't about to start an argument that day.

"Come here then, come here," she waved László towards her, despite Károly's looks of objection. He bounded into the kitchen and practically fell into her open arms, clinging to her nightdress. He watched his two older brothers tentatively, afraid to make a sound.

By that time, József and Károly had already wolfed down their breakfast. They stood from the table and donned their knapsacks and were ready to go; they couldn't waste time because the day would break soon, and they'd lose the cover of darkness.

Their father reminded them again, "You have relatives there, they can help you. And you must write to us when you get there, you must not forget, your mother will be up day and night waiting for news of your safety."

He firmly believed that emotion was weakness and that was not the time or place for weakness, but his sons could see the pain in his eyes. László was trying to prove his masculinity by holding back his tears, too, but it was more obvious. László had always been trying to live up to his brothers, to act older than he was, and they were usually annoyed with him for it. Their parents told him that he was too young to join his older brothers and had to stay, the Soviets didn't want anything to do with him anyways. László would spend the next few months sulking and plotting ways to escape on his own, wishing to prove to them that he was mature enough.

As the eldest brother, Károly felt compelled to mend the hurt László felt for being left behind. He rubbed his arm and said, "Look, you're going to have a lot more responsibility around here, you've got to act like a man now, alright?"

Tears welled up in his eyes, he tried to wipe them away as they rolled down his flushed cheeks. He nodded in agreement and leaned into Károly's chest for a hug. For the first time in many years, they hugged each other, not knowing when they might get to do that again.

Ilona couldn't hold back her tears, her chin quivered, and she reached for József. She held him tightly and stroked the back of his head as she did when he was just a small child. She opened her other arm and welcomed Károly in and László in. They held each other like that for a moment, even their father, typically an impassive man, hugged his children for the last time. His eldest son wasn't even a child anymore, and the second oldest was practically an adult, as well.

They let go of each other slowly, sniffling and wiping their tears.

"Wait," Ilona swallowed, she turned away into the kitchen and returned with a paper sack, "I've packed you some food, please take it." She handed them a paper sack of some food she'd prepared: some boiled eggs, apples, and sandwiches made with butter and ham. Food that could travel reasonably well. They'd rarely been able to get a ham or a roast at the market, usually the good food was reserved for the communists or sent out of the country, but during the revolution the grocery stores were able to carry a decent variety of food because food exports halted.

"Dodika. . . Karolika, my boys," she cooed softly. Her eyes shined with love and tears.

They smiled weakly at her, not knowing what to say and walked towards the door slowly. Their father gave them each a firm handshake and a pat on the back, and Mama gave them a kiss on each cheek. Károly opened the door and shuffled outside, eager to leave, but József remained in the doorway, holding onto Mama's hands.

"Be careful," she begged them.

They had more bravery than they did life experience, and they were anticipating the escape to be easy. Still, they hesitated in the doorway.

Their father looked at his sons and gave them a single nod as if to say, "It's okay to leave."

Ilona told them she loved them once more, and László murmured a meek goodbye. József pulled on the doorknob as Ilona pushed from the inside and together they shut the door. Both young men hesitated on the stoop, breathing in the cold morning air, then they walked through the courtyard.

They looked back at their house, suddenly it seemed smaller than ever before. There was nothing left to do but leave. Their neighborhood was silent, it seemed ominous; they could hear the blood rushing behind their ears, like they were underwater. Pécs felt deserted as they left home, it was a surreal experience.

The landscape was covered in snow as far as they could see, József thought about how lucky he was to have his thick winter boots which his uncle had made for him. He made the boots two sizes too big so that József would have room to grow.

Chapter 2
"Until The Russians Came"

I was born on August 22nd of 1940. I was born József László Kutnyak. László was a very, very common name for boys. When I came to America and the judge asked me if there was anything else he could do for me, I says, "Well, you know, I would like to change the spelling of my name," so then I became Joseph and I felt more American.[9]

My parents were Károly and Ilona. My mother's maiden name was Biro. Ilona Biro. Her grandmother, my great-grandmother, called me Dodi. How she come up with it, I have no clue, but everybody in the family called me Dodi.[10] I hated it, I thought it was such a silly nickname. When I came to the United States I thought, "Man, I'm gonna get rid of this nickname, I don't want it, I just want to be called Joseph."

But then when I came to Portland, the family I was staying with had four boys already and one of them was named Joseph, and they says, "Well, we can't have two Joes in the house, do you have a middle name we can call you?"

And I says, "Well, I have a middle name but I never gonna answer it. I have a nickname, you can call me Dodi." So, I never got rid of the name, it stuck with me forever. All the family and close friends call me Dodi, you know, even Linda still calls me Dodi. But to everyone else, it's Joseph, or Joe.

My earliest memories go back to when I was really little, maybe 3, 4

---

[9] The spelling of his name was changed when he became a naturalized citizen in 1966, not when he first arrived in 1957 as a refugee. For 9 years he was "stateless" and his status as a refugee was as a "parolee."
[10] "Dodi" was an old rural nickname for the name József.

years old. We lived in Hird, a small town, more like a village, in the southwestern part of Hungary. That's the town I was born in. It was in Baranya County. My father owned a ranch out in the country, and my eldest brother and myself had the run of the whole place. We could go out whenever and wherever we wanted, it wasn't so dangerous for kids like it is now, our parents never worried about us.

We had two great big Saint Bernards, named for Thunder and Lightning. When I was a small boy, I would go out playing or walking and one of the dogs was always with me, just following by my side. We had many acres, and the countryside was big rolling hills of green; green for as far as you can see. There were cows and chickens and a whole bunch of animals. The animals were pretty noisy, the kind of noise that you have to get used to or else you can't sleep. I didn't mind it though, not like some people.

My father was pretty strict. Typical European male. That's, "I'm the head, you do what I want, if not then the belt comes off and you get a whoopin'." My father was strict with everybody. You don't say anything what make him angry. But my mother, she took care of us. She was a good cook, too.

Then, the war came to Hungary and changed life for us. After that, I grew up in a topsy-turvy country. Meaning, we did not have a stable government, and we did not have control of our own country. My father moved us into the city of Pécs, after my younger brother was born. We rented a house there and we stayed until I left in 1956.

I remember the Germans coming into Hungary; the soldiers would always stay with families. They would just come in and says, "OK, so many of us are going to stay over here, and so many of us are going to stay over there," and that was that.

The Germans came in with their foreign language and foreign attitudes and forced Charles and I to leave our room so they had a place to sleep; after that we slept in the family room. They were big brooding men, it was something like 13, 14 of them in our house. A house only big enough for our own family, not for all the extras using our water and eating our food and sleeping in our beds. And they all needed food of course, and lots of it. So, my mother would cook their meals, and clean up after them, and all of us was trying not to step on any toes in there.

I remember behind our house there was an Officer's Club for the

Germans. Officers only, no soldiers or anybody else. There were restaurants in there, and even a bowling alley. Us kids, being the neighbors and being a little rebellious, always jumped the fence and snuck into the bowling alley and since we were there we helped set the pins. We were not employees, kind of like volunteers actually, but they never kicked us out and they gave us tips for setting the pins. Whatever tips we got from them was very appreciated by the whole family.

Back in the early twentieth century, before the war, Hungary was part of the Austro-Hungarian Empire. It went as far North as the German Empire, as far East as the Russian Empire, and straight South to the Mediterranean Sea. It was massive, Austria and Hungary were one empire working together, and you know, it was one of the greatest world empires. The land is great for growing stuff; most of the land is flat between the hills, and the rivers provide all the water, and the temperatures are really warm in the summer and really cold in the winter, so you never have to worry about things like your crops failing or not having enough rain. But the empire, it collapsed in 1918, after the first war.

Another thing you have to understand is Hungary goes back a thousand years, and its history is very messy. The people from Mongolia, from the far East, invaded Hungary, they came in and says "Well, hey, this place is pretty good for living." Then the country fell to the Turks from the Ottoman Empire, they were in control for a pretty long time. They had taken the land in between Turkey and Hungary and controlled everything. Then Hungary was controlled by the Germans, and then the Russians. I guess you could say that the national mindset was "here somebody else is occupying us, here's another goddang language we gotta learn."

When the Germans were leaving, we had a break from borders for a little while until the Russians came.[11]

---

[11] He always referred to them as Russians, so I have left the verbiage the same in his memories and in his dialogue throughout the book. I use the term "Soviets" most often, but sometimes I use "Russians," not in place of the word Soviets, but instead to be more specific, because not all Soviets were Russians.

Many, if not all, of the Soviet Union and Eastern Bloc countries were forced into collectivized civilization of almost every part of daily life.

The "collective," as it was sometimes called, was when farming became a state operation rather than an individual one. Farmers were forced into the collective and if they didn't want to conform, they were forced out of farming entirely. Collectivization also contributed to urbanization because those who were run out of their farming business often moved to the city where they could live in apartments and participate in careers within energy and heavy industries that communism valued. The Soviets would also requisition land and animals without giving much, if any, compensation to the farmers, and landlords became richer when people moved off of the property they owned and into a rented apartment.

In communist countries individual business was prohibited or heavily restricted and farmers couldn't sell their goods on their own. Some farmers chose to leave their profession rather than become completely controlled by the Soviets, and some even slaughtered their own animals so they didn't have to join the collective, and killing their own livestock became a crime. The collective farming system wasn't beneficial for the farmers or the consumers, it was mostly for the benefit of the Soviets and their puppets. The majority of the produce that Hungarian farmers grew was exported, and the best produce and meats were reserved for the highest members of the government.

I suspect that my great-grandparents moved off of their farm and into the city of Pécs after the Soviet takeover for one of two reasons: they didn't want to join the collective farming system, or they were forced out of it to give their property and animals to somebody else.

Not only were their farms collectivized, but their paychecks were highly taxed to support the collective, their land and homes were sometimes split or given to the Soviets when they occupied Hungary.

CHAPTER 3

LEAVING

They walked in silence for nearly ten minutes, shuffling through the alleys and forgotten paths to avoid unwanted attention. They were well versed in how the AVH operated and knew that they could be on somebody's radar at any moment. Nobody could be trusted because you never knew when somebody was spying for the communist regime.

Soon, they reached the spot where they had planned to meet their friends, near their old high school. The knot in his stomach felt heavier when he stood still so József shifted his weight anxiously. Károly watched him silently, he didn't want to admit it, but he was nervous, too. The temperature was below freezing, and their body temperatures dropped drastically as they stood still waiting for their friends to meet them.

They had all agreed to meet at that corner only last night. In the darkness the night before, József and Károly had run to Gellért and Amós' houses to tell them of their plan and ask if they would join in the escape. Amós and Gellért had also gotten the letters and mused over the idea of leaving before, so they agreed without much persuasion.

Much like the Kutnyaks, Gellért's family was supportive of the plan, even if it broke their hearts. Amós truly had every intention of telling his parents after his conversation with Károly in the garden of his home, but he didn't have the courage, fearing they might try to talk him out of it. Instead, he left a note on the kitchen table for his mother to see in the morning. The pain she felt, knowing she might never see her child again and hadn't even gotten to say goodbye, was unbearable.

Everybody knew that they were risking their lives by escaping, but it was the only chance they had of survival. Everybody in Hungary knew that people were leaving every day, but nobody spoke about it, fearing that the AVH would find out. You didn't want the secret police or the Soviets to have any reason to look in your direction twice, especially if you were doing anything nefarious or illegal.

Amós and Gellért lived near each other, so they caught up with each other as they walked. It wasn't long before they arrived at the meeting spot where József and Károly waited for them.

Amós was Károly's friend, he would turn 19 that winter, his constitution was weak, he was quiet and apologetic, and very cautious. Gellért was József's friend, 16, and quite a character.

Gellért sang a greeting, "Fine day, isn't it?"

They ignored Gellért's sarcastic comment but nodded to greet them. Károly, ever the leader, said, "We should go before we're seen."

Without wasting any more time they headed towards the train station. The fundamental difference between Gellért and the others was that Gellért didn't fear for his life and that's what made it all an adventure to him. To everybody else, it was quite literally life or death, and they couldn't mask their fear with humor. He continued to crack jokes as they walked while Amós sighed heavily, half-way between exasperation and worry.

They walked to the train station in relative silence, everyone either in deep thought or dissociating from their current situation. They did arrive at the train station safely, but they still held their breath, they weren't out of the woods yet. The sun still hadn't risen, and shadows lurked everywhere, fear played tricks on them and sometimes showed hidden figures among the trees.

The landscape was unforgiving, and the forest sometimes did harbor enemies, but other times it was just the mind playing its tricks. They, except for Amós, had experience in those woods working with the Partisans. As young children, József and Károly began volunteering with the Partisans who were stationed in the forest. They needed guards and it was an easy job for young kids to do, even if it could be a deadly job. Guarding a camp meant walking the perimeter and giving a warning call if the Soviets or somebody unknown got too close, it was usually a boring job. They were taught not to trust shadows and told to shoot anything that moved.

The first train going west to Austria would arrive at 5 a.m., which gave the boys a few minutes to buy their seats from the ticket master. There were no direct lines to Austria from Pécs, so they would be making several stops and a switch from one line to another during the trip. They each bought tickets to take them 400 kilometers closer to Austria. They wouldn't take the train all the way over the border, they planned to get off at the last station before the border and walk the rest of the way. They thought it would be safer that way, because if by chance the Soviets were checking passengers at the border, they would be able to circle around the border station and bypass the Soviets entirely. They knew they wouldn't be using the return ticket, but it was safer to appear as if they were going to return home. Their father had insisted that it was the best way to leave without being noticed. The hardest part would be blending in with the snowy landscape.

The platform outside was completely deserted, but it was so cold that they stood nearly shoulder to shoulder while they waited. Amós mumbled something to Károly, clearly hoping to keep it between them, but if József had learned anything from having an older brother it was how to eavesdrop without being completely obvious.

"I didn't tell my parents, I. . ." Amós stuttered softly, "I left a note, but I didn't tell them." He hung his head in shame. Unbeknownst to him, even though it tore their hearts out, his parents were immensely proud of their son and supported his decision to leave, they knew it was his best chance at survival. Amós wasn't the only one that winter who left in secret, for some it was easier to avoid the tearful goodbye.

"They will understand. You can always come back home later," Károly offered with a half-smile, "When those assholes are gone."

He scoffed slightly, "What if they never leave?"

None of them wanted to believe in that possibility. They had grown up under the occupation and hadn't known anything else. It was entirely possible that the Soviets would remain in power forever, but that scared them more. The most reassuring part of leaving was that they would one day be able to return to a sovereign country, back to their families who couldn't leave with them. They hoped that at least the children wouldn't have to grow up in a county controlled by the secret police and communists like they had to.

While the boys waited for their train to arrive, they worried and wondered about the future. All they could do was hope that once they got on the train that it would be smooth sailing from there, and that once they got to Austria, they'd become untouchable to the Soviets.

CHAPTER 4

"IT WAS JUST HORRIBLE"

When the war started to turn against the Germans in 1944/45, when the Russians were pushing the German forces back, they came through Hungary. Everybody hated them, and I mean everybody. They were underhanded, they robbed the country blind and bled it dry. There was always somebody destroying our country and telling us what to do. So, when the Russians invaded our land, we thought "Well, the Mongols didn't last, the Turks didn't last, the Germans didn't last, so these guys won't be here long." They were pushed out of Hungary when the wall that was dividing Germany fell down in 1989.

The Russians were completely different than the Germans. The Germans had darker uniforms, they were clean smelling, they had better manners, and they spoke more languages. The Russians had brown uniforms, they were dirty and smelly, their bathing habits were pretty lax, and they only spoke Russian. The Germans usually knew other languages, and were better about learning the language of the country they lived in. The Germans could talk to us, but not the Russians. And because the Russians never showered, their smell just got worse and worse and pretty soon it stunk up the whole house, it was all you could smell. . . it was just horrible.

It's funny, out of all the things you remember, the smells really stick with you. I remember the first time the Russians came to our house. Here again, you had no say whether to let them in or not. They knocked on the door and says, "OK, so many of us are going to stay with you" and that was it, no ifs ands or buts.

One of the soldiers come in and looked at our house, looking at all our belongings and he saw a clock in the hallway; an old-fashioned clock with a bell on either side, at the 11 and 1 o'clock positions. And he seen that and pointed, and he says, "Burzhuaziya?" [bor-zjwa-zia].

OK, so the Russian language is one of the Slavic languages and my father spoke one of them, not Russian, but it was the same family of languages so if you knew one then you could understand the rest and speak it pretty well. He was from what is Yugoslavia originally, so he knew that language.

My father says, "No, no, we not rich," because burzhuaziya *means rich, or upper class. He says, "Sorry, but we don't have any food or anything for you, so if you want to eat you have to bring your own."*[12]

And one of the sergeants or officers says it's not a problem and commanded the other guys to go get some food from town. Pretty soon they come back with bread, cheese, meat, and a barrel of wine. Where they got the wine, who knows. It took a couple of them to haul the barrel out of the truck and put it at the front of the house.

Luckily, the front of the house was in a courtyard hidden behind a wall and big gate, so it was not like this barrel of wine was sitting in view of the streets. What our neighbors would have thought! When the Russians opened it up my father noticed that there was oil on the top of the wine, obviously, the barrel had fuel in it before. These Russians, they just go right ahead and dip their hands in and flush out the oil, then they dipped their cups in and drank. It was always 5 o'clock in Russia.

You know, I was just 4 or 5, memories are just certain things that were really out of the ordinary, like they bringing a big 55-gallon drum with wine in there. For a little kid, you remember that.

One captain kept them in line, they usually never bothered us. And they took care of us as far as food and whatnot, we didn't worry too much, but like I said, they never bathed. Day after day the sweat got worse.

Just like the Germans, they kicked us out of our bedrooms and almost had full control of the house. The Russians, they stayed with us for many years.

---

[12] The Soviets hated the bourgeoisie, the wealthy and capitalist class. That moment was probably more sinister than my grandfather realized as a young kid; the Soviets didn't inquire about the clock because they were curious, they were trying to determine if the family was in the class of people they hated and if they should be liquidated or exiled.

CHAPTER 5
THE AVH

The AVH, the *Államvédelmi Hatóság*, the State Protection Department, was the highly feared and hated intelligence agency and political police, otherwise called the secret police. Originally the *Államvédelmi Osztálya,* the AVO, the organization changed its name in 1950, but Hungarians continued to call it the AVO (Ah-voe) which rolled off the tongue easier.

The Soviets, still occupying Hungary after World War II, created the AVO to serve as a subsidiary to the KGB (the NKVD at the time). The AVO and its directors cut away at the existing political parties within Hungary, imposed Stalinesque purges and policies, arrested Hungarians who criticized communism and accused them of being or collaborating with fascists, and began a decade-long rampage in which they arrested, tortured, and killed people for fabricated crimes.

According to the people of Hungary, the AVH had a simple and horrifying task: to hunt, torture, and kill, any citizen who showed even the slightest disobedience to the new Soviet regime and communist way of life. By the autumn of 1956, the secret police had created such a hostile climate in Hungary that when the revolution broke out some of the freedom fighters began killing officers of the AVH with zeal.

Contrary to their name, they were less like a law enforcement agency and more akin to thugs. Anybody who even so much as verbalized dissatisfaction with the Soviet Union, the Russians, the Hungarian government, collective farming, taxation, and any other facet of communism, was likely to find themselves in an interrogation room and possibly in a gulag or a grave.

They served the ruling communists of the Hungarian Working

Peoples' Party by performing political persecutions and purges of anyone who opposed, or might stand in the way of, the communists. They had a total force of about 48,000 employees and a vast network of up to one million paid informants who would *regularly* double-cross their fellow countrymen by turning them in to the AVH for money or immunity.

For perspective, Hungary had a population of just about 9.85 million in 1956, and it's estimated that about one million people, or 10% of the population, were regular informants for the AVH. Citizens with knowledge about others would be bribed for information, which included bankers, real estate agents, teachers, repairmen and chimney sweeps, to name a few.

For example, if a chimney sweep were in somebody's home, they'd be able to eavesdrop on conversations, perhaps they'd hear Radio Free Europe on the radio (which was highly unlikely, because people wouldn't play an illegal broadcast while strangers were in their home, but it's just an example), or they'd notice behavior or belongings that the AVH might deem as suspicious, or maybe they'd try goading people into a conversation of anti-Soviet rhetoric. The informants were paid to tell the police what they saw, and it's not unreasonable to suspect that the informants would sometimes lie in order to get the payment.

Those citizens are separate from the ones who weren't paid to inform but were instead coerced into ratting somebody else out while they were under investigation, and often under torture. One of the easiest ways to get a better deal while being interrogated by the AVH was to give the secret police the names of other people whom the AVH could arrest. People didn't always tell the truth in interrogations; they'd sometimes lie and give names of people who had done nothing wrong.

In the eleven years between the end of WWII and the Hungarian Revolution, the AVH arrested an estimated 1.6 million Hungarians for a crime against the regime; 1.3 million of the arrests were between 1950 and 1953 alone. They interrogated and beat nearly all whom they arrested, and they imprisoned or deported many of them. Almost half, an estimated 700,000 of the people they arrested, were imprisoned for the crime, whether real or imagined. Crimes ranged from stealing small amounts of money or food to high treason, and often were fictional or trumped-up charges. At the time, Hungary had less than 10 million citizens, so approximately 16% of the population had been arrested in 11 years' time and about 7% of the population had been imprisoned. One of the best ways to ensure one's own safety, if being questioned by the AVH, was to rat somebody else out so the AHV had more people to arrest (Korda, Molnar).

They didn't need evidence of a crime to arrest or imprison somebody, sometimes it was a false charge, but even when there was a crime it was often as petty as listening to the radio, or not hanging a photo of Stalin in their classroom. But if one were found guilty of a crime, individuals and their families suffered.

The AVH also began going after religious leaders in order to suffocate religious influence during the Rákosi years. They arrested the head of the Catholic Church in Budapest, Prince Primate József Mindszenty, on fallacious charges of espionage.

Mindszenty was a great source of irritation for the communists ever since 1945 when he began preaching to Catholics to vote against the communists. By Christmas Day, 1948, Mátyás Rákosi, then First Secretary of the Hungarian Working Peoples' Party (the ruling Communist Party), had decided it was time to finally eliminate the burden of that Catholic Priest. Not only would they get rid of him, but they'd also demonstrate to everybody else that any resistance, especially religious resistance, would be dealt with accordingly. They arrested Mindszenty's secretary first as an intimidation tactic, and he knew he was next.

After being tortured he was given a show trial (a trial in which the goal is not to seek truth, but only to "justify" punishment, because the minds of the judge and jurors have already decided the defendant is guilty of a crime, whether or not they did it) and sentenced to life in prison in January of 1949. People who listened to the show trial or read the confessions quoted in the newspapers instantly knew that he had been forced to confess, the wording was entirely out of step with his natural voice and writing style.

A few months after Mindszenty's sentence, the Church's number two, Archbishop Károly Grosz was arrested for sedition and sentenced to five years. Then several Jesuits and Lutherans were arrested, and the Greek Orthodox Bishop János Ödön Péterfalvy, whose torture was especially brutal.

In 1949, priests and church leaders of all denominations were made to swear an oath to the constitution and therefore to the communists; if they refused, they were jailed. The religious persecutions certainly made the point very clear to the Hungarians—if it could happen to the Church, it could happen to anybody. In 1951, a statue of the Great Teacher Stalin was unveiled on the site of the destroyed Regnum Marianum, a church that was built in 1931 to symbolize the appreciation for the collapse of the short-lived Soviet Republic of 1919. The communists had demolished one of Budapest's most important churches and then erected a statue that would remind everybody of who is in charge. The freedom fighters tore that statue down on October 23, 1956.

The AVH utilized any method they wished on their victims, including torture, and they were allowed to get away with it because they didn't have to face a judicial review of their actions. Their methods were condoned by the government, and their headquarters was a location of the former Arrow Cross Party (the far-right party that was willing to collaborate with the Nazis during WWII). In the basement of 60 Andrássy Avenue was one location of torture: the House of Terror. They used many torture devices ranging from whips, to truncheons, to nail presses and electrodes, and sometimes they dissolved bodies in an acid bath that drained into the city's sewers.[13]

Gábor Péter, a man with a thick mustache and an M-shaped hairline, looked average and almost approachable, but he was the absolute leader of the AVH, and he was one of the most abhorred men in Hungary. His chief torturer, Gyula Prinz, was another. Prinz, a former Arrow Cross member, worked in the same building doing the same thing in the fascist regime as he did in the communist regime. He

---

[13] The House of Terror was transformed into a museum under the leadership of Viktor Orbán, Prime Minister of Hungary from 1998-2002 and again beginning in 2010. The museum is not only meant to inform, but also to evoke emotions and Hungarian patriotism for visitors who are guided through each room of the House with words like "TERROR," "Double Occupation," "Gulag," "Soviet Advisors," "Resistance," "Deportation," "The Torture Chamber," and "Hungarian Political Police" hanging overhead until they finally descend into the basement on a slow elevator. The basement was the torture chamber, it was fully reconstructed and designed to make visitors feel the claustrophobia and fear of torture and death. People are allowed into the torture cells which have been recreated as they might have looked, but no records were made (or remained) about the torture house. Some of the torture rooms are too small to stand up in or too narrow to sit.

tortured an estimated 25,000 people in his career.

Shortly before Stalin's death, on January 3, 1953, Péter was requested to Rákosi's villa. It wasn't out of the ordinary for them to meet in person to discuss business—most business wasn't ever written down—but it was unusual that the Hungarian Defense Minister, Mihály Farkas, was already in Rákosi's office awaiting Péter. They claimed to have evidence that Péter was an enemy spy and arrested him. He was sentenced to life imprisonment, a mild sentence compared to others who got death, but was released in 1959.

The arrest of Péter, a vicious torturer and the boss of the secret police, wasn't very surprising. People were quite accustomed to the Communist Party's infighting and petty arrests; a large portion of the Party had been in prison or on trial at some point before and/or after becoming a popular figure within the Hungarian Communist Party. Both the Soviets and Hungarians were subjected to repeated purges and political witch-hunts looking for people who could be an enemy spy. Nobody, no matter their position, was safe, and evidence was irrelevant. Anyone who had left the country during the Horthy[14] era from 1920 to about 1945 (which was a significant number of communists), could have become a spy for the west; but anybody who stayed during the Horthy era could have been an informer for the anti-communist Horthy government, thus a traitor. Everybody was afraid, but they couldn't let it be known that they were afraid because then they'd look suspicious.

If the leaders of the Party and the chief torturers within the AVH were arrested on forged (sometimes nonexistent) evidence of a crime against the regime, the regular citizens absolutely would not be spared. Hungarians had a saying, "There are three types of people: those who have been in jail, those who are in jail, and those who will be in jail."

---

[14] Miklós Horthy was the Hungarian admiral and regent of the Kingdom of Hungary from 1920 to 1944. His administration was conservative, antisemitic, and fascist. He banned the Communist Party and many of the communists fled Hungary during that period, and it was Horthy's foreign policy which led Hungary into an alliance with Nazi Germany.

CHAPTER 6

THE TRAIN

There weren't many people on the train but they assumed that many, if not all of the passengers, were escaping. Austria was an independent country—finally, after the hellish sequence of events following World War II—and the government was offering asylum to political refugees fleeing Soviet persecution in Hungary, and that train was headed straight for Austria.

They found four seats together without difficulty, stowed their modest bags under their seats and relieved their feet. József glanced at the other passengers, trying to be inconspicuous, he couldn't shake the feeling that somebody was watching him.

The train took off shortly after everybody boarded, trees and bushes started flying by, and it wasn't long before they were out of the city. Once the last image of their city had completely vanished from sight, they finally tore their eyes from the window. They were tense and quiet, not wanting to draw attention to themselves, but soon their bodies relaxed a little and they settled in for the long journey. József was exhausted but just as he started to close his eyes, he saw the shoulder of a Soviet soldier, his stomach dropped.

He leaned into the aisle a little to get a better view of the two Soviet soldiers who sat at the front of the train car with their backs to the wall so they could see the whole car. Everyone knew that if they were caught trying to leave, they were likely to be taken, beaten, and never heard from again. The secret police were probably also on the train, they were always monitoring all modes of public transportation, but they were on high alert during and after the revolution.

Actually, they'd been on high alert since the summer, after the protests in Poland and the July 13 plane hijacking, the world's first civilian hijacking of a commercial plane. Seven Hungarians wanted to escape, and they knew they wouldn't have much luck crawling under the Iron Curtain, but they could fly over it. Twenty-five-year-old laborer, Frank Iszak, his wife Anais, and their co-conspirators, made the decision to commandeer a plane after its take off from Győr. It was risky and they were scared to death, but they dreamed of freedom from tyranny. A fight ensued between the KGB agent onboard, four crew members, and fifteen passengers including the seven escapees. They nearly crashed while fighting for control of the cockpit, Anais' leg was broken in two places, and on top of all that, the door was slightly cracked so they had to stay around 10,000 feet while flying over the Alps otherwise the cabin would depressurize. The clouds obstructed their view, and they eventually began to run out of fuel so they needed to land as soon as they could.

They came out of the clouds and miraculously saw a runway below them. They needed to land the plane but if they landed in Czechoslovakia, East Germany, or even Austria, they'd be returned to Hungary and executed, so they were prepared to commit suicide instead. A Jeep with a mounted machine gun appeared on the runway, it had stars and stripes on it and the Hungarians knew they'd made it. They'd flown about 600 kilometers, the runway was actually on a NATO air force base that was being constructed in Ingolstadt, north of Munich, it was inexplicably good luck to land there. Upon landing, the injured were taken to a hospital and the escapees weren't returned to Hungary, they'd found their freedom. Iszak wrote about his experience in his memoir *Free for All to Freedom.*

Hungarians were all dreaming of escape and the fact that some made it out from the iron grip gave many the courage and hope they needed to escape, too. Not only that, but just a few months earlier in 1956 the border fence and landmines that were scattered between Hungary and Austria were removed after land disputes between the two countries were settled. They even talked about connecting flights between Budapest and Vienna, because in the Eastern bloc people were heavily restricted from traveling to free western countries, even before the hijacking incident. By happy coincidence, the landmines which would have exploded and potentially killed thousands of people, and the wire fences that trapped people inside, were removed. The Soviets and the AVH knew all of this, and they were always on the lookout.

József knew they were vulnerable, but he didn't want to react too suddenly or loudly and draw attention to himself. He looked around slowly, trying not to move his head too much, to see if he could identify anybody who might be part of the secret police. AVH officers dressed in civilian clothes, but most had a certain look, a menacing wickedness behind their eyes.

Do we jump off the train? No, we'd die trying. And if we lived, Russians would be out there waiting. We could move to the next car, but that would draw attention to ourselves. Could we make a run for it at the next station? No, they would definitely suspect something then.

The soldier on the aisle said something to the other and they both chuckled. It seemed so strange to József that the Soviets had the ability to laugh and smile. The funny one must have felt József's gaze, he looked over and their eyes met briefly. His brows were thick and narrowed to the center which made him look perpetually angry, it contradicted his smile. József tried to keep a straight face to hide his fear but he felt his mouth salivating and a tingling sensation rise to the back of his throat. He turned away from the soldier, fearing that he might vomit.

Luckily, the soldier didn't think twice about József. He was only a flower on the wall, a kid unworthy of a second glance.

He nudged Károly and motioned nonchalantly in the general direction of the soldiers. "Up there, on the right," he murmured.

Károly, on the window seat, had to lean over József to peer around the seats to catch a glance. Gellért made a lot of commotion turning around to look, which was stupid and could have drawn unwanted attention to them.

József admonished him, "Don't turn around, they'll see you!"

"Should we get off at the next station and switch cars?" Károly whispered.

"Don't bother," a stranger across the aisle advised.

That gave them pause, they didn't know if he was speaking to them, they thought they were being quiet.

They eyeballed him, noting his unshaven face and dirty clothes, he sat next to another disheveled man. Neither one looked like a spy, but they could never be too sure. Neither of them made eye contact with them across the aisle, knowing that sudden movements could draw the Soviet soldiers' attention. They did not seem threatening, but they were nosy and József didn't like that.

"There's no need to switch cars, there's scouts on all of them. They can't do nothing here anyways, there's too many people." His voice was guttural, but soothing. "Markos," he introduced himself, "This here is Zádor. He doesn't speak much." He gestured to his traveling companion who nodded his head.

All four young men looked at each other cautiously, all thinking that the strangers could be AVH officers. They didn't want to talk to strangers, but they didn't want to seem suspicious by ignoring them. They introduced themselves quietly, trying not to make direct eye contact with them.

"You boys can't be older than 18," he said.

"Me and him are 16, sir," József slightly pointed towards Gellért, "And they're 19," indicating Károly and Amós.

Markos raised an eyebrow at the young men across the aisle, he didn't ask, but it felt like there was an implied question about where they were going.

They were quiet for a moment, then József lied, "We're going to Lake Balaton for some work," hoping it would get the strange old men to back off. He didn't give too much explanation, but just enough to seem acceptable. The worst lies have too much detail.

Markos chuckled and glanced over to them, "You don't have to lie to me, son. We're going to the same place," and he winked.

They didn't want to say anything else. They examined the pink scars that littered Zádor's face and wondered why he hadn't said a word. Zádor had been imprisoned and tortured, which explained the scars. They took him in 1945, and again in 1954 for speaking ill about communism and the USSR. The second time, they cut out his tongue.

The train crept to a stop at a station a few hours away from Pécs, but they still had many more hours to go. József told the others that he needed to relieve himself.

"Don't get lost, I'm not coming to find you with your pants around your ankles," Gellért smirked.

József ignored him and stood, holding on to the seatbacks for stability as the train came to a complete stop and lurched forward. When the doors screeched open, the chill hit his eyes, making them water. The morning sun was the most unfiltered at that hour, having just begun to peak over the horizon, but it was still below zero.

They stopped near a small village, the train station was a miniscule building; it could hardly be called a whole station, it would be more accurate to call it a stall. József knew that the trains on this line customarily stopped for at least three minutes at each station; he jogged nearly fifty feet into the trees, down a little slope, and behind a tree to relieve himself with some privacy. He could barely see the top of the train.

It's too damn cold, József thought, as he unbuttoned his pants and relieved himself. But not even a minute after it had come to a halt, the train started screeching away. Normally the trains stayed for several minutes at each station, even the short ones.

He panicked and fumbled for his pants, furiously scrambling out of the woods as the train gained more speed. He tripped on roots and fallen tree branches hidden beneath the snow as he struggled to gain speed up the hill. The fear of being left behind propelled him forward faster than he had ever run, hoping against the odds that he could catch up to the train. It was already passing him by, he pumped his legs as hard as he could to keep up.

He screamed out for his brother, knowing that he couldn't be heard but not knowing what else to do. Károly was already on the move, to József's surprise the back door to the last train car slid open and Károly yelled, "Dodi!" which was hardly audible. József sprinted faster as Károly leaned over the railing howling, "My hand! Grab my hand!"

József's feet hardly touched the earth, he was moving so fast on top of that gravel and ice. He misplaced his step, it could have been fatal, but he regained balance quickly and Károly stretched farther.

"My hand!" he yelled again.

He was barely able to grab his brother's hand before his feet slipped beneath him, Károly pulled him up just enough for him to grip the railing with his other hand. With their combined effort, they were able to draw József up onto the deck where they both collapsed.

Károly turned his head towards him, clutching his chest like he was in pain, and said, "Damn, Dodi, don't do that!"

Completely consumed with adrenaline and at least a smidge of brotherly love, they laughed and pushed each other around. When they had absorbed the situation, they pulled themselves together before going back inside. József knew that he was saved by the grace of God.

CHAPTER 7
THE LONG WALK

There was not much to do or say on the train so eventually the slow rocking of the train eased them all to sleep. József dreamed, as he always did, of something horrific.

His nose led him through the doorways and hallways of his house and into the kitchen where his mother prepared a stew—rabbit, if he were to guess. Her hair, usually tied tightly at the nape of her neck, flowed like a silky waterfall, and when she turned to smile at him her cheeks lit up the room and illuminated people that were not there before. In a voice as smooth as honey she told him to sit, but he saw that the table was overflowing with Soviet soldiers, clad in winter gear and Kalashnikovs.

The captain gave him an order, "Sit, boy, we have good news. You are recruited for the Red Army. You must come to Russia to complete your duty."

József turned to his mother, he wanted to beg her to stay but he couldn't speak.

Without hesitation she said, "It's the only way. You must say goodbye now."

He panicked, he wanted to cry out to her "How could you do this to me?" but the words wouldn't come out.

He woke up startled, sweat beading up on his forehead, his hands clenched in fists, and his heart beating ferociously. Neither Károly nor their friends noticed, for they were all still asleep. József tried calming himself but he could not shake the feeling that they were in danger. He knew his dream was just a manifestation of his fears and that he was escaping the Soviets, but he was anxious and thought of every worst-case scenario.

The train ride was long, he had much time to dwell on the negatives and worries. It was late afternoon by the time the train approached the last stop before the border. They'd been riding the train for many hours and were stiff, ready to get off. All but two of the passengers stood to gather their luggage and fix their clothing. The Soviet soldiers took notice, it seemed suspicious that everybody was getting off at the same station.

The soldiers stirred in their seats, stretching their limbs and adjusting their coats. József froze where he stood, but the soldiers did not stand. The boys watched them for a moment, hesitating to make another move because the deer that cannot be seen cannot be shot; but their desire to escape outweighed their fear of being caught in the act and they made their way to the door, which was luckily in the opposite direction of the Soviets.

Once they were through the threshold, Gellért asked, "Smell that?"

Sniffing at the stale air, József detected a hint of pine mixed in with the burning coal but couldn't figure out what he was supposed to be smelling. "What?" he asked suspiciously.

"Freedom!" he beamed.

Amós tried to hush him so that people wouldn't suspect them, and József rolled his eyes, as usual when listening to Gellért's ramblings. The scruffy older gentlemen from the train walked close to them which at first made them uncomfortable.

Markos spoke softly, "Stick with us, kids. I've been through these woods before, I know where we're going."

With a strange mix of uncertainty and excitement, the boys graciously accepted this offer of guidance. József still wasn't so sure that he could trust them, but at the very least he thought they couldn't be a physical threat to them or put them in any more danger than they were already in.

Several people from the train went inside the station to pretend they were waiting for another train, but they were planning to cross the border, too.

"Should we wait for a while?" Károly wondered out loud.

"No, the sun is going down, we don't have a lot of time to waste," Markos explained. He kept walking, rather briskly for such an old man.

They all agreed to keep going. They saw some of the people go to the train station to wait for a while, and they even saw people begin walking in the other direction, back the way they came, to throw the Soviets off if they were watching.

The weather worked against them; it would have only taken them an hour to reach Austrian ground from where they were at, but trudging through the slush and ice, and fighting against the freezing wind made the trek a lot slower. Following the train tracks would have taken them on an easier path, but they couldn't risk running into the AVH or Soviet Army at the border, so they were going to circle wide to avoid it.

While the six of them discussed the easiest and most discreet route through the forest, a trio of young men cautiously approached them.

"Do you mind if we join you?" He jerked the hand that held his knapsack to show that he was doing the same thing, escaping. They all figured that they were all safer in larger numbers.

Károly looked at them cautiously, he was about to question the new people before Markos, the self-appointed spokesperson, said, "We're all going to the same place, I see no reason why not."

"Excellent, thank you!" one rejoiced.

Everyone introduced themselves and shook hands, and together they set their sights on the west.

They walked in several small clusters so they could hold private conversations while they marched toward Austria. József and Károly had the quickest pace due to their long legs and they found themselves at the front of the pack.

It wasn't long before Amós stopped dead in his tracks, which caused a ripple effect of everyone staggering to a halt. "Stop, stop," he warned, "There's people behind us, they're following us."

Everyone in Hungary was cautious, and some people were quite good at gauging who or what was a threat. Amós wasn't one of them; he thought everything was a threat, even when it wasn't. They all turned around quickly to see who Amós was talking about.

"Ah kid, they're doing the same thing as us, can't ya see?" Markos said, pointing to their luggage.

Amós still seemed wary, but Károly said, "We should wait for them," which seemed reasonable to everybody else.

"Hey!" he called out.

He waved his arm in the air as if the strangers in the woods could not see the nine people standing in a barren field. They picked up their pace and nearly jogged to reach the group quicker.

The group of strangers was a motley crew: a pair of identical and classically handsome young men, one short and peculiarly rhombus shaped man, a tall and lanky man with shoes that could double as skis, and one young woman with a stern expression and piercing blue eyes.

She stood tall and proud, she didn't step down for anybody, and she was the first to speak, "Who are you?"

József was instantly enamored with her, she was beautiful. She was also intimidating, so when he opened his mouth to speak but only babble came out, "I'm, uh, we're-"

Gellért intercepted, "I'm Gellért, this is József, a straggler we picked up along the way. Poor thing was all alone, begging for scraps, unable to talk!" He held onto József's shoulders and feigned a sympathetic frown.

József was too embarrassed to say anything to save face. Gellért had always embarrassed him in front of girls, he was irritated but he was used to it.

She was not amused, József hoped it meant she didn't believe the lie about him. Markos told the newcomers that they were welcome to join, and they could travel together. She questioned where they were going exactly, but her brother—one of the twins—cut her off and accepted the offer.

He placed a gentle hand on her arm to calm her down, she was visibly annoyed. "Not everyone is an enemy, Iren."

"Fine, walk with us, but keep your distance. It's a good idea to stagger ourselves, and if we're seen, run in different directions for Christ's sake," she instructed them.

Iren was a hard pill to swallow but her beauty and confidence captivated people. József wondered if she'd always been that callous or if the revolution changed her. Almost everybody had been changed by the circumstances and, for the most part, they would never return to their old selves.

They all introduced themselves as they walked, except Zador, he simply nodded.

"Hey, I'm Emil. This is Elias," the gentle young man gestured to his twin brother, then nodded towards their older sister, Iren, "Sorry about Iren, she's just protective. . . Where are you coming from?"

"Pécs," Károly and József chimed together.

"We left this morning," Károly finished.

"And you've already made it this far?" Emil asked, a little taken aback, and perhaps a little jealous. "We came from Budapest three days ago."

Everyone's ears immediately perked up to listen.

"How'd you end up all the way down here then?" somebody interrupted the conversation, he seemed suspicious of Emil's story.

To wind up down there, nearer to where Hungary, Austria, and Slovenia all meet, they had added about 150 kilometers to their trip than if they were to have gone straight to the west from Budapest to Austria. Refugees coming from Budapest usually traveled through the northwestern city of Győr, another major city in Hungary, about 120 kilometers away from Budapest. From Győr they still had about 50 kilometers to go until they reached the Bridge at Andau, the popular name for the bridge that crossed a canal in the northwestern corner of Hungary.

The bridge could hardly be called a bridge, it was more like a rickety raised footpath, not sturdy enough for a motorbike and not big enough for a car, but it became the key to escape for a large portion of the refugees. The bridge was entirely in Hungary, and they still had a few hundred meters more to go until they reached the Austrian border. Its name is also a misnomer; the village of Andau is actually in Austria, several kilometers away from the border. Nevertheless, the bridge at Andau became a popular location for escaping refugees.

"We got a few rides with some truck drivers and a farmer to get here. We took the first opportunity that came our way, it was either ride with the truckers, even if they weren't driving straight to Austria, or wait to see if anybody else would come along offering a ride that would be quicker. Waiting any longer was dangerous, so we took whatever we could get."

"So, were you there when. . .?" József tried to change the subject but couldn't find the words to finish, fearing that he may have over-stepped.

Emil didn't need more than that to know what the end of that sentence was. He gave one sharp nod and bit his lips. "Yeah. Elias and I are students at University. Or, at least, we were students. I guess we're not anymore." Emil laughed hollowly.

"It took us a few days of jumping trains and running at night before we got here. We couldn't get out of Budapest until after the majority of the fighting ended, the whole city was blocked off by Russian tanks. We couldn't even leave the apartment."

At that point, Iren scowled over her shoulder at Emil for even opening his mouth. All eyes were on him now, he ignored her.

"So. . . You were there? At the protest. . . When they came?"

All he said was, "Yes," and he kept walking as if he didn't just drop a grenade. The gravity that laid on them silenced every mouth for a few seconds while they walked in agonizing anticipation.

Only Gellért, always the provocateur, dared to probe, "And?"

"You want to know the truth?" he asked sharply, suddenly on edge. "Some of my best friends were killed."

Taking a breath, he continued more calmly, "We all helped plan the protest, us students. We sat down one day and made a list of demands, then organized the demonstration at the Parliament. At first, it was just students, then all of a sudden there were like a hundred thousand people there, it was unbelievable. When some troops showed up, they even threw their hats and joined us—took the red star off their clothes and everything.[15] I even helped tear down the statue of Stalin, some of the welders went and got oxygen tanks and blow torches and we tore that son of a bitch down, all that was left was his boots. I thought it was the beginning of a new era, it was incredible, the feeling that we were changing our nation. We all had this feeling like we were making history, there was a brief silence after Stalin's head fell, but then everyone yelled and clapped, it was fantastic.

"Some students had loudspeakers and they were saying what our demands were during the protest in the streets. At first, Radio Kossuth agreed to let them go on the air, but at the last minute we realized that they'd tricked us, and the radio wasn't broadcasting anything, so they

---

[15] The Hungarian military personnel who deserted and joined the freedom fighters were, for the most, part young men of the same age as the majority of the civilian freedom fighters: late teens and early twenties. They may have been enlisted, but they held the same core beliefs as the resistance. Guided by their moral compass, they abandoned their duties to the oppressor and joined their compatriots. It boosted morale to see the military join their side, and without the military to open munitions warehouses the freedom fighters wouldn't have been able to acquire many weapons and the Soviet troops and 700 tanks that were ordered in on the first night would have crushed the resistance quickly.

marched to the Radio and demanded to go on air. And it started out as a peaceful protest, you know, until the AVO held the students in the radio building as hostages, we demanded for them to be released and then the police started firing into the crowds and throwing tear gas.

"We left to gather guns and ammo to protect ourselves from the AVO after they killed a bunch of people at the Radio. And after midnight, the Russians ordered tanks to come into the city. We started gathering and organizing, it wasn't just a protest anymore. Some of us bounced around from group to group, fighting here and there. They declared martial law and there was supposed to be a curfew, so we'd fight until the curfew began and pick up as soon as it was over in the morning. We thought that we were in the lead, that the revolution was going in our favor, people had hope.

"On Thursday, two days later, there was a demonstration in the square outside the Parliament, there were several thousand people there, we demanded that Gerő leave his position and the protest was going well. Then suddenly, we heard shots from up above the buildings and then the tanks fired at us, and people started dropping dead. We tried to get into the Ministry of Agriculture building, but I think the police were shooting at us from inside the buildings, and they wouldn't let us in. I swear there were AVO disguised in the crowd as well. We were basically cornered, there were tanks and soldiers surrounding us, I thought I was going to die." He took a deep, shaky breath and walked quietly for a few seconds. By then everybody was walking close together, listening, utterly horrified and entranced by his story.

He continued, "I know what I saw that day. There were bodies and shells everywhere, bullet holes all over the building. I saw hundreds of people shot dead, most of the time in the head or chest, they were killed on purpose. I was shot in the shoulder; it barely grazed me. The shooting finally stopped and some of us laid on the ground, afraid to move. I tried to see who was still alive, I lifted their heads or turned them over to see their faces, there were so many dead. I saw them, and I knew lots of the people who died, there were hundreds. . . Hundreds. A few of us escaped and we watched a tank roll over the bodies in the street, and soldiers started throwing bodies in piles, we left before they could catch us.

"After that, we spent days holed up in our apartment in the city, afraid to leave, and then a few days later we heard on the radio that other cities formed a resistance, too, and the Soviets were beating them down like they did to us. We also heard a Russian broadcast say that there were only twenty people killed at the Ministry of Agriculture, and that was a goddamn lie! We saw it with our own eyes!" he almost yelled; he was getting worked up over it.

"They lie about everything. Even Nagy lied, he's just like the rest of the communists. After our protest, Nagy was the Prime Minister again and he was going to offer us protection, going to let prisoners go, going to exit the Warsaw Pact and remove the AVO. Those were all things we wanted, it seemed like our protest worked, but I saw hundreds of dead bodies in Budapest. They killed thousands, and thousands more began to go missing. I knew the revolution was over, that they'd win, but people kept fighting. There were some who believed that change would come no matter what, and some who probably believed that we could win if we just kept fighting. But. . . nothing is going to change." He had to stop, he needed to breathe.

Emil continued, "Our father also died. He joined the resistance because I asked him to. Our father believed the Soviets should leave, and we should fight for a free state, but he didn't want to march at first. I convinced him because we needed more people to join, so I asked him to join the protest and then he got caught up in the fighting. He died because of me.

"There were those few days when we thought that the ceasefire would hold. We watched as the Soviet tanks left the city, we celebrated in the street, but then the tanks came back, and they attacked Budapest on the 4th. They'd made a big show about leaving just to trick us. They didn't hold back at all; they destroyed half the city, and we gave up.

"We had to wait for an opening to get out of the city, they had thousands of tanks and tens of thousands of men standing guard all over, every way out of the city was blocked off and they were capturing people who tried to escape. Then we finally had a chance to sneak out after some tanks left their positions. Iren said she was going to Yugoslavia, she knows some people at the university there, but before he died our dad told us to go to Austria if we ever got out, and to stay together. She gave in and came with us, and I guess she's still ticked about it," he finished, referencing Iren's obvious disdain.

The weight of the air around them was suffocating, they couldn't say anything for a long while. They simply watched their feet stomp through the snow with heavy hearts.

Several minutes later Emil apologized, "Sorry, I didn't mean to bring you all down."

That broke the tension, a few chuckled but somebody said, "I'm really sorry about your dad."

They continued walking in silence. Emil grew pensive and stared at the ground before his feet as he walked. Everybody minded their own business, even Gellért, listening to the whistle of winter wind.

The Soviets were ruthless, many boys and men had already disappeared, but there would be no stopping the Soviets in their revenge for the rebellion, and no telling what would happen to them. The revolution may have started strong and unified many Hungarians to fight for the same cause, but by early November they knew the fight was lost against the Soviets. People fled to the borders in droves.

During the revolution, phone lines going in and out of Budapest were cut, the radio played recorded communist propaganda, and people weren't getting information quickly or accurately. Despite eyewitnesses who said that citizens made hundreds of telephone calls a day (except for in Budapest) because while the government and secret police were occupied elsewhere, they felt secure catching up and spreading information on the phone because the AVH wasn't listening.

CHAPTER 8

"THE GOVERNMENT WAS FULL OF RUSSIANS"

During the revolution, there was rumors going around that all the high school kids and kids who just graduated were getting letters that they have to go back to the school on such and such day and all that, and then whole classes full of kids disappeared. The rumors was that the Russians was taking these young men away. Kids would leave home one day, and then they just disappeared. And the kids who got these letters and went to the school, were never heard from again.

I knew it was true because I got a letter too. It says to go to the high school, with a day and time to be there and all that. That was one of the reasons that we says, "OK, it's time to get out of dodge." I had the choice to go back to the school and being taken away and sent to Russia. Or, you know my father always say, "Young men go west."

My friend who I worked with at the trade school got one too, and my brother and his friend, and we all decided "OK, we gonna leave, or if we gonna stay then they gonna kill us."

So, we left one day at 4 in the morning. We had to leave. Not that we wanted to, but we had to. If we didn't, then our chances of surviving were not very good. Charles and myself told our parents, talked it over with them, and they says that they would kill us if we didn't; everybody knew it was the best thing we could do—the only thing we could do. We left with our parents' blessing, that was lucky.

Even though we knew it was the Russians taking these boys away, the letter came from the high school, it had Hungarian stamps and all. Basically, it says "You were in the class of such and such year and we would like you to come back for whatever." The reason was very vague, but it was implied that you should be there. Before I got that letter, I had already heard the rumors so I definitely wasn't going to the school for anything.

And it was a weird thing, to be asked to go to school at that time. I mean, there was a revolution going on, things kind of quit. We had no school, people stopped working, everybody stayed indoors. We thought this would be a war! But even with that, some kids went when they got the letter. Not 100% turn out, but pretty good, and those kids just disappeared. They went to the school and then nobody ever seen them or heard from them again. Just gone.

We don't say it was the Russians, even now. It was the Hungarian government. But the Hungarian government was full of Russians. It was a secret police, not soldiers out in the streets with guns telling people where to go. The secret police rounded the kids from high school up and whoever they got, they were shipped to Russia – or probably to Siberia. Coal mines or led mines or salt mines. There were vast resources in Siberia and labor camps was the easiest way for the Russians.

Here it is, 60 years later, and in that time, not one of the people who disappeared come back. So, what happen to them? I believe, and many people believe, they were taken to Russia.

———

Through my research, I couldn't find any reported evidence of similar letters to the ones they received stating that they had to report to their school, however, a few other Hungarians stated in their memories or to their families that they received a similar letter or knew of people who had gone missing under really suspicious circumstances (which wasn't uncommon). Young Hungarians were conscripted to the Hungarian military and sometimes to the Soviet military, and the letters could have indicated that young men would be sent to the military. The Soviets covered up or destroyed evidence that incriminated them, or they just never recorded evidence of their deportations of *millions* of people all over the continent, and in the Soviet Union and in satellite states such as Hungary, all published media was censored and propaganda was pushed, but one would think that somebody would save saved a letter like that at some point. So, take the anecdote of the letters with a grain of salt, but this was part of my grandfather's memories, therefore it's included.

Chapter 9

Almost There

Everybody in their troupe had broken off into pairs or trios and held private conversations. Some talked about how much they hated a man named János Kádár. Kádár was a traitor and many Hungarians despised him. He was a Hungarian, but he was in bed with the Soviets, a proud communist; at first, he was the minister of the interior in Hungary, then some issues arose between him, and other Stalinist communists and he was removed from his position and the party and imprisoned.

József was eavesdropping and he heard one man who called himself Csaba say, "The Russians, they opened fire on the city the next morning. The radio was broken, all that was playing was the national anthem, over and over. It was like the world was ending. . . Then Nagy came on and told us that we must stop the fighting. He was probably forced to say this by the Russians, that's what we all thought."

"The entire country is falling apart. I hate to leave but it's the only option now," one lamented.

Another man chimed in with, "Everything happens for a reason," which ticked József off, but he held his tongue.

It didn't make sense to Jozsef how anybody could think that all of the Soviets' cruelty and the devastation of the revolution happened for a reason. The idea that this was part of the divine plan wasn't rational.

József and Gellért walked side-by-side for a while; they talked, trying to keep their spirits high. They reminisced about work, it was a mundane topic, but it seemed easier and more familiar to them than talking about the future. They had gone to a trade school together where they learned skills in general construction. They had the option to choose to study any of the trades that were offered.

In Hungary, high schoolers could choose to study a trade outside of pen-and-paper education, and their options ranged from mechanics, ironworks, brickworks, and even mining. József figured that any trade would be just as good as the next, so he went into construction with his best friend. The plan for all trade school students was to receive training, graduate, and get a decent job after high school to serve the state. József and Gellért were close to graduating before they fled, and they were worried about having to go to school all over again in another country.

They recalled some of their best and worst memories in their shop, including one time one poor kid they worked with became the butt of a joke for a few weeks.

"What about when Nikola started hollering inside that storage drum? Banging on the walls and screaming 'It's too loud, it's too loud!'" Gellért roared with laughter, "Ahh!" he screamed, mockingly, to imitate Nikola's fear. They'd all taunted him for weeks like that, then pretended they couldn't hear him.

József laughed, but that memory felt oddly distant as he listened to it. As time passed, he would remember the story fondly, though. The construction shop was commissioned to build a large container to store sunflower seed oil for a nearby farmer. It needed to be large, so they were required to build it on site; they spent two whole days in the heat of summer building that container on the farm. Nikola was the smallest boy in their class, he had the privilege of getting inside to hold the walls together so that the others could finish welding the edges shut. The noise from the welding echoed terribly inside the container and the poor kid couldn't hear for the rest of the day.

While Gellért continued laughing at the memory of Nikola's pain, somebody noticed a small group of people at least 100 yards away, walking parallel to them, and announced to the others, "Hey guys, stop for a minute, I see some people."

Iren, who liked to keep herself as the head of the pack, turned to examine the strangers across the way and then looked back at the rest of her group. She glowered and declared, "We don't know them. They could be Russians, or the AVO, or spies. We need to keep going."

Iren was right, it was true that for more than a decade you could not trust anybody in Hungary if you didn't know them. It was safer to assume that anybody you met had ill intentions or could at least be bribed. Whether they were being paid or threatened, your friends could one day turn on you. Neighbor turned on neighbor, friend on friend, son on father, and so on, until the entire country had split into two groups: those who spied, and those who kept their mouths shut.

"Iren, come on, they aren't spies or police. Look at them, their clothes, their baggage. I bet my life that they're fleeing, too," Elias told his sister. He was the voice of reason, which bothered Iren to no end.

"Spies always try to fit in, but whatever you say," she rebuked. Elias sighed, as did a few others, but she was right. Iren was harsh, but she was considerably calmer around her brothers.

A young man in the group across the field waved, he didn't want to call out in case someone else heard them. He and his group paused and looked at each other before advancing, likely debating the likelihood of danger in the cluster of strangers before deciding if it was safe to approach, they began shuffling through the unbroken snow towards József's group.

When they were close enough to hear each other without shouting they stopped walking and both groups sized each other up.

Ilya, one of the strangers, spoke first, "Where are you going?"

Iren answered cryptically, "Through the forest."

"Mind if we join you?"

"That's no problem," Elias stepped in to offer before Iren could say something snarky.

Ilya was a fair-haired and pale man, he was traveling with his friend, Jozsua, who looked worn and beaten, an older couple, and two young men who also fled from Budapest. They were called László, a very common name, and Cain, an uncommon name to say the least.

Ilya explained that he and his friend Jozsua had left a few days before and spent three days walking west across Hungary. They met the others on the way and began traveling with them; it seemed everybody knew that they were safer in numbers. Several of them said they left without a plan, they had not packed anything or carried enough money, and one hadn't even had time to get his identification before he left.

It was not rare for the Hungarian refugees to have left their homes with nothing but the clothes on their backs, but it wasn't common for them *not* to carry their identification since the AVH frequently stopped people to randomly check their papers. Nevertheless, many Hungarians still crossed the border that winter without their identification because they didn't have time to grab it or their apartment in the city had collapsed or been bombed out, and their papers lay somewhere in the rubble.

They walked on and soon snow began to fall, and the cold bit harder. Everyone's feet were so frozen and wet that they felt as if they were burning. The sun was setting, and they'd already been walking for at least two hours, but they had to keep going until they made it into Austria. They knew the border was close, but they didn't know how close or if they'd gone astray and started in another direction by accident. In any case, they had to keep walking in a vaguely westward direction until they could find Austrians to help them get to a refugee camp.

Emil and Elias were in the lead and soon Emil put out a hand to signal for everybody to stop for a break. Iren started walking towards a thicket of trees.

"Where's she going?" Someone spoke, he sounded angrier than concerned.

"Lady business," Emil replied.

The middle-aged married woman from the last addition took the opportunity to follow Iren. She'd had to hold her long peasant-dress up the entire journey so that it didn't drag in the snow. The men in the group only had to walk a few feet and turn their backs to relieve themselves, but the chances for women to have privacy were few and far between. Within seconds they were out of sight behind some trees and József had the strangest feeling of unease, perhaps from nearly missing the train earlier that day. He was glad that Iren had not gone alone into the woods, but something still didn't feel right with him.

Cain pulled out a map from his pocket, unfolded it, and studied it carefully. He announced that it was not far off, maybe half an hour. He pointed towards the southwest slightly, through a thicket of trees rather than through the barren field slightly more north.

"If we go through the forest, we'll be there before we know it," he grinned. He folded his map and put it away, when somebody else asked to see the map, just to double check, he said "Don't worry about it, I already looked."

Károly and Amós exchanged curious glances.

Most of them sighed with relief but some were more caught up on Cain's slightly odd behavior. Without any street signs or landmarks it was remarkable that Cain knew how far away they were from the border, and that he hadn't referenced the map until just then. József tried not to pay attention to the bad feeling in his gut and only focus on how close they were to freedom. He was so close, he thought he could taste freedom, but he wasn't sure what freedom tasted like.

"Not long now, Dodi," Károly nudged József's arm and tried to give him a reassuring smile.

The knot in his stomach was still there and it made him feel sick. He knew—they all knew—that worrying too much would not help them. The first step was to get into Austria and then they would figure out what to do next.

It had been a few minutes since the ladies retreated into the woods when somebody stood up from sitting on their suitcase and pointed to the distance.

"What's that thing, way out there in those woods?" He was pointing in the opposite direction toward a shadowy thicket of trees.

"Animal, maybe?" somebody suggested, unconcerned.

"No, no, it's gotta be people. . . Look, see how many there are now?"

Everyone turned to look at the human shadows that emerged from the darkness. It was not an unusual sight that day to see people appearing out of nowhere, so when two dozen more people hiked toward the herd of travelers it seemed quite ordinary and didn't disturb anybody. In fact, even the most anxious travelers seemed relatively unbothered; and when Iren returned, she didn't comment, or even give the newcomers her signature sharp eye. Everyone watched as the newest people climbed the small hill to cross the distance between them.

"Hey fellas," one man waved his arm and called out. He waited until he was closer before asking, "Are you all going?" It was an odd way to phrase it but it's better to have the benefit of the doubt when asking questions about illegal activity.

His name was Karl, he was at least 40, well-groomed, and he carried a hard, brown suitcase which showed signs of old water damage. Behind him, a small bespectacled boy with a clean gray pea-coat and expensive winter boots; his name was János, Karl's 5-year-old son. All the members of their group varied in age and social class.

Everyone had gotten weary of fighting against or hiding from the

Soviet invaders, they needed to put their needs first. The elderly, in particular, who had seen the worst half of the century, were fed up enough to risk their lives during the exodus. There were even young children who'd left without the rest of their families because leaving was safer than staying. Some parents told their children to leave, and others left in secret. Every parent who took their children across the border, rich or poor, was only hoping to build a better life. Some had been traveling on foot for upwards of a week, while others had only left that day. Some wanted to go to America, but some thought that it was better to stay closer to home in case they could return later.

They introduced themselves, shook hands, and exchanged pleasantries. They were polite with the small talk even though they all knew that in a few hours' time they would go their separate ways, and never talk to those strangers again.

They'd separated into small groups of two or three to hold private conversations as they trekked through the final leg. A mother and her little girl walked parallel to József and Károly. She was no older than 4, she wore her hair in plaits tied off at the end with pink ribbons, her name was Isla. She was sneaking glances at József from behind her mother's legs. He gave her a smile and she blushed. Her mother wasn't paying attention to Isla, she was only determined to continue walking. József saw the little girl peek at him again so he turned his head sharply and stuck his tongue out at her. She giggled and grabbed onto her mother's coat tail, causing her to stumble.

"Stop that!" her mother scolded, but Isla paid her no mind.

József and Isla had made a game out of it. He pretended not to notice her when she looked at him but just as she was about to hang her head in disappointment, he would stick out his tongue, puff out his cheeks or cross his eyes, and she would laugh. She danced around and hid her face until she was brave enough to peek at him again, then he would stick his lower jaw out and make a soft sound like a monkey. Isla burst into wild laughter and held on to her mother's coat again, which her mother did not appreciate.

"Stop that, I said!" Her mother reached down and swatted at the girl's hand, and that was the end of their little game.

Isla looked around to József one last time, but her eyes were filled with sadness, he felt bad about making Isla's mother angry. By then it was dark, and the temperature dropped rapidly, he had gotten used to the cold, and no longer felt the wind's sting but his nose was icy to the touch. They needed to get out of the cold soon though or they'd risk hypothermia or even frostbite on feet from walking in wet socks. The trees that towered above them swayed gently, the wind whisking through the branches occasionally made an eerie sound.

Time wasn't passing quickly enough and after walking in silence for a while, they heard somebody shout through the trees.

"*Stoy! Stoy!*" the voice commanded.

"It's the Russians! Run!"

There were faint lights in the distance, the Soviets shouted and fired their guns several times, and the refugees scattered.

CHAPTER 10

"I'M GONNA SHOOT!"

Before the revolution, in the day time, you could walk around on the street, wave to the Russians, say hi (most people could talk to the Russians, not fluently, but just enough); but when it grew dark, everything changed. That's when the guns came out, and when they took people away, and if any Russian truck was going by a building or a bridge you could send bombs down to blow up the truck. The next day you're out walking around like nothing happened.

There was a bridge near Pécs, the bridge went over a pretty deep ravine and a steep hillside. You could drop those Molotov Cocktails on the Russians, and we did. Even us kids did it. We took a wine bottle, put some gas inside, stuck a rag into it, lit the rag on fire, and threw it over. Any trucks or tanks going by – with half a dozen bottles thrown at it – was over.

The Russians started to be more cautious, and meaner than at the beginning. They wouldn't go anywhere alone or even in pairs, but only in groups so they had enough back up. And there were some routes they wouldn't go, but that one bridge was the main way to get to Pécs, you couldn't avoid it, and that was difficult for them because whoever had the high ground had the upper hand, and the tanks could not raise their guns high enough to shoot at us up there, so we had that advantage.

During the revolution the freedom fighters who fought against the Russians were stationed in the woods. In the day, we got food together and took it to the men who stayed in the woods all the time. A lot of the times we had to put messages in the food for them to communicate with other people, it was all very secretive. And we had to pull guard duties a lot too for those guys in the woods, to keep the Russians out of the area.

One night I heard a noise, so I stopped, my heart just hammering.

I heard the noise again, I was scared, and I called out, "Who's there?" I heard it again and screamed "You better say something or I'm gonna shoot!" Still no answer, but more noise. So, I shoot. I stood behind a tree and I shot, you know, aiming so I was hidden. No more noise. "OK," I thought, "All clear." The next morning, I went to see who I hit, or what I hit, and I saw a deer head. Only the head, I had blown the hind end completely away.

Well, sometimes we hit people, and that's where we got the guns. We picked them off dead soldiers, Russian or otherwise. You had to keep stealing because you never know when you gonna run out of ammo.

PART TWO:
THE REVOLUTION

Talpra magyar, hí a haza!
Itt az idő, most vagy soha!
Rabok legyünk, vagy szabadok?

—Sándor Petőfi, "Nemzeti dal"

Arise, Magyars! The country calls!
Now or never - the time has come!
To be free men or prisoners?

—Sándor Petőfi, "National Poem"

Sándor Petőfi was considered a national poet
and revolutionary hero of the 1848
Revolution.

CHAPTER 11
EVENTS THAT INSPIRED THE REVOLUTION

The spark that ignited the resistance didn't begin overnight, even though it may seem that way. Hungary had been ruled by extremist regimes since 1920, first with the fascist Horthy regime and then the communist Soviet regime. Many who resisted the fascists also resisted the communists, and most of those who grew up under the oppressive regimes didn't favor the government.

When East Germany rose up in defiance of the Soviets on June 16, 1953, they showed the other countries what a popular uprising could accomplish against the dictatorship. The uprising began with construction workers going on a strike against the production quotas the communists wanted them to achieve without extra pay, and by the next day the uprising consisted of at least one million people demonstrating in around 700 cities or villages across East Germany. The demonstrators were protesting the worsening living standards and production expectations without appropriate compensation, and some of the protests became violent and were described as riots. The East German government felt the protests posed a threat to the government so martial law was enacted and the Soviets and the Kasernierte Volkspolizei violently suppressed the protests.

The United States supported the East German uprising by providing food relief for East Germans to keep the uprising going and undermine and destabilize the government. However, the government tightened its reins on their people by preventing them from receiving the United States' offer of aid and cutting off transportation from East Berlin to West Berlin. Western governments didn't want to provoke a Soviet military invasion of West Germany, which seemed like a possibility, so they didn't intervene further. The food relief campaign ended in October, but the courage to resist spread and showed the other satellite states that they, too, could revolt.

Three years later, on June 28, 1956, roughly 100,000 Poles began protesting in Poznań, which sparked several months of political reform. The industrial employees were disgruntled, to say the least, about the recent changes in policies that required them to work more to reach higher quotas for the same, or less, compensation, and the tax increases. They demanded fair wages for the work demand, as well as lower prices for food and necessities, and for the government to reverse some of the recent laws that diminished working conditions.

What started out as industrial workers going on a spontaneous strike in the early morning grew to 100,000 in a few hours. Employees at other industrial plants, students, and even some police officers joined the protest on a whim, and the local police couldn't tame the crowd, so it turned into a violent uprising quickly. The riots were easily stamped out within a day by the Soviets, but Poles throughout the country were encouraged to resist the Soviet Union and demand freedom. The Polish United Workers' Party (the Communist party which ruled in the one-party state from 1948 to 1989) realized that political reform was necessary.

Polish communists were either Stalinists or moderate anti-Stalinists, and over the next few months change was clearly on the horizon. The Polish communists chose a new Party Boss, Władysław Gomułka, a moderate communist who'd been in jail from 1951-1954 due to Stalin's purges. Gomułka's election worried the Soviets so much so that Khrushchev flew to Poland to confront them; he said that the Soviet Union wouldn't recognize Gomułka's leadership, but it was a bluff, and the Poles knew that. After a few days, Khrushchev relented, he recognized Gomułka's right to lead Poland and withdrew the Soviet soldiers he'd brought with him. The Poles didn't want to eliminate communism, they wanted moderate reforms; they promised that the reforms wouldn't impede the Communist Party or the balance within the Eastern Bloc.

The Poznań protests and the transitional period afterwards are regarded as pivotal moments in Poland's history. Perhaps because of the significance and the impact it had on countries like Hungary immediately afterward, the communist authorities did their best to conceal and censor historical documents about the events, effectively deleting any mention of the riots and the subsequent transition. The communists, like they did in Hungary, persecuted people who participated in the riots for years afterwards.

As mentioned earlier, a plane hijacking occurred on July 13, 1956, a few weeks after the protests in Poland began. Seven desperate Hungarians made a risky escape and were granted asylum in West Germany, but if the plan had failed, they would have been executed. Freedom from Soviet tyranny seemed like a pipe dream, but when Frank Iszak and his co-conspirators made it over the iron border the possibility of escape seemed within reach for many.

The 1953 East German Uprising was the spark the entire Eastern Bloc needed to think resistance was a possibility, the 1956 Polish uprising confirmed that they could attain more freedom from the Soviets, and Iszak's escape showed the slim prospect of freedom, but there were still more factors at play. There was also a revival in Hungarian nationalism in the fall of 1956. They felt more patriotic after the reburial of László Rajk [Rike] in early October, which was a complicated matter.

Firstly, Rajk was a communist who was hated by most citizens of Hungary who didn't favor communism. Rajk helped organize the despised AVH, and he held several positions within the government including the Minister of Foreign Affairs, Minister of Interior and was a member of the High National Council. He prohibited (or outright liquidated) almost 1,500 religious, nationalist, and maverick groups and establishments. Rajk even initiated some of the first Hungarian show trials, which were trials in which the judge and jury had already decided that the defendant was guilty without regard to evidence. Show trials were basically theatrical productions with rehearsed and memorized lines and were of course popularized in Russia and implemented all over the Soviet Union.

Rajk was popular among the communists, but when Rákosi felt threatened by Rajk's power or influence, he accused Rajk of being a western spy, held him in a prison camp, put him on a show trial, and executed him on October 15, 1949. The communists' constant betrayal of their own comrades (Rajk was not the only one) put a bitter taste in the mouths of many Hungarians.[16]

Rajk's wife, Julia, who heard his execution from her prison cell while she was imprisoned in the same facility, petitioned the government to give Rajk a state funeral and to have his body reburied in the Kerepesi Cemetery, the last resting place for Hungarian heroes. Initially, the government refused and offered her a payout of a handsome amount of money instead, but she refused the money, she just wanted respect for her late husband.

Despite being a hated figure during his life, he'd become a well-known victim of the communist regime and thus was transformed into a patriotic hero. He was reburied on October 6, 1956, and about 100,000 people attended to mourn Rajk in the pouring rain. There was an overwhelming sense of nationalism during and after the service. Proud Hungarians yearned for change; the fire of revolution was lit that day.

After the service, about 500 students marched to the Batthyány monument in Buda to protest against the communists. The monument was a memorial to the first Prime Minister of Hungary whom the Austrians executed in 1849, after the first Hungarian revolution. The student demonstration was mostly just shouting anti-communist rhetoric, and it was quickly deescalated by police, but it foreshadowed what would transpire later.

---

[16] Miklós Molnár, Hungarian author and professor who fled following the revolution, states that Rákosi kept a tape recording he had secretly made of Kádár while he interrogated Rajk during his imprisonment and torture, he kept the tape as "insurance" against any future issues that might arise with Kádár. The entire political system thrived on treachery.

CHAPTER 12
OCTOBER 23 - DAY ONE

Students from the Technical University of Budapest were eager to make change. They were invigorated by the recent success Poland had in gaining a little more freedom from the Soviets (they were still a satellite state, but they were granted a few concessions) as a result of the protest in the industrial town of Poznań.

On October 22, thousands of students congregated in a lecture hall to discuss their ideas for change, and during that meeting they created the Sixteen Points; a list of political and social reforms.[17] They planned a demonstration for the next day, and they wanted to recite their Sixteen Points on the radio for the whole country to hear during the protest.

In short, on October 23, the university students appealed to the citizens of Budapest to join them in a protest against the Soviet domination of Hungary. The protests began with about 20,000 student demonstrators in the afternoon and steadily grew throughout the day as more people heard about the protest. Just like in Poland, the spontaneous protests gained momentum rapidly by word-of-mouth. Impromptu and hastily planned demonstrations rarely grew so quickly, but the fact that several spontaneous demonstrations *had* formed in recent years deeply frightened the Soviets and threatened their control. It was a major oversight to underestimate the popular uprising.

An estimated 200,000 people joined the protest that had only been planned the day before in an age without instant access to spread and seek information. Soviet troops who witnessed the statue of Stalin being torn down said they thought there were about 100,000 people in the square around 9:30 p.m., but the protest continued growing. For reference, the population of Budapest in 1956 was about 1.7 million

---

[17] A complete description of the Sixteen Points can be found in the appendix.

people, therefore the protest had a turnout of up to 14% of the city's population.

On the morning of October 23, a short message announcing that the students were holding a demonstration later that day was given. Ernő Gerő, a slender man with a prominent nose and emotionless eyes, was the First Secretary of the Hungarian Workers' Party and thus the most powerful man in Hungary at the time. Gerő arrived back from his trip to Belgrade and was immediately informed about the radio announcement earlier that morning and he became enraged, as usual, and at first, he didn't want to allow the protest. His council convinced him that banning the demonstration may incite violence or that they might ignore the ban, seeing as how they were already in the midst of preparation. Gerő was encouraged to give more consideration to the Sixteen Points, which infuriated him further.

At 12:53 p.m., the music was interrupted, and an announcement was made on the radio that all public gatherings were prohibited in Budapest.

Precisely one and a half hours later, the radio was interrupted again with another announcement that public demonstration was no longer banned.

At about 3:00 p.m. the student protesters began their march. A group of about 8,000 students marched from the Buda side of the river Danube, and another group of about 12,000 from the Pest side,[18] and they met in front of the Hungarian Parliament Building on the east side of the city in District V.

As the evening progressed people marched through the streets and told anybody they saw, "If you're a Hungarian, join us!" People left work and school and saw the demonstrations and marches growing and joined them without any more information. It was simply the electricity of such a spontaneous and patriotic protest that made people want to participate, and when they found out it was a demonstration to demand reforms and try to drive the Soviets and the AVH away, they were glad they joined.

That evening, with the protesters gathered outside in the streets, a small group of student delegates met with Valéria Benke, a politician and the head of Kossuth Radio, accompanied by members of the AVH.

---

[18] Budapest is actually two separate cities, separated by the river Danube. Buda and Pest are on the west and east side of the river, respectively.

They said the radio should "belong to the people" and asked for time on the air to list their Sixteen Points, and for microphones in the streets so that protesters would be able to voice their opinions.

Benke communicated with her superiors in the Party who told her to negotiate with the protesters so they could avoid a riot, and eventually she agreed to letting them read aloud their demands. However, the crowd knew they'd been tricked by Benke (who acted alone, without orders or permission from her superiors) when they couldn't hear the student on the radio but could clearly see her speaking in front of them. She read the Sixteen Points into the microphone, assuming she was on the air, but those who were far away or on balconies above the crowds didn't hear the speaker on the radio, they heard music instead. The protesters became enraged by Benke's deception.

Gerő, uncompromising and capricious, went on the air to berate the protesters in an aggressive speech. Gerő called the young revolutionaries a mob that was trying to cause national subversion and provocation. He insisted that they wouldn't succeed, saying that the government condemned the protesters who wanted to "poison" the youth with "chauvinism."

Communist Party Members would later bicker with each other about who was to blame for provoking the protesters into becoming violent. Gerő believed that Nagy directly instigated the revolution in his speech given around 9pm on October 23 to the protesters, outside the Kossuth Radio building. Nagy insisted that the protests and uprising would have been preventable if only Gerő had handled the situation better.

Unsurprisingly, no newspapers reported on Nagy's speech and no official record exists, but a journalist in the crowd later recounted what Nagy said. He began with a greeting of "Comrades!" to the protesters, who shouted and booed at him. The communists had implemented the word "comrade." Nagy was unsure what to do, obviously upset by the initial reaction. Nagy, although moderate and anti-Stalinist, was still a communist at heart.

Imre Nagy was a bespectacled man with a receding hairline, a full mustache, and absolutely no sharp edges on his soft oval face. He began trying to change the political system and liberalizing Hungary when he was sworn in as the Prime Minister in his first official term in 1953.

Because of his previous attempts to make changes, and because he'd released political prisoners from Rákosi's time, the revolutionary college students wanted him to be the leader of the revolution. Nagy was too radical for the Stalinists within and abroad though. He and Rákosi continued to struggle with each other for power, and by 1955, Nagy was removed, and a man named András Hegedüs, a stooge for Rákosi and the Soviets, took office as Prime Minister. Hegedüs was yet another man with little hair on the top of his head, and very little neck. Unfortunately, Nagy was held responsible for Hungary's economic issues by many folks, but when the uprising began, he stepped in to lead the revolution.

His speech continued:

> Citizens, I affectionately salute those who are present here. All my esteem goes out to you young, democratic Hungarians who, by your enthusiasm, would help to remove the obstacles that stand in the way of democratic socialism. It is in negotiations in the bosom of the Party and by discussion of the problems that we will travel the road that leads to the settlement of our conflicts. We want to safeguard consti-tutional order and discipline. The government will not delay arriving at its decisions. (Sebestyen)

The crowd did not respond. His speech clearly was not what they wanted or needed to hear; it was a politician's way to tell the citizens to be complacent.

Nagy urged the quiet protesters to go home, but they heckled him, telling him that *he* should leave, and they'd all stay. He became flustered, the protesters were not happy with his speech, and not happy with him—the man they wanted as their leader.

Because he was stumped, Nagy began singing the Hungarian national anthem in a disastrously poor attempt to redirect the situation. Even his most ardent supporters knew that Nagy failed to rise to the occasion and completely missed the mark.

Nikita Khrushchev was a bald man with a weak jawline and small eyes, and he was the First Secretary of the Communist Party in the USSR after Stalin. Late at night on October 23 he organized a meeting of Soviets at the Kremlin in which they discussed what to do about the Hungarian protesters. By then, the violence (instigated by the AVH) had already begun at the radio building. The Soviets wanted to enact martial law and send in troops to control the situation, they thought it was going to take more force than the Polish uprisings had earlier that month which were not nearly as volatile.

Khrushchev agreed with the Minister of Defense, Georgy Zhukov, politician and diplomat, Vyacheslav Molotov, and First Deputy, Lazar Kaganovich that the Soviets should intervene in Hungary with force.

Only Anastas Mikoyan, the Deputy Chairman of the Council of Ministers of the Soviet Union, believed they should "let Imre Nagy into the Hungarian leadership and let him try to restore order." He warned, "if our troops go in, we will ruin things for ourselves. The Hungarians will restore order on their own," (Sebestyen).

Khrushchev agreed to put Nagy back into power and to remove Rákosi because it was clear that one of Hungary's main grievances was Rákosi, and by removing him and appointing Nagy they hoped to appease the protesters. Mikoyan, whose nose was both crooked and flattened and whose laugh lines were so deep he looked friendly, was sent to Budapest in order to supervise that transition of power and to report back to the Kremlin. Several other communists were sent as well, some were incognito to spy on the others, to make sure that everybody would do their job correctly. Spying on each other was par-for-course with the Soviets.

Meanwhile in Budapest, protesters tore down the statue of Stalin the Great Teacher. The bronze statue was 8 meters tall and sat atop a large limestone plinth with several stairs leading up to a carved relief of Hungarian working-class people welcoming Stalin. The entire monument stood 25 meters tall and about the same in width. Students and industrial workers at first tried to tear the statue down with rope and brute force, then by tying the rope to trucks, neither of which worked. Then, welders went to fetch their supplies and returned with acetylene torches and oxygen tanks to melt the bronze enough to topple over. They began torching the statue's knees and soon were able to pull the statue's body down enough to snap at the knees, leaving only the boots behind on the monument. Stalin's body fell, his head broke off and rolled, and the crowd surged. They began calling the monument "Boots Square." Protesters tied the statue to a truck and dragged Stalin's body around the streets to further desecrate his memory.

Unfortunately, when protesters go rogue and begin vandalizing statues or buildings, it ruins the reputation of the revolution. Some protesters broke into the *Szabad Nep* (Free People) offices, the communist propaganda newspaper. University students broke into the official bookstore for the *Szabad Nep* and began destroying the printed rubbish they'd grown tired of being fed. They threw the communist propaganda into a pile in the street and set fire to it.[19]

Several blocks away, enraged protesters tried breaking into the Kossuth Radio building in order to go on the air like they were promised, but the secret police were waiting inside. The students who got inside the building first were apprehended and held hostage by the AVH within. Students outside started demanding for their classmates to be released, but the AVH only spoke in violence. At first, the protesters tried bashing in the door, but resorted to throwing bricks into the windows, which worked.

The secret police threw teargas at the protesters, which backfired on them when the smoke went right back into the building they were inside through the broken windows. Then they fired warning shots into the sky, and soon fired at the protesters and several unarmed protesters, most of whom were students, were killed almost instantly, some were shot in the back as they were running away.

When the AVH began killing protesters in the streets, hell began to break loose. Hungarian troops were ordered to the scene to crush the resistance and restore the peace, but they did the opposite, the revolution had already begun.

Colonel László Zolomy's company arrived first and when he realized the protesters were unarmed and there were several casualties already, he gave the order to his men to do nothing unless the protesters tried entering the radio building after it had already been vandalized. He was later imprisoned for his actions, or lack thereof, during the "Battle for the Budapest Radio."

Lieutenant-Colonel Janos Solymosi who commanded the Piliscsaba Tank Regiment brought 14 tanks and 17 trucks of troops and

---

[19] After the first night of protesting, a handful of independent "newspapers" popped up, some said there were upwards of a dozen. The independent newspapers distributed information about the freedom fighters and the labor strikes to the population in order to spread accurate, non-communist controlled, information.

upon arriving at the scene declared that his troops would not fire upon the protesters. Several soldiers joined the protesters and fought against the AVH, which helped the resistance immensely. The soldiers who defected risked death or life imprisonment when the revolution was over, but truth be told they didn't have much to lose in the first place. The People's Army of Hungary was loyal to the people, not to the regime.

The demonstrators were unarmed, but after the Soviets began firing, they quickly gathered weapons and returned to the streets to fight for their freedom. The Hungarian soldiers who abandoned their duties to the military and became freedom fighters did so because in reality, they were just young people who'd been conscripted to the military, but they had the same sentiments as the protesters. And, since they had access to the munitions warehouses, they helped supply the other fighters with weapons.

Sándor Kopácsi, the Chief of Police in Budapest who commanded 1,200 officers, also played a pivotal role in the revolution. Kopácsi was an average looking man with a full head of hair and he would later be named Righteous Among Nations by Yad Vashem for his anti-fascist activism and his family's work in assisting Jewish people during WWII. The Minister of the Interior, Lászlo Piros, asked how the police would contain the protests earlier that afternoon, he explained that his men weren't equipped with riot gear and that if the students really wanted to protest there would be no stopping them—that wasn't what Piros wanted to hear. Kopácsi secretly sympathized with the resistance, he knew that he would disobey the orders to suppress the protests as long as they were peaceful (which, the vast majority of the 200,000 protesters were until the AVH began killing them).

Kopácsi abandoned his duty to the Party and joined the revolution. Since he had access to the weapons storage that the police used, he began handing out guns and ammunition to the freedom fighters. There were also two military academies in Budapest, the Zrinyi and the Petőfi, and they also emptied out their munitions stores which included a fair number of guns and grenades and a handful of submachine guns. On Csepel Island in the Danube River there was a building called the United Lamp Factory, it was a cover for an arms factory, and later in the evening, industrial employees took control of the factory and distributed at least 1,000 rifles to the freedom fighters.

CHAPTER 13
OCTOBER 24 - DAY TWO

Nobody should be under the impression that the revolution was waged solely in Budapest, nor should they forget that nothing happens in a vacuum. The revolution didn't just happen out of nowhere by "counterrevolutionary reactionaries" as the Soviets claimed, even if the warfare was spontaneous.

Workmen in industrial jobs and peasants in the countryside joined the revolution immediately upon hearing about events in Budapest. In fact, on October 23, the residents of Debrecen heard the news of the uprising beginning, and they too began ripping the red stars off of buildings, flags, trolleys, and anywhere else they would find the emblem. At some time during the first few days in Miskolc some Russians were attacked by protesters and an army car was pushed into the river. In Cegléd, about 5,000 joined the resistance and disarmed the police. People everywhere found their courage and in places like Lovas, Balinka, and Szombathely the industrial workers demanded that the Russians leave.

On October 24, the factory workers in Győr protested and demolished a war memorial that the Soviets had erected, and they broke into the prison to release political prisoners. The AVH killed four of the protesters when they began firing and they wounded many more. The Győr police and locally stationed Hungarian army troops joined the resistance and forced the AVH to surrender.

Demonstrations were held in all major cities and many minor ones, too, and the general strike which began on the second day of the revolution spread far and wide.

On the morning of October 24, the burning radio building was won by the revolutionaries after battling all night. During the night the Soviets sent in thousands of troops and stationed them outside government buildings and blocked streets and bridges that accessed Budapest. The resistance fighters created barricades of their own out of random things like barrels and pallets, overturned cars, really anything they could find that could hold up when stacked. From behind those barricades, they threw Molotov cocktails[20] and fired at the Soviets, and for a few days it looked like they were in the lead even with their rudimentary machinery and simple tactics.

Throughout the day the Soviets sent in a total of 20,000 troops, 1,100 tanks, 185 heavy guns and 159 planes. The Soviets were completely unprepared for the guerrilla warfare they were about to face. A disorderly band of rebels with nothing left to lose and little memory of freedom, who gathered weapons from dead bodies and made Molotov cocktails in a few seconds, fearlessly waged war on the Soviets. The Hungarians had the advantage of knowing the city better than the foreign troops and knew that the tanks couldn't navigate many of the narrow streets or alleyways where the freedom fighters barricaded themselves. The Soviets didn't order their troops to combat the insurgents on the streets face-to-face which would risk casualties on their side, so they fought from the relative safety of their tanks, and they weren't as quick or nimble as teenagers with an incendiary bomb who could make a mad dash from a hiding spot and disarm a tank with an explosion.

It was a highly disorganized revolution, with very few leaders, very few plans, and the only battle strategy many of them used was fearlessness. Many of the freedom fighters were teenagers or young adults in their twenties, some kids still in elementary school even built barricades, ran messages between groups, or assembled Molotov cocktails if they couldn't lift a rifle. The battles they engaged in were

---

[20] Molotov cocktails are named after Vyacheslav Molotov, an Old Bolshevik Soviet foreign minister who started the propaganda during the Winter War of 1939 in which he stated that the incendiary bombs the Soviets dropped over Finland were actually "airborne humanitarian aid" of food packages for the starving Finns. The Finns coined the term Molotov cocktail to describe the type of incendiary bomb created from a glass bottle, fuel, and a string or rope sticking out of the cap which would be lit on fire before throwing and would explode and ignite the target. The Finns called the "airborne humanitarian aid" food packages "Molotov's breadbasket," and the incendiary bombs made from (usually) a wine bottle were dubbed Molotov cocktails, which paired with the breadbaskets.

small, and the main goal of the revolution wasn't to win battles or cause harm to the opponent—although that did play a part—it was to keep fanning the flame of resistance. They fed off each other's energy and simply holding out just a little bit longer against the Soviets gave people hope that the revolution was worthwhile.

At 4:30 on the morning of October 24, the Budapest Radio played a message:

> Fascist and reactionary elements have launched an armed attack against our public buildings and against the forces of law and order. In the interests of re-establishing law and order, all assemblies, meetings and demonstrations are forbidden. Police units have been instructed to deal severely with troublemakers and to apply the law in all its force.

This message was repeated every half an hour. Later, they put an addendum on that message: "The Soviet soldiers are risking their lives to protect the peaceful citizens of Budapest and the tranquility of the nation," (Sebestyen).

Overnight, the terms freedom fighter and revolution began circling. In Pest, the Hungarians had already gotten their hands on thousands of rifles and several machine guns from the munitions factory and military compounds. In Buda, a group built barricades to fortify Széna Square, a busy area of the city which would become one of the main locations of the revolution. There were several bases where the freedom fighters convened but there were four major bastions: Széna Square, Báross Square, Tompa Street, and the Corvin Cinema and adjoining Corvin Passage.

The Corvin Cinema was an impeccable location to use as a stronghold for guerrilla warfare. The street, Corvin köz, was a loop, and therefore blockaded easily at the entrance and exit, and the Corvin group freedom fighters acquired up to twelve tanks to surround their fortress with. They also had access to secret passageways and tunnels underneath the cinema which connected to other streets in the area; it gave them a major advantage over the Soviets who couldn't drive their tanks close enough and wouldn't get out of their tanks to fight face-to-face. The freedom fighters were able to pop up out of the corridors to make a quick attack, then disappear again. The Russians literally could not see them coming, and having that advantage boosted morale among revolutionaries.

Another advantage of the Corvin stronghold was the fuel pump behind the Cinema which they could use to make Molotov cocktails and refuel their vehicles. Not to mention the Kilián Barracks was located directly across the street from the cinema. The Kilián Barracks was a four-story, 30,000 square meter building that was built in the 1840s as a barracks for the military. It was a fortress in the middle of the city. At the time, it housed about 900 military conscripts, who allowed the freedom fighters into the barracks and supplied them with weapons (witnesses said there were hardly any weapons there, perhaps 30 pistols and a dozen machine guns).

The fact that the Hungarian military was welcoming and joining the resistance alarmed the Soviets. Colonel Pál Maléter of the Hungarian army was sent in to take control of the barracks, but that backfired.

Colonel Maléter was 39, he had a prominent jawline, an incredibly wide forehead, and heavy, expressive eyebrows, which combined gave him one of the most unique faces in all of Hungary. His men, and most people who met him, admired him. When he arrived at the Kilián Barracks with 5 tanks and his men, he saw dead teenagers on the streets, disabled Soviet tanks blocked his way, and he heard gunfire everywhere. He realized that the freedom fighters weren't fascists, they were mostly teenagers and students, and they lay wounded and dead on the streets, so he ordered his men to use whatever doors they could remove as improvised stretchers for the wounded.

Maléter told the Minister of Defense that he was joining the insurgents, and many criticized his decision. He said "This was the moment I knew I would have to make a decision that would change my life. Once in the barracks, it was clear to me that those fighting for their freedom were not bandits, but loyal sons of Hungary," (Sebestyen).

After being shot at, the protesters went on the defensive; some immediately joined the fight, but some would join a group for a battle or two and then go home. The strength of the freedom fighters is unknown, eyewitnesses say there were up to 26,000 civilians who participated in the Hungarian Revolution at some point, and nearly 2,000 military conscripts who joined the revolution instead of supporting the communist regime.

Budapest had about one fifth of the entire population, but the revolution didn't stop at the city limits. Soon, Hungarians everywhere began protesting and formed a general strike in solidarity with the resistance. In industrial areas, the workers who were supposed to be the foundation of the communist society were quite determined to support the revolution, as well. Most workers went on strike, but the transportation, gas, and electric employees continued working in order for the revolution to continue.

In an area called "Red" Csepel, a southern district of Budapest, the industrial employees took over the factories, and witnesses said all but 240 of the 15,000 workmen from the Csepel industrial district joined the revolution. Out of those 240, about 200 of them were assigned to guard the factories against sabotage, but they may not have directly participated in the fighting; therefore, only about 40 industrial workers remained loyal to the communists.

Farmers outside of Budapest even arranged food deliveries to the freedom fighters and managed the collective farms on their own without the farm managers whom the Soviets appointed. The social and political reform they hoped for included the ability to control their own farms and sell their own products and goods as cooperative farms, rather than having the Soviets force farmers into a state-run farm. They passed along messages to each other and organized the resistance almost immediately; they told each other not to be fooled if the Soviets wanted them to surrender and lay down their arms.

Chapter 14
October 25 - Day Three, "Bloody Thursday"

Between October 24 and 25, 14,000 more Soviet troops arrived along with 250 more tanks, by then a small army of at least 34,000 troops and 1,350 tanks had been sent in. During a stand-off between the Russians in their tanks and a group of nervous protesters on the ground, a few students bravely climbed onto the tanks to speak with the Russians. They'd printed out flyers to distribute which said: "Russian friends. Do not shoot! They have tricked you. You are not fighting against counter-revolutionaries. We Hungarians want an independent, democratic Hungary. You are not shooting at fascists but at workers, peasants and university students," (Kovago).

Remarkably, the Russians were convinced, they agreed not to fire upon the Hungarians, and they talked amicably; they felt that the revolutionary demands were justified. The Russians offered to escort them to the Parliament where a protest was being held, so students climbed onto the tanks, and they proceeded towards Parliament. It was one of the most unique and awe-inspiring sights of the revolution, a Hungarian flag had even been mounted to the front tank of the procession.

There was already a demonstration of several thousand people happening in Kossuth Square, outside of the large neo-Renaissance Ministry of Agriculture building, and the even bigger neo-Gothic Parliament building. Even though demonstrations were banned under martial law, the government and police did not seem concerned. The Russian tanks guarded the building, sharpshooters sat on the roof of the Ministry of Agriculture, and the AVH tried to disperse some protesters, but the effort to stop the demonstration was minimal. They were peaceful, but they were calling for the dismissal of Gerő and other Stalinists which the Soviets labeled as a direct threat and incitement to terrorism. Survivors said the mood of the demonstration on October 25 was hopeful and light, and then without warning it became a bloody massacre.

It is speculated that the crowds from several simultaneous demonstrations had been corralled into that square on purpose. They were packed so tightly in and Russian tanks and armored cars blockaded the streets around the square. The crowd was so large that not everyone heard when the first bullets were shot at them. The AVH officers were likely the first to fire their machine guns from their positions on the roof of the Ministry of Agriculture into the crowd of unarmed civilians, and then the Russian tanks began firing at them from at least two points on the ground. The protesters were surrounded, many were crowded up against the walls of the buildings around Kossuth Square and tried entering the buildings for shelter only to find that the doors were locked and shots were coming from within, as well.

Some of the Soviets mistook the firing from within the buildings as enemy-fire, and they fired back. Survivors from the crowd remembered seeing a Russian machine-gunner aim at the top of the Ministry building and toward the ground-level of the building. It is also possible that some of the Soviets did not participate in the massacre, whether or not they were omitted from the plan, not all were shooting at the protesters. Nevertheless, the massacre of unarmed peaceful protesters was planned and executed with the participation from the Soviets, the AVH, and possibly the Hungarian border guard units.

Witnesses say they fired on the crowd for about a half an hour, in two fifteen-minute bursts of heavy fire. All the surviving civilians had fled, but some hid and watched from afar as the Soviets and Hungarians worked together to get rid of the bodies. They saw tanks drive over bodies, trucks plowing the bodies to move them, Soviets stacking bodies in heaps behind the buildings. Eyewitness estimates were consistent with at least 800 to 1,000 dead. They buried people in mass graves in the cemetery, they took people's identity papers away so that the dead couldn't be accounted for, and some may have been cremated as they were piled up behind an old crematorium.

It's referred to as "Bloody Thursday" and it was one of the largest public massacres in Europe after World War II. Published estimates of the number of people killed range from about 20 to 1,000, but the best estimate is between 800 and 1,000. There are a lot of reasons why an exact number isn't possible to settle on, but the most important thing to remember is that the Soviets were in charge, and the Soviets always tried to hide rather than publicize the truth about their actions.

The Hungarian government wouldn't even talk about the massacre, they pretended it didn't happen and then they walked by the bullet holes in the walls for years.[21] However, a report prepared during the revolution by László Toth, the Chief of Staff of the Army, declared, "The Soviet troops received the order to liquidate the protest in front of Parliament. This they did. . . Soviet soldiers opened fire on the rebels," (Sebestyen).

Most of his communications to the Kremlin were public, but that report remained a secret for decades. The Soviet troops most likely received their orders to liquidate the square from Ivan Serov, the feared head of the Russian KGB. Serov had piercing ice-colored eyes, a tall forehead, wrinkles between his eyebrows that made him look deep in thought, and a habit of snapping his fingers in irritation. He wasn't far away from the massacre, having a meeting at the Communist Party headquarters, he was already irate that day about reports of the Russian soldiers giving the students a ride on their tanks, they were fraternizing with the enemy. A report about the demonstration at Parliament sent him over the edge and the report identified Serov as the one who ordered the Soviet soldiers to "clear the square."

The news of the massacre spread and changed the mood of the freedom fighters from excitement to rage. Protesters who survived the massacre became militias overnight, the fire was lit under them, and many went straight to the nearest group of freedom fighters, armed themselves with weapons, and began waging war on the Soviets and AVH. A few hundred other protesters marched to the American Legation building two blocks away from the site of the massacre and began shouting, begging, for American support and weapons to fight with, but their cries fell on deaf ears.

The freedom fighters went on the offensive; they acquired new locations for their bases, small streets or squares that they could defend easily, and developed new tactics to fight the Soviets. A banner was

---

[21] Today the wall has been replaced but silver bullets have been placed on the wall, at head height where they were originally, to memorialize the victims.

put outside the Corvin Cinema stronghold with the words "There are three Great Powers—the US, the USSR, and the Corvin group," (Sebestyen). At first, the Corvin group and Maléter's soldiers (he was in command of the Kilian Barracks across from the theater) argued about who would make decisions about operations, but when news of the massacre known as Bloody Thursday reached them, they put aside their differences to work together.

Within hours on October 25, the freedom fighters were able to take down three Russian tanks and capture two more tanks and an armored vehicle through a series of attacks using the passageways underground. Soon, Soviet tanks moved to the Corvin Cinema and Passage for the first large street battle, and when the Soviets retreated in defeat they left behind armor and equipment. Their loss raised the freedom fighters' hopes that they had the possibility to come out victorious, even if it was a remote possibility.

CHAPTER 15
OCTOBER 26 AND 27 - DAYS FOUR AND FIVE

As the revolution progressed everybody fell into a position that suited them best. Some carried messages back and forth between groups, nursing students and pharmacists tended to the wounded fighters, families made food for the fighters on the streets, and people who lived in apartments in Budapest welcomed fighters in for a rest or for a tactical position to shoot from.

Young children participated in the revolution by building road-blocks and barricades and making and distributing Molotov cocktails. In many of the groups the average freedom fighter was a teenager, very few were older than 25, most were in their late teens and early twenties. Leaders like the revered "Uncle" Szabó who commanded the Széna Square group were of the mindset that "if they want to fight, they are old enough," (Sebestyen). Szabó was respected and people praised him for how much he truly cared about the kids who joined his group.

A leader of the Corvin group, Gergely Pongrácz, was later interviewed in the "Cold War Interviews" published on the National Security Archive. He said:

> The average age didn't reach 18, but we had over there 12-13-14-year-old kids. Many times I sent them home, and they didn't want to leave. . . the patriotism keeps them over there, the ideals keep them over there, because they want a free Hungary. That's why they stayed with us. . . We had a few older fighters. . . it was maybe only a dozen older than me. I was twenty-four. (Pongrácz)

Nagy failed to rise to the occasion, and he greatly disappointed the Hungarians with any actions he took because they were too little and too late. By Saturday, October 27, more than 325 civilians had died in the fighting (excluding the massacre outside of the Ministry of Agriculture which took 800-1000 people), 2,200 were wounded, and hundreds of Soviet tanks and thousands of troops still roamed the streets of Budapest. Negotiations and conversations between communists and the freedom fighters, including the Hungarian military leaders like Maléter who had joined the revolution, got them nowhere.

The Soviets and freedom fighters both won and lost battles, and there were a few in which nobody emerged victorious. However, any battle in which freedom fighters survived felt like a victory. The Soviets were also low on supplies and morale, they had to get food and supplies from local shops which made them targets out in the open, all of which contributed to their poor performance.

About 2,000 men from the Hungarian military joined the resistance, but the Minister of Defense (during the revolution only) Lieutenant-General Károly Janza, wanted his soldiers to "liquidate the troublemakers" and would have court-martialed any troops who disobeyed. Unfortunately for him, his troops would not have obeyed his orders. The Hungarian troops were, for the most part, loyal to their people, not to the puppet-government.

Colonel-General Lajos Gyurko pledged to the communists that he would command his troops to fight the rebels and suppress the revolution. He commanded his men to shoot demonstrators who planned a march, but luckily the protest was called off. However, a few days later, about 500 people demonstrated in Tiszakécske [Tiza-kech-ka], a small township. They, like many other protesters, tore down communist symbols around the town, they had a revolutionary flag and they sang the national anthem. Gyurko ordered a MiG fighter jet to strafe the civilian protesters. Seventeen were killed and 110 were wounded, and later that day Gyurko ordered two more aerial attacks on other towns that may have been planning a protest.

The majority of the fighting happened in Budapest in several main locations throughout the city, but the protests happened across the country, even in little townships. The citizens were on the freedom fighters' side, and that scared the Soviets.

The Nagy government hadn't made much of a difference, but on Saturday, October 27, Nagy met with Soviet emissaries and János Kádár, the newly elected General Secretary of the Hungarian Workers'

Party. Kádár looked perpetually dejected, but he was a snake in the grass; he was a bald man with a wide dimpled chin and deep wrinkles. The emissaries wanted a ceasefire, but Kádár then offered a solution of a political deal in which everybody would get more of what they wanted. They wanted to dissolve the AVH but keep Soviet troops in Hungary long-term, and they said they were willing to offer amnesty for all of the freedom fighters. This seemed like the best possible solution, and they agreed to it, but they also needed to get Khrushchev to agree to it. But they were unaware that the Soviets were planning one last large assault on Budapest.

CHAPTER 16

OCTOBER 28 - DAY SIX

Over 50 Russian tanks moved into place on the morning of Sunday, October 28, with the goal of quashing the resistance once and for all. They planned to destroy two of the revolutionaries' main fortresses, and the locations of much of the fighting in Budapest: the Kilian Barracks and the Corvin Cinema across the street. They had secondary targets on several more strongholds; they hoped that their attack would defeat those strongholds and demoralize the rest of the freedom fighters.

Nagy was adamantly against the destruction of the revolutionary bases, as it would have also destroyed the apartments and business in Budapest, as well. He even threatened to resign as the Prime Minister if the assault was carried out. Officials discussed the matter and the Russians wanted to make a deal, like they did in Poland; a compromise at best. Their negotiations achieved very little.

Many Hungarian soldiers were also opposed to participating in the destruction of the city's buildings just to seek out the freedom fighters. The Hungarian military withdrew over one third of their troops, then unexpectedly, they proceeded with a deliberately weak attack against Maléter's small army at the Barracks for two hours. The Hungarian soldiers who had not officially defected to the revolutionaries took the loss, retreated, and a ceasefire agreement was made.

Agreeing to a ceasefire was embarrassing for the Soviets, they blamed the Hungarian army, primarily, for their lack of loyalty. The world's second leading superpower, the USSR, had been humbled and defeated by ragtag groups of guerrilla fighters, most of whom were students and the working-class. The Russian troops and tanks retreated, leaving their dead soldiers in the streets. By then, about 500 Russian soldiers had been killed. Meanwhile, the Hungarians began giving the fallen freedom fighters funerals in the streets.

Nagy, always a day behind, praised the freedom fighters and embraced the revolution after the ceasefire was called. He had to keep his reputation as a leader of the people, one who would make sacrifices for the cause of freedom. Nagy still had the trust of the Communist Party at the Kremlin, but he needed to perform a juggling act in order to maintain that trust, *and* to maintain the trust of his people.

Yuri Andropov, the Soviet ambassador to Hungary from 1954 to 1957, tied up one loose end. On October 23, it was Gerő who called for Russian troops to reinforce Hungary to quell the protests. They were willing and ready, but Khrushchev needed an official request in writing saying that Hungary asked for Russian troops to enter. No written request was made, but the Russians had still entered Hungary. Without that written request, the Soviets couldn't have legally sent Russian reinforcements; they would otherwise be invading unlawfully as an aggressor. Even more, the United Nations Security Council was convening soon to discuss these recent events. Andropov tried to convince Nagy to sign a letter, backdated to October 23, requesting Soviet intervention; Nagy refused, and he hadn't been appointed as Prime Minister until later that night so it wouldn't have made sense for him to sign the letter. So, Andropov went to András Hegedüs to collect a signature on the letter. Hegedüs was the Prime Minister from April 18, 1955, until October 24, 1956, when Nagy took over, and he wasn't well liked within Hungary. Hegedüs signed the letter, then he immediately fled to the Soviet Union for sanctuary.

CHAPTER 17
OCTOBER 29 - DAY SEVEN

On Monday, October 29, life almost looked like it was back to normal; the fighting had died down to just a few shots that rang out here or there, people went to work and to the grocery stores, and, except for a few pockets, even the capital seemed calm. It almost looked like they'd gotten away with it. Maléter even put his faith in the new government and stood behind the ceasefire, commanding his men and the freedom fighters to lay down arms against the Soviets and not to stir up any trouble.

The Hungarians needed to devise a plan to keep the peace so the ceasefire would remain in place. Sándor Kopácsi, Budapest's Police Chief, was delegated the task to create a National Guard that would replace the AVH but would be made up of a mixture of the freedom fighters, police and military. Kopácsi wanted Béla Király to be the new commander of the National Guard, and so did Király's old students from the military academy.

Béla Király, a 43-year-old with an average build and beady eyes, was a former Major-General in the Hungarian military and had spent five years in prison after being sentenced to death for being a spy by the Rákosi regime.[22] He'd been released from prison in September, and in October he'd had a surgery and was confined to a hospital bed for several weeks where some of his old students from the military academy would go see him. On October 22 they told him of the plans for the protest the next day, and later that week they told him of the

---

[22] It must be reiterated that whenever the communists accused and convicted somebody of being a spy it wasn't likely that they were actually a spy. In order to sabotage their adversaries (and even their "friends") they would accuse them of being a spy for the west, and evidence wasn't required in order to convict them.

destruction and chaos that had ensued. On October 29, he snuck out of the hospital with a few armed freedom fighters and was escorted to the police headquarters where he accepted the position of commander -in-chief of the Revolutionary army from Kopácsi. There were some in the room who opposed Király's ascension to the position, one man who'd even been one of the judges at his trial and still believed him to be a spy and a disgraced ex-Major-General, but still more vouched for him.

Kopácsi and Király began planning the National Guard, and interestingly, Maléter was not exactly thrilled about the idea of letting the freedom fighters into the National Guard in order to replace the AVH. He'd led the freedom fighters, he knew their passion and some of their abilities, but it was risky business.

An important moment during the revolution was when hoards of AVH files were discovered. The secret police destroyed many of the incriminating files that existed, but they couldn't destroy it all and they left thousands upon thousands of files. Many people sought out the files on themselves or on their friends or family to know what had been said about them. Not only did many find files about themselves, but they also learned who in their family or circle of friends and acquaintances had been paid informants for the AVH. Informants could make good money by spying for the secret police, some were paid about 1,500 fornits a month for spying, which was much more than most working-class people would make from their salary.

CHAPTER 18
OCTOBER 30 - DAY EIGHT
THE REPUBLIC SQUARE MASSACRE

The most notorious battle of the Hungarian Revolution happened on Tuesday, October 30, as the Russian tanks and troops were evacuating Budapest. Crowds lined the streets to watch as the detested Red Army left the city, it was a joyous occasion, and many believed it signified their victory.

A queue was forming outside of a small grocery store to collect their rations, and as they waited, they watched a truck make a special delivery of fresh meat to the Communist Party headquarters across the street in Republic Square. Ironically, food was more available during the revolution than it had been before because food exports from Hungary halted, but the sight of the communists still receiving special treatment angered them.

The shoppers told the nearest group of freedom fighters about the special delivery, and the fighters promptly marched into the building. They demanded to know why the communists were still getting the same favoritism, and inside the building they recognized AVH officers, which ignited the fight. The AVH had disbanded, per the agreements made the previous day, but they were still hanging around the Communist Party headquarters and receiving special treatment. By then, the tanks that had been protecting the building had already left, leaving it defenseless.

After the first shots, the freedom fighters retreated when they realized how outnumbered they were, but they returned with more support for the battle. At first, they tried negotiating for a surrender, but it soon turned into a shootout. All of the civilians in the headquarters called every government office they could to beg for help.

Five tanks from the Hungarian military were sent in to control the situation, but two never arrived. The three tanks which made it to Republic Square, later than expected, saw one tank already on the scene and shooting at the building. Not realizing that the tank was operated by freedom fighters, the three tanks also began firing at the Communist Party headquarters, assuming that that was what they'd been sent there to do rather than protecting the building. It was the largest blunder of the revolution.

The building was crumbling as the battle ensued, nearly every window had been shot out and there were gaping holes in the walls. Freedom fighters had been holding AVH officers and Communist Party staff hostage inside the building as it was being assaulted by several confused tanks. A man by the name of Mező managed to escape the building with a white shirt on a pole, saying he surrendered and begging not to be shot, but was promptly executed.

A French journalist, Jean-Pierre Pedrazzini, one of several Western journalists who'd flocked to Budapest to document the war zone, was shot by accident when he stepped out in front of a tank for a photo—he did not live. A Czech-born American photojournalist for Life Magazine, John Sadovy, and Italian photographer Mario De Biasi were on the scene as well. They witnessed AVH officers running from or being escorted out of the building for their execution. Twenty-three AVH officers were killed in front of the Communist Party headquarters that day, some swiftly, others in brutal beatings. Many civilians in the building managed to escape, but several had been in the battle and taken to the hospital by the time the lynchings were over.

When the three-hour siege was over, the freedom fighters acquired construction vehicles and began digging holes in the streets. They were certain that there were secret dungeons and tunnels underneath the street and the Communist Party headquarters where political prisoners were being held. It wasn't an altogether unreasonable suspicion, but they spent several hours digging, made it nearly 10 meters deep, and came up empty handed.

After the massacre, Khrushchev and other senior officials in the Communist Party thought that it had been a mistake to withdraw from Hungary and didn't wish to maintain the ceasefire. The unrest in Hungary might have spilled into other Soviet satellite states, and they didn't want to appear weak by withdrawing from Hungary.

In Warsaw, Poland, about 300,000 people had organized a demonstration to show support for Hungary's Revolution, which was by far the largest protest, but other demonstrations happened in various cities in Romania, Czechoslovakia and Transylvania. Not to mention that throughout the summer and fall of 1956, several countries were expressing dissatisfaction with the Soviet Union, even within the USSR. Georgia, a satellite state, had been put under martial law to quell the riots, but when the Hungarian Revolution began, Georgians rioted yet again.

The Russians formed a plan for the Soviets to remain in power in Hungary by invading again, and they decided who to choose as the puppet-leader for after the revolution. Nagy was appointed Prime Minister on the first night of the revolution, but the Russians needed somebody more loyal to them. They believed that they'd only need three days to completely disarm the revolutionaries and establish their control once more.

Reportedly, Khrushchev had trouble sleeping that night, worried about his position and the Soviet Union's grasp on power in the Eastern Bloc. Mikoyan, the only Soviet who believed that Nagy was the right man for the job of Prime Minister, and several other communists, were still on the scene in Budapest and their reports back to the Kremlin were grim. They reported back about the bloody massacre at the Communist Party headquarters and of growing anti-Soviet rhetoric in the country, they feared that Hungary would break away from their grip, leading other countries in the Eastern Bloc to do the same. They urged the Soviet magistrates to send military reinforcements, which greatly pleased those who had always wanted a full-scale invasion of Hungary, such as Ivan Serov, the man who ordered the massacre on Bloody Thursday.

Hungarians watched as tanks left Budapest heading back to Russia on October 30, then they watched as more tanks rolled in not too long afterwards. People also saw tanks heading towards the western border with Austria, which was curious to them; the Soviets were mobilizing troops to the border in order to control it.

Also on October 30, the Prince Primate József Mindszenty of the Catholic Church was released from his confinement—he spent five years in prison and two under house-arrest. Cardinal Mindszenty was one of the most famous political prisoners of the time and he returned home quietly without any fanfare to avoid inciting violence in a crowd or angering the anti-religion Soviets.

There were between 7,500 and 8,000 more prisoners who were released throughout Hungary during the revolution. Vác was one of the most notorious prisons, a fortress in northern Hungary, where many had died due to mistreatment; liberating the prisoners from Vác during the revolution was a high point for their achievements. Many foreigners, some of whom Hungary never admitted to having, were locked up in prisons across the country, including Vác, and after liberation they were able to escape. One notable prisoner was Edith Bone, a British doctor who'd been arrested while at the airport trying to go home in 1949. Her father was Hungarian, and she was a communist, but after realizing the horrors of Stalinism and Rákosi, she wished to leave. She was charged with espionage, put in solitary confinement for years, and stripped of her identity—she wasn't even given a prisoner ID. When the British inquired as to her whereabouts, Hungary proclaimed that Bone had left on her flight and was not in Hungary anymore.

CHAPTER 19

OCTOBER 31 - DAY NINE

In Hungary, the new cabinet of ministers met to discuss their next course of action amidst the rumors that the Russians were moving their troops back in instead of retreating. The Russians' tactics confused the Hungarians, and their meeting didn't get them anywhere. Nagy didn't want the press getting a hold of the rumors that the Russians were invading so as not to scare the public. Soon, Nagy went to see Mikoyan and his partner Suslov off, they were leaving for Moscow. He asked them point blank why the Russians were seen coming back into Hungary and they explained that the military's movements were routine, it wasn't an invasion, and there was nothing to worry about. Nagy believed them, he believed each time the Russians lied to his face, and he believed that the Hungarians had come out victorious in the revolution.

Once back in Moscow, Mikoyan tried in vain to change the decision to invade Hungary, he argued with senior officials of the Soviet Union about stopping the invasion; he was completely against it. He thought it would be a mistake to invade and was a little bitter that he'd been made to spend a week in Hungary to oversee and negotiate all for nothing. Instead, he advocated for finding another way to come to peaceful terms because a full-scale assault on Hungary would tarnish the Soviet Union's image and would stir up new tensions in the Cold War, but they wouldn't listen. In fact, some of them revelled in Mikoyan's misery, some within the Kremlin disliked him and thought that the display of humanitarianism was weak.

In Budapest that night people celebrated with parties and danced in the streets that had been a war zone just hours prior. They rejoiced thinking that they'd won and that the Soviets would no longer oppress them. It was the calm before the storm.

CHAPTER 20
NOVEMBER 1 - DAY TEN

The country woke on November 1 to find that Russian tanks were returning, troops were flooding across the border from Ukraine and a line of 850 tanks was coming from the Czech border. They were about to face the Soviets' wrath, to become a lesson for any other Soviet-occupied country.

Nagy tried siphoning answers out of the Kremlin, but they were evasive, they ignored his calls and the ones who would speak to him were dodging questions about the invasion. Nagy threatened to withdraw Hungary from the Warsaw Pact and declare itself neutral, which was one of the goals the revolutionaries wanted anyways but doing it in a hasty scramble was tricky. The Warsaw Pact was signed in May of 1955 by the Soviet Union and seven Eastern Bloc republics, including Hungary. That pact was in direct opposition to NATO and bound the satellite states to the USSR.

Nagy announced that Hungary was leaving the Warsaw Pact, which was ultimately a long-term goal of the revolution. The Soviets knew that the growing unrest in Hungary was leading to their withdrawal from the pact, but they couldn't allow it, for it would give other countries within the Eastern Bloc the precedence to leave as well. Leaving the pact and declaring neutrality was a desperate attempt to seek help from western powers. If the Russians were to invade any one of their colonies that had signed the pact, it would be considered an internal affair, a family squabble, and no other country could come to their aid. However, as a neutral country Hungary might have received international support.

After the announcement that Hungary was leaving the Warsaw Pact, Khrushchev and other Soviets vacillated on their decision to invade while others continued to advocate to proceed with the planned military assault. Before the invasion, Khrushchev went on a confidential tour of Eastern capitals to meet with other communist leaders to discuss the situation. Even Mao Zedong, the First Chairman of the Chinese Communist Party and founder of the People's Republic of China, agreed that a quick military response was necessary to shut the Hungarian Revolution down and prevent other countries from revolting as well. Khrushchev then went on a "peacekeeping" mission to the satellite states to discuss the situation in Hungary, but also to reinforce the idea that if any country rebelled against them, they would not get away with it. He visited with the leaders of Poland, Romania, Czechoslovakia, Bulgaria, and Yugoslavia. Antonin Novotny of Czechoslovakia and Gheorghe Gheorghui-Dej of Romania offered Khrushchev their own troops to help crush the Hungarian revolution, but he refused. Josip Borz (Tito), the communist Prime Minister of Yugoslavia, persuaded Khrushchev to place János Kádár in the Prime Minister's position rather than Ferenc Münnich.

The Soviets were confident they could pull off the invasion without intervention from the west. At that time, the United States, Britain, and France were distracted by the Suez Canal Crisis in Egypt; their troops had invaded, and a war had begun. Not only that, but the United States was opposed to any confrontation with the Soviet Union and helping Hungary—neutral or not—could lead to another war with the Soviets.

Nagy hadn't thought to ask for international intervention until that point. He appealed to the United Nations to recognize Hungary as a neutral nation, which would mean that the great western powers of the world *could* defend its neutrality. Nagy also communicated with the United States, pleading for their intervention, but the requests were ignored because the US was preoccupied with the Suez Canal Crisis.[23]

That night, Nagy announced to the country that they were withdrawing from the Warsaw Pact. It was hopeful and emotional, but he wasn't optimistic that they could avoid the Russian invasion.

János Kádár recorded the following message to the population earlier that morning:

In their glorious uprising, our people have shaken off the

---

[23] Suggested reading: *Failed Illusions* by Charles Gati, and of course, *Twelve Days* by Victor Sebestyen.

Rákosi regime. They have achieved freedom for the people, and independence for the country [and the Hungarian Socialist Workers Party] would take part in elections and would break away from the crimes of the past once and for all. It will defend the honor and independence of our country against anyone. (Sebestyen)

But by the time the citizens heard his speech play on the radio that evening, he had already left the Parliament building, lied about where he was going, and gone to the Russians. He and Ferenc Münnich, another Hungarian communist, decided together to betray their people and side with the Russians. They both had high ambitions and were rewarded by the Soviets with high positions in politics, both served as Chairman of the Council of Ministers of the Peoples' Republic of Hungary[24] (Kádár served two terms in that position, before and after Münnich's term).

---

[24] "Chairman of the Council of Ministers" is the official title for the Prime Minister, otherwise known as the Premier.

CHAPTER 21
NOVEMBER 2 - DAY ELEVEN

Hungarians still wanted to believe that they had come out on top after the Revolution. The Russian tanks moving in were suspicious, but there was hardly any press coverage or official announcement that the Russians were invading so many didn't realize, or didn't want to believe, that they were about to be attacked. People went back to work, the strikes ended (temporarily), and officials assured the public that everything would be back to normal on the following Monday, November 5.

Nagy and Andropov continued arguing back-and-forth about the Russian military campaign, Nagy hurled accusations at Andropov who kept insisting that Hungary was not under attack—he was stalling, buying time. Nagy also spoke to Sándor Kopácsi that morning regarding the whereabouts of Ferenc Münnich (Kopácsi's boss) and János Kádár, but nobody could locate them because they had defected the night before. Things became more and more suspicious each day, but they had to keep the peace and make sure the public didn't do anything that might be construed as "anti-Soviet" so that negotiations could continue.

The Soviets at the Kremlin had to decide whom they were going to replace Nagy with after they crushed the Hungarian Revolution. Some thought Münnich would be a fit replacement, but ultimately Kádár was chosen by the Russians with the advice from the Yugoslavs who believed Kádár would resonate more with the Hungarians because he had been imprisoned and tortured while Münnich had lived a comfortable life.

Meanwhile, Russian tanks were approaching Budapest and the Soviets prepared for Operation Whirlwind which would completely stamp out the rebellion.

CHAPTER 22
NOVEMBER 3 - DAY TWELVE

The Russian tanks were closing in on Budapest and other towns where battles had ensued between the freedom fighters and Soviet troops. In Budapest, the center of the revolution, most people were carrying on with their lives like normal, unaware or unconcerned with the tanks that were closing in. November 3 was akin to a dying man who seemed healthy and happy the day before his death, but to everybody's surprise, his body gave out the very next day.

Back at the Kremlin, Kádár was interviewing for the position of Prime Minister in Hungary.[25] The interviews were essentially only a formality, as the Soviets had already chosen Kádár, and they could appoint anybody to any position they wished anyways. Kádár didn't want the government of Hungary to operate in the same way as before—as a puppet of the USSR. But he ultimately had no say in the declarations to establish a new government, everything was written by the Soviets including the speech Kádár would give to Hungarians upon his ascension.

In Budapest, the Soviets and the Hungarians negotiated for much of the day, and it seemed to be going well. Béla Király smelled the deception, and he warned Nagy, who still wanted to trust the Soviets at their word. Király fled to the United States after the revolution and in February of 1957 he told Life magazine about Russia's trickery:

---

[25] Kádár served as Minister of the Interior from 1948 to 1950, in 1951 he was imprisoned as a result of the political purges during the Rákosi regime, and Imre Nagy released Kádár from prison in 1954 during his first term as Prime Minister. When the Soviets removed Ernő Gerő from his position as General Secretary of the Party on October 25, 1956, Kádár replaced him and thus was a part of Nagy's government during the revolution, which he would betray by defecting to the Russians.

First, Russia will evacuate all her armed forces from Hungary. Second. . . the Russians want to leave by degrees. . . Third, the Hungarian garrisons must cease denying the Russians food and fuel. Fourth, the Russians are not prepared for a winter movement and the Hungarians must be patient; the troops will not be able to move until January 15. Lastly, they say the Russian army did not want to attack the Hungarians but only did what the Hungarian government asked. Therefore, the evacuation must not only be peaceful but friendly. The troops must leave in a festive air and the Hungarians must cheer them as they leave. (Aczel)

Maléter was also short-sighted, although less so than Nagy, and he trusted the Soviets at their word when he was invited to attend another round of negotiations in Csepel, the southern industrial district of Budapest, at 10 p.m. Several people warned him, including his wife, that it could be a trap—luring him out of Budapest at night to arrest or execute him so he couldn't lead the revolutionaries. Maléter didn't believe that there was anything to worry about, and even spoke on the phone to Király back in Budapest during his meeting with the Soviets and assured his colleagues that the talks were going smoothly. Then, around midnight, Soviet soldiers burst through the doors and placed Maléter and the other Hungarian officers there under arrest. Ivan Serov was behind the arrests.

At the very moment they were negotiating with Maléter for a peaceful resolution, the Soviets were organizing a barricade of thousands of tanks around Budapest in preparation for their full-scale invasion. It was Soviet treachery at its finest.

CHAPTER 23
NOVEMBER 4 - DAY THIRTEEN

General Király woke after midnight to the news that the Soviets were ready to attack, they'd been issued the order to move into Budapest at midnight. He rang Nagy to warn him that the Russians were about to begin a war with the Hungarians; he insisted that either he or Nagy make an immediate radio broadcast to tell the troops that war was imminent and to prepare themselves. Nagy refused to make the announcement and only he could give Király permission to make an announcement of war in his stead, but he also refused to permit Király from making that call.

Operation Whirlwind was already underway, but the Hungarian troops and freedom fighters weren't prepared to face the Soviet army that time. 150,000 Soviet troops from 10 divisions and 2,500 tanks were sent in to "restore peace," and up to 60,000 more were reportedly on stand-by just in case. Not only that, but 20,000 troops had been stationed up and down the Hungary-Austria border to prevent military aid from western powers getting in *if* they chose to (but it was unlikely they would intervene, and the Russians knew that). They went in equipped with anti-tank guns, each soldier had a submachine gun, they had everything they could possibly need including bazookas, walkie-talkies, armored vehicles, newer, more agile tanks, and even flame-throwers.

At 4 a.m. the codeword "Thunder" was given and then people began hearing explosions.

Király again called Nagy and "begged for the orders to open fire," but Nagy again refused.

"Calm down," Nagy said, "The Russian Ambassador is here in my office. He is calling Moscow right now. There is some misunder-standing. You must not open fire," (Aczel).

He rang Nagy again to let him hear the shelling outside his building, again urging Nagy to make the declaration that the Soviets were attacking. And again, Nagy was dismissive.

He called Nagy a fourth time a little later with information about the Russian tanks' movements in Budapest; they'd gotten past the defensive barrier to the capital. Nagy was curt and asked Király not to update him with any more reports, even though just hours before he had asked Király to continue updating him. Király thought it was strange that the Prime Minister didn't want reports from the commander-in-chief of the military about the invasion. Nagy wasn't concerned with the updates because he was on his way to the Yugoslav Embassy where he'd already taken up the offer of sanctuary. The Yugoslavs had agreed to "neutralize" Nagy and keep him isolated so the Soviets could invade, but he'd believed they were acting out of kindness rather than an ulterior motive.

By 5:20am, Nagy agreed to make a broadcast. "This is Imre Nagy speaking. Today at daybreak Soviet troops attacked our capital with the obvious intention of overthrowing the legal Hungarian democratic government. Our troops are in combat. The government is at its post," (Sebestyen).

Nagy's message to the people wasn't completely true though. The troops weren't in combat because they were largely unaware, because Nagy had refused to tell the troops to prepare for war. Not to mention that the military couldn't organize since the Soviets had arrested Maléter and his senior officers a few hours prior. And the government wasn't at its post, the government was splintered, and its head was going straight to the Yugoslav Embassy after his last broadcast to the people.

Andropov's bosses were pleased with his performance, he'd strung Nagy along by beating around the bush and lying in order to keep Nagy in the dark so that Hungary could be completely disarmed by the time the Soviets got there.

The Soviet soldiers began disarming the remaining groups of revolutionaries, who were desperately outnumbered. Small pockets of freedom fighters put up a decent fight for nearly a week, trying to give as much hell to the Soviets who thought they'd be able to crush the revolution in just a few days. The Hungarians had begun the revolution because they had everything to fight for, but by the end they had nothing left to lose. They were valiant, but the Soviets were brutal, and they knew the freedom fighter's tactics, so the element of surprise was lost. The Soviets demolished buildings and razed entire streets just to search for a few insurgents who remained in hiding, they would stop at nothing.

Many of the freedom fighters had already abandoned the fight on October 28, when the ceasefire was announced, so there were fewer to look for. Certainly, a task that 150,000 Soviet soldiers could have handled on foot, but instead they used their tanks to destroy the city. The tanks they'd brought for the finale were newer, smaller, and with heavier reinforcement than the ones that had been trying to maneuver in Budapest before; they were able to drive down smaller alleys whereas before the freedom fighters counted on tanks not being able to use those streets. The Soviets strafed the city from aircraft while blowing it to bits from the ground without any regard for the collateral damage.

Nagy's deputy Zoltan Tildy remained at the Parliament that morning, determined not to let the building fall to rubble.[26] The guards at the building asked what they should do, he told them that only the Defense Minister could give them orders to fight, he couldn't, but he did give them advice to send an officer holding a white flag to the Soviets.

Around 8:30 a.m., Soviet officers arrive at the Parliament to speak to Tildy, demanding that the Hungarians sign a document of surrender. The document needed to be signed by Istvan Dobi, a communist, a former Prime Minister and Chairman, and the President of the People's Republic of Hungary from 1952 until 1957. His position was purely ceremonial, much like a king or queen in a Monarchy. He signed the official surrender.

Back at the Kremlin, Soviet officials argued again about who they should place in certain positions in the new Hungarian government. Kádár had already declared to Hungary that he was the new Prime Minister, but some Soviets were still wary of that decision and fought

---

[26] The Hungarian Parliament is a gorgeous neo-Gothic building, it is still the largest building in Hungary. The groundbreaking began in 1885 and the building was completed in 1904 and remains a cultural icon of Hungary.

to reconsider. The staunch Stalinists in the Kremlin (such as Molotov and Kaganovich) argued with Khrushchev that they should place a Stalinist back in power in Hungary. Khrushchev knew that the Hungarians hated the Stalinists like Rákosi and that's why communism failed in Hungary, causing the uprising; if they placed people with the same political ideologies in positions of power again, nothing would change, and they needed to keep Hungarians complacent so they could keep them under the thumb of the Soviet Union.

After Moscow announced their victory in crushing the resistance, the Hungarian secret police came out of hiding and began arresting the freedom fighters. There are some accounts of the AVH hanging groups of freedom fighters, including the student organizers, on bridges over the Danube River.

CHAPTER 24
NOVEMBER 5-11 - DAYS FOURTEEN TO TWENTY

Most of the freedom fighters had surrendered on November 4, realizing quickly how outnumbered they were, but isolated groups of the resistance kept burning until November 11. On November 6, Széna Square and the Corvin Cinema fell, and the freedom fighters who were still alive made a run for Austria.

When the Soviet troops defeated groups of freedom fighters, they would execute any who were left standing and hadn't been able to run away. Freedom fighters who surrendered to the Soviets were also executed after surrender.

Freedom fighters continued to resist the Red Army for a week with very little supplies, without a commander, and no means to communicate with other groups about coordinating their attacks. They were still able to take down several Russian tanks, kill a few hundred troops, and wound upwards of 1,000 more, but they knew they weren't fighting to win.

At Móricz Zsigmond Square, the freedom fighters constructed barricades to slow the Soviets down. A few fighters ran to the roofs of the buildings and shot at the tanks and cars that got held up at the barricade; the fighters recalled that 67 Russians were killed in that attack. The Soviets had to turn back to regroup, and when they did, the freedom fighters turned over the cars in the streets and made the street impenetrable by placing logs strategically in between cars on either side of the street so that tanks couldn't just push the logs out of the way, and they couldn't roll over them. The Red Army came back for a retaliation attack; they sprayed the buildings with bullets, intending not to take any prisoners. The freedom fighters thought they would all die there that day, but, miraculously, they disabled several tanks and drove the rest off. The freedom fighters held that square for 36 more hours after that battle, they fought until they were finally subdued, and the entire block was in ruins.

After the battle at Móricz Zsigmond Square, which proved more arduous than the Soviets anticipated, they turned their sights towards the Castle District. They acted as if they were going to bat with a powerful army instead of a group of barely armed kids. First, they shelled the district from the nearby Gellert Hill for an hour, it seemed unlikely that anybody could have lived through that, but the Soviets then sent in tanks to scope it out and execute any remaining freedom fighters.

Imre Geiger,[27] a 20-year-old freedom fighter who'd narrowly escaped the battle at Móricz Zsigmond Square, went up the hill to the Castle District to continue the fight. He recalled how their first main objective to defend the area was to destroy tanks. They could destroy tanks in several ways, and many were easy jobs for young kids to do. First, they could spread oil or soap on the roads and as the tanks tried to drive uphill, the tank's tracks would slip, sometimes they'd slide into a building and get stuck. Or they could fool the tanks into stopping for a moment so they could pounce.

Geiger explained it best to Michener:

> One clever girl spread brown plates upside down, and they looked exactly like landmines. The Russians would come up to them, hesitate, and then start to back up. . . From a soda water plant [a workman] got a truck load of empty oxygen tanks. He spread these on the street, and you should have seen the tanks rolling around. Some little boys strung grenades on strings and jockeyed them back and forth until they came under the tracks of the tanks. The explosions stopped the tanks, and we killed them. But the bravest were the young boys and girls

---

[27] Imre Geiger was not his real name. James Michener wrote and published *The Bridge at Andau* in 1957, where Geiger's actions are detailed, but Michener changed many of the freedom fighter's names in order to protect their identities and their families who had been left behind in Hungary. Michener's book is a historical narrative of the Hungarian Revolution as told by survivor testimonies, but because composite characters had been created (like how I have created several characters, such as Emil) to tell the story of the revolution and because names had been changed for protection, some have labeled *The Bridge at Andau* as a historical novel. Michener cited no sources for the book, and Geiger's testimony isn't verifiable in any other way. This doesn't mean that *The Bridge at Andau* shouldn't be believed, but it should be taken with a grain of salt.

who just dashed out and stuck lengths of plumber's pipe into the tracks, making them jam. You never saw such kids. (Michener)

Another way to trap a tank was to lure it into a dead-end street. Geiger said that they'd prop up empty guns in a doorway or young girls would hold broomsticks out of windows down a street, the tanks would take the broomsticks to be sniper's guns and drive towards them, nosing itself into a trap.

They filled depressions in the cobblestone roads with fuel and when a tank drove over it, they'd throw a grenade into the fuel and the tank would go up in a blaze. Somebody put an electric wire onto a tank and electrocuted the Soviets inside. A trolley driver sped his trolley up and jumped off at the last second before it ran into a tank and went up in flames. Some young girls even took up the dangerous task of darting out as tanks passed by to throw Molotov cocktails at them, and many were killed in the act.

A young boy, twelve or less, sacrificed himself and those who witnessed it and lived didn't even know his name. He strapped himself with grenades, holding more in his arms, and ran out in front of the first tank in a long column. The grenades exploded, killing him and destroying the tracks of the tank, buying the freedom fighters down the road more time to prepare to take on the rest of the tanks.

After three days of fighting in the Castle District the remaining 30 freedom fighters there surrendered to the Soviets and were promptly executed. The Soviets executed the children who fought for their freedom as well as the adults. They killed many civilians in random attacks on the streets, Red Cross workers, and ambulances tending to the wounded.

The Kilian Barracks continued the fight until November 9. Their goal was not to win or overcome the Soviets, they knew they didn't stand a chance, the goal was just to resist for as long as possible. The Soviets apparently didn't realize when the fight was over, the freedom fighters had abandoned their post and escaped during the cover either by making a run for it on the streets or through the passageways underneath the cinema.

The freedom fighters in Csepel were able to fight until the 11th. "Red" Csepel, the industrial district which should have been the backbone of the communist regime, fought valiantly against it until the final hour. Nearly 15,000 workmen went on strike, joined the resistance, hid in their factories, and attacked the Soviets without a leader or a plan. They had a burning hatred for communism and the AVH, which they used to fuel their fight; and the Soviets attacked the workmen with the same hostility.

Imre Geiger, who'd escaped two battles thus far, arrived in Csepel with his rifle for the final battle. He was filling Molotov cocktails next to another freedom fighter who looked a little odd to him. At first, Geiger thought he was a Russian who'd infiltrated, but it turned out that he was a North Korean who'd been sent to Hungary after the Korean War in order to study in Budapest's factories.[28] Then Geiger met two Greek teenagers who couldn't speak Hungarian but wanted Geiger to mail letters to their families for them if he managed to get out. There were several Greek kids who'd been deported during the Greek civil war by the Russians and sent to Hungary to study communism.[29] Even the foreigners turned against the Soviets during the Hungarian Revolution.

The workers on Csepel Island did everything they could to fend off the Soviets, they even ignited the entire fuel plant, but they knew they'd lose in the end. They didn't surrender though because they knew that surrender meant death, instead they slipped out and swam across the river—like the fighters from the Kilian Barracks had—and Geiger was among them. They invented a crude "armored car" to fight the Soviets with; it was a three-wheel wheelbarrow carrying a machine-gun, propped up with sandbags. They'd taken over the factories and worked to replenish their own supplies of ammunition throughout the

---

[28] In the 2010s, Mozes Csoma, a professor, began researching the Hungarian Revolution and interviewing survivors in order to uncover the role that North Koreans played in the revolution. His book, *From North Korea to Budapest: North Korean Students in the Hungarian Revolution in 1956*, published first in Hungarian and Korean and later in English, recounts the oral history of survivors and archival data that had been hidden or forgotten. About 200 North Korean students, many of whom were military veterans from the Korean War, fought alongside and taught the Hungarians (many of whom had no experience with weapons and machinery) how to use the guns and tanks they acquired during the fighting. The North Koreans had grown to like their Hungarian classmates and friends, and some had disdain or hatred for the Soviets.

[29] The Soviet Union forcibly relocated 70,000 to 80,000 total Greeks to other communist countries in three waves: 1942, 1944, and 1949. The Greek civil war ended in 1949.

revolution and after.

Parts of Budapest were in complete ruins, reminiscent of the Siege of Budapest from November 1944 to February 1945, in which only about a fourth of the city's buildings *hadn't* been bombed. The areas the freedom fighters had used as their fortresses were ruthlessly shelled and all that remained was debris. Photos from the beginning of the revolution showed excited young Hungarians waving flags, demonstrating, and smiling, and at the end photos showed buildings with entire walls collapsed and dead bodies lying in piles of rubble throughout the streets.

Official reports say that between 2,000 and 3,000 Hungarians died in the fighting, with up to 20,000 more who were wounded, and around 700 Soviet soldiers had died, some of whom were executed by their own command for not participating in the slaughter of Hungarians. However, survivors of the uprising testified that up to 30,000 Hungarians were wounded or killed, and up to 8,000 Soviets; they also believed that no less than 160, but no more than 480, Russian tanks had been destroyed by freedom fighters.

Official reports from the USSR and their satellite states often try to hide the truth, and it would make sense that the Soviets wished to hide the true scope of the Hungarian Revolution and to downplay the casualties. Keep in mind that the 800-1,000 people brutally massacred on Bloody Thursday hadn't been accounted for, and officially the lowest estimate is about 20 deaths, and that the government hadn't acknowledged the event for 30 years.

The government continued to arrest, imprison, torture, and execute Hungarian revolutionaries until November of 1957. Tens of thousands were arrested, imprisoned and/or deported to the Soviet Union and held in gulags. Estimates will never be accurate, but the highest estimate is that up to 50,000 people were arrested and/or imprisoned for participating in the revolution.

Chapter 25

The Aftermath

Kádár had arrived in Budapest on November 7 in an armored Soviet car, accompanied by tanks, to the sound of isolated shelling in the distance. Budapest was still under martial law, the Soviets were still in charge of the country, and of Kádár himself—he was still under probation, being new to his role. Hungarians all throughout the country began resisting passively, a general strike was formed, and posters were posted all over the city disparaging Kádár.

The Soviets had already begun arresting the freedom fighters but, in another attempt to fool the population, Kádár repeatedly proclaimed that nobody would face trial for participating in the uprising. He knew that the Soviets might replace him if he couldn't get control of Hungary, and the general strike that started again after the Soviets invaded was very damaging. Kádár tried negotiating with the leaders of the Central Workers' Council of Greater Budapest who organized the strike, but they were only willing to agree to restoring heat and food deliveries. They said that the Central Workers' Council was the true representative of the working class.

The workmen of Csepel returned to work on November 11 and the communists tried to convince the workers to resume fulfilling the pre-revolutionary quotas with a promise of food and their full wages (which weren't enough compensation in the first place for the recently increased labor and productivity increases). The leaders of the strike were threatened with death and knew that AVH spies would be planted within their factories, but they didn't care. Communists were afraid that if the factories and heavy industries weren't producing anything then their economy would come to a standstill and inflation would spike even more, but the strike continued.

No matter how much the government pleaded with the workmen, the strike continued; it was obviously effective. Truck drivers stopped delivering food to the communists, cleaning ladies stopped going to work for the communists, city workers limited the electricity and heat, and in Tatabánya the coal miners stopped collecting the coal, which was vital for heating and electricity. The Soviets sent troops and tanks into Tatabánya and cut off food to tens of thousands of residents and began plucking people off the streets for interrogation, deportation, or both, but still the miners continued striking.

In Csepel, the workmen laid traps in their factories and told the Soviets that they'd blow up the buildings if the Soviets tried to take over the factories or force them back into work. To the dismay of the oligarchs, the general strike went strong through January 1957, and phased out over the next several months.

Maléter and Kopácsi were arrested and reunited in the dungeon of an Embassy building where the noose was just meters away from the ballroom—fitting for the Soviets. Király and Pongracz were among the freedom fighters who fled to the west in order to escape the inevitable death penalty. The refugees began trickling over the border to Austria in late October, but the masses began leaving early in the morning on November 4 and continued for several weeks. The Soviets deployed tens of thousands of troops to the Austrian border in order to keep it secure from western powers that might try to aid the revolution, but they left stretches of the border unguarded so refugees walked right through. Many walked for days, some caught rides as far as they could go, and others took a train to the closest station they could manage and then walked the rest of the way through to avoid run-ins with the Soviets who did sometimes catch refugees.

Until the first week of December the government was tolerant about the mass exodus, but then Kádár tightened his grip on the nation and escaping became more dangerous. Hungary was back to being a prison.

Soon Kádár's facade dropped, and he revealed himself as a Judas. He repeatedly promised Nagy that he wouldn't be harmed or prosecuted and could return to his home if only he would come out of hiding from the Yugoslav Embassy. A written guarantee that Nagy and the other 41 Hungarians who had taken refuge at the embassy could return to their homes unharmed, with immunity, was given on November 21. Nagy's naïveté never failed, he truly believed that Kádár wouldn't be so unwise as to try and pull a fast one during his first month as Prime Minister.

On November 22, he said his goodbyes and gave thanks to the Yugoslavs (who had only offered him sanctuary as a favor to the Soviets, but they failed to get Nagy to formally resign as Prime Minister and devote loyalty to the Kádár government) for their hospitality. A bus with obvious KGB officers onboard arrived to take the Hungarians home, it wasn't Serov's idea to arrest the Hungarians, but he did enthusiastically approve of the plan. The bus driver even warned Nagy that not all was as it seemed, he was a little spooked and he got off the bus, but the Yugoslavs persuaded him that the KGB were there as protection, and Nagy got back on the bus along with the other Hungarians. The bus took off and a few hundred meters later, the driver was ordered to pull over, and the Hungarians were pulled out and arrested. The trickery and abduction were planned, and the Yugoslavs were in on it even though they denied it. Nagy was tried for treason and eventually hanged on June 16, 1958.[30]

It was clear that Kádár had a penchant for deceit and used that tool to ensnare victims. He deceived Nagy (although an argument could be made that Nagy was easy to deceive because he was so willing to trust), then Sándor Rácz and Sándor Bali of the Central Workers' Council, both of whom had been promoting the general strikes which were destabilizing the country, then freedom fighters like József Dudas were all tricked into coming out of hiding or attending a meeting which resulted in their arrest.

It shouldn't come as a surprise that Kádár also went back on his word that no punishment would be doled out to the freedom fighters. For the next few years, the new Peoples' Courts convicted over 22,000

---

[30] Imre Nagy, Pál Maléter, a journalist Miklós Gimes, the Chief of Staff József Szilágyi and the Minister of State Géza Losonczy were all buried in a prison courtyard after their executions (Nagy, Maléter, and Gimes were executed on the same day). In 1961, their bodies were exhumed and reburied in unmarked plots in a Budapest Cemetery; the exact location was an official secret and wasn't discovered until 1988 after an investigation. On June 16, 1989, 31 years later, all 5 men were exhumed once again and buried in Budapest's New Public Cemetery At least 250,000 people attended the reburial ceremony.

people for participating in the revolution, 330 of whom were executed.

History often looks at revolutions as "failures" if they don't end up with the dramatic change that the revolutionaries were fighting for, while the Hungarian Revolution didn't achieve everything they hoped for, and it ended up with more arrests, it was successful in a few measures. Most importantly, the AVH was disbanded and the secret police never reorganized in Hungary. Even the Kremlin magnates realized that the AVH was where much of the anger in the country stemmed from. Another successful outcome was that between 7,500 and 8,000 political prisoners who'd been convicted on wrongful charges were released, including several foreign nationals, and political persecutions dropped dramatically in the years following—except for the freedom fighters.

In 1957, the UN General Assembly organized hearings in five cities over the course of five months in which they interviewed 111 refugees, including military commanders, government officials, medical staff, students, peasants, and freedom fighters. They reviewed newspapers, radio transcripts, film, photos, and written testimonies of two hundred other Hungarians to piece together the events of the revolution. Hungary and Romania refused to allow UN officials to enter their countries, and of course the Soviet Union ignored the UN's appeals for information. A 268-page Committee Report documented the revolution, and the conclusion was that the "Kádár government and Soviet occupation were in violation of the human rights of Hungarian people," and the UN deplored "the continued repression in Hungary," (*Report of the Special Committee on the Problem of Hungary, The Situation in Hungary*). Unfortunately, no further action was taken by the UN except to detest and condemn the USSR and Hungarian government, but it was at least a step in the right direction for the UN to document it.

The success of a revolution is not measured only in its tangible outcomes, it must also be measured in the way in which it morphs public opinion. Within Hungary everybody was aware of the horrors they faced, and the youth were breaking the cycle of indoctrination by participating in the revolution. Outside of Hungary, particularly in the west, the revolution opened up many people's eyes to the evils of the Soviet Union as public support for the Hungarian underdog prevailed. Support from the popular music artist Elvis Presley helped sway public opinion when he appeared on the Ed Sullivan show on January 6, 1957; he dedicated a gospel song "Peace in the Valley" to Hungarians, he said that he felt so strongly about Hungarian relief and urged the listeners to donate immediately. By the end of 1957, contributions amounting to about six million dollars (in 1957) had been donated, thanks in part to Elvis telling his audiences about the revolution. When public figures spread information about a topic it brings awareness to a larger audience and starts the dialogue with people who may never have heard of Hungary's plight before. It's not unreasonable to theorize that some Americans were influenced to offer housing and/or employment for the refugees specifically because of Elvis' appearance on the talk show.

The Hungarians didn't overtly ask the United States for support and intervention between October 23 and November 4, even though rumors spread throughout Hungary that the United States was coming to the rescue during the revolution. István Bibó, who had been appointed to the Minister of State on November 3, typed a plea begging President Eisenhower to help Hungary. They needed political help moving forward, not military help, it was already too late for that.

The uprising was international news and the United States was fully aware (as they are aware of every international conflict, revolution, and genocide, even when they don't take action), especially after the protesters pleaded for help outside of the American Legation building after the massacre on Bloody Thursday. When President Eisenhower heard about the armed uprising in Budapest in October, he immediately knew he didn't want to interfere and risk an issue arising between the US and the Soviet Union. Not to mention that the Presidential election was right around the corner, and he didn't want to lose his popularity, and his attention was on Egypt and the Suez Canal Crisis, so he didn't want to spread resources too thin.

On July 12, 1956, after the Poznań protests in Poland broke out, the Eisenhower administration, including the Secretary of State John Foster Dulles,[31] met to discuss a confidential policy which the National Security Council was creating regarding Soviet satellite states. To put it plainly, the policy's goal was to *allow* resistances to form in countries that were occupied by the Soviet Union, but not to incite the resistance

[31] John Foster Dulles' brother, Allen Dulles, was the director of the American Central Intelligence Agency during the Cold War until 1961.

or any violence. Inciting a rebellion would negatively affect the United States' relations with the Soviet Union and would simply be negative PR for the US.

Anti-communist insurgencies or demonstrations would also give the United States and the Eisenhower administration positive PR because American citizens would see how hated the communists were in the satellite states, thereby confirming any negative beliefs about communism and in turn confirming positive beliefs about the American way of life. During 1956, America was in the throes of the Red Scare, public hysteria over the real and perceived fears about the rise of communism worldwide,[32] and publicity that displayed the evils and threats of the Soviet Union benefited the United States.

For the United States it was always about self-preservation, maximizing their own benefit and minimizing the risk, even at the expense of human life. The consensus within the Eisenhower administration was that letting uprisings in the satellite states play out was how they needed to "play the game" with the Soviet Union. The final draft of the US Policy Toward the Soviet Satellite States in Europe, created on July 18, 1956, stated:

> Avoid incitements to violence or to action when the probable reprisals or other results would yield a net loss in terms of U.S. objectives. In general, however, do not discourage. . . spontaneous manifestations of discontent and opposition to the Communist regime, despite risks to individuals, when their net results will exert pressures for release from Soviet domination. Operations which might involve or lead to local violence will be authorized only by the Secretary of State with the approval of the President on the basis of feasibility, minimum risk, and maximum contribution to the basic U.S. objectives. (*Document NO. 4*)

Vice President Richard Nixon stated that an uprising in the Eastern Bloc which might fail and be quashed by the Soviet Union would help America and the public opinion. The administration agreed to keep their silence about this resolution to effectively abandon or ignore resistance movements in satellite states out of fear of public

---

[32] Over 50 countries had been a communist state at some point, the majority of which were either influenced by the USSR or directly consumed by Soviet colonialism.

disapproval; Nixon couldn't think of anything "worse than a leak tending to indicate that we at the highest levels were agreeing on a policy of national communism under any circumstance," (*Document NO. 2*).

When appealed to, the United Nations was also reluctant to get involved, fearing a global confrontation—perhaps the beginning to World War III—but by November 4, the UN resolved to demand the Red Army end the fighting and evacuate from Hungary. The Soviets eventually stopped the bombardment, but they didn't leave Hungary once and for all. Without military aid and interference from western powers, it was a suicide mission for the revolutionaries who continued to fight for a free nation.

CHAPTER 26
HEROES OF THE HUNGARIAN REVOLUTION
(NOT AN EXHAUSTIVE LIST)

Sandor Alex Boldizsar, 22, was an industrial apprentice when the revolution began, but he fought bravely and was severely wounded. He fled to Austria with friends, running by night and sleeping in barns offered by kind strangers during the day. After rehabilitating from his wounds in a refugee camp, he was flown to the US on the first flight.

József Éder Árpád, 19, was working as a movie projector operator when the revolution began but he fought bravely until the final moments, primarily with the Corvin Group. He gave up his dreams and his secured spot on the Hungarian Olympic Team and fled the country, fearing the revenge the Soviets would take on Freedom Fighters. He later enlisted in the US Army to continue upholding and protecting the freedoms he longed for.

József Dudás, 44, had spent a quarter of his life in prison, first being part of the anti-fascist underground, then for opposing the Stalinists' takeover of the Hungarian Communist Party. At the time of the revolution he was a factory worker, the group of revolutionaries he led were mostly colleagues of his. He and about 150 people occupied the office building of *Szabad Nep,* the communist newspaper in Budapest, for several days. He was arrested and executed in January.

József Mihaly Ertavy, 26, was printing and distributing pamphlets of information about the freedom fighter's Sixteen Points. His wife, Katalin Ertavy-Barath, 34, was a volunteer ambulance driver who tended to the wounded fighters. They both fled the country when they realized that József would be executed for his crime of distributing the pamphlets. Katalin, already a published author, later wrote a book about her experience titled *A Teaspoonful of Freedom*, and several more books about Hungarian history.

László Fülöp, 22, was a coal miner who was drafted into the army in 1954, after which he worked in a textiles factory. He participated in the first protests and stayed involved until the end; he wasn't an armed fighter, despite his military experience, but he helped build barricades and tended to the wounded. He fled in early January.

Éva Horváth Kiss, 43, always wanted to be a doctor but her family only allowed her to be a pharmacist. She worked at the Szent Imre pharmacy at the Móricz Zsigmond Square, which became one of the strongholds for the freedom fighters. Éva gave the fighters fuel for the Molotov cocktails, shelter, and medical aid to the wounded.

Éva's daughter, Edith, just 14 years old, participated in the demonstration on the first night; she yelled, "Russians go home!" and sang the Hungarian national anthem with pride, she felt like change was on the horizon. She arrived home to hear on the radio that the AVH shot protesters at the radio building—which she was not near that night—and that the protest turned into an all-out rebellion. Éva, her husband, and two daughters left Hungary after the revolution was crushed.

Dr. Imre Latkóczy, 66, a lawyer and member of the Hungarian Social Democrats, had been imprisoned by the communists during the purges, and was released just a few months before October 1956. He immediately joined the resistance, and both he and his son László fought with the other freedom fighters. Imre, who had prior experience with weaponry, was able to train the young fighters to use guns. He fought bravely to resist the Soviets until he was killed on November 7.

His son, László Latkóczy-Osváth, 31, worked at the railroad station when the revolution began, and he provided metal rods to the protesters who used them to topple Stalin's statue over. He fought alongside his father and fellow countrymen until the revolution was crushed and his father was killed, then he fled to the west.

Gyula Medgyessy, 29, was an enlisted soldier in the Hungarian Army when the revolution began and as such, he should have owed his loyalty to the regime, but when the fighting broke out, he joined the resistance. At one point, Medgyessy pulled Imre Nagy out of a truck in the rear of a convoy and moved him further up the line, fearing that a Soviet tank would strike the convoy and kill Nagy. After the revolution he fled and immigrated to the US.

Leslie László Megyeri, 15, was a student who participated in the demonstrations on the first day. He and his father, who had previously been jailed for being an anti-communist, joined the other freedom fighters. Afterwards they fled and made it to Ireland where Leslie later joined the Irish Army.

Gergely Pongrácz, 24, was an agricultural engineer and when he heard about the revolution, he left his farm and traveled 80 kilometers on his tractor to join the fight. He became the leader of the Corvin Group, and using underground passageways he was able to knock out three Soviet tanks and capture two, and an armored vehicle. He evaded capture and escaped to the west.

Tibor Sarkady, 20, was a student at the Technical University in Budapest when his classmates organized the first protest. He fought courageously until it was clear that no hope remained. He escaped and immigrated to the US, but the Hungarian government sentenced him to death in absentia for his participation in the revolution.

János "Uncle" Szabó, 59, was a truck driver and became a rebel commander in the resistance. He was well liked among the young fighters, and he led one of the main armed groups of freedom fighters, the Széna Square group. He was caught trying to escape to the west and hanged in January 1957.

Sándor Taraszovics, 25, helped set up a communication system to warn the freedom fighters of the Soviets' movements and strength, and he tapped into lines which the Soviets used for the military intelligence communications and disrupted their ability to communicate with Moscow. After fleeing to Austria, he was sent to the US to testify before the United Nations on the events that transpired in Hungary.

Vazul Végvári, 27, had been trained at the Zrinyi military academy before becoming a Franciscan Monk and when the revolution began the abbot of his monastery forbade the monks from joining the revolution. Végvári left almost immediately for Budapest and the next day was holding grenades and wearing a machine gun around his neck. He became a leader of the Castle District, where the 13th century Buda Castle was located, and fought until his group was overrun by the Soviets. He was caught by the Soviets twice as he tried to escape into Austria but was let go both times because they couldn't identify him.

Thousands of freedom fighters died without recognition, many of whom were children and teenagers.

CHAPTER 27
THE REPUTATION

Hungarians turned into radical militias overnight and some of their tactics gave them a bad name, but the Soviets also did their best to tarnish the freedom fighters' reputation. Their warfare tactics included capturing and lynching communist leaders and AVH officers. The sporadic murders of secret police, which were committed by several of the various groups, gave the impression that nobody was truly in control of the uprising. They sometimes put on an impromptu mock-trial of the AVH officers they caught and hung them or beat them in a fit of rage, and the crowds would quickly disperse afterwards. In 1957, the government calculated that 289 AVH members were killed in the revolution, but that most were killed in the fighting, not in calculated murders. Between 90 and 100 AVH members were lynched. Nothing else did as much damage to the revolution's reputation as the lynchings did.

János "Uncle" Szabó, leader of the Széna Square group found his group of freedom fighters participating in the destruction of public property and vandalism, he put an end to it himself. Later, he prevented freedom fighters from lynching a few AVH officers that they'd captured. Gergely Pongrácz, leader of the Corvin group, wouldn't allow his group to execute AVH officers they found either, and in general most freedom fighters didn't participate in the lynchings. However, those who did participate had many reasons to hate the AVH and the communists, and people try to get revenge for injustices because they assume they can get away with it while the country is in utter chaos.

Király was disgusted by the cold-blooded killing, he shed light on the situation when he explained that:

The revolution was not characterized by brutality. Quite the opposite. It was characterized by moderation, mainly. If you think of the thousands who perished under the Rákosi regime, the hundreds of thousands who were interned or imprisoned, there was really very little violence against the oppressors. The Hungarian Revolution was moderate compared to the regime it was attempting to topple. (Sebestyen)

All of that aside, the lynchings could be quite brutal. Sometimes they beat the secret police, kicking them until they died, and other times they hung them by their feet and beat them that way. Some were given the mercy of a quicker death by hanging from a tree or scaffolding. At least a few times the revolutionaries stuffed money into the dead man's mouth or left the body to rot in a pile of cash, and those actions only helped propel Soviet propaganda that the revolution was spurred by uncontrollable fascist insurgents hellbent on killing communists rather than on seeking change within Hungary.

The shortsighted myth that anybody who opposed communism must therefore be a fascist has carried itself since the early 1900s, and it's part of the rhetoric that modern communists still use to discredit the revolution. Communism is as far left as the spectrum can go, it is socialism on steroids, and most people of the world like most aspects of socialism; but communism appeared more like fascism in practice. The two are supposed to be diametrically opposed, which is why the communists use "fascist" to describe the revolutionaries who fought against them, and why the Nazis conducted political purges and slandered communists in Germany. The Hungarians weren't even looking to destroy communism completely, they wanted moderate communism and policy changes to reflect a legitimate socialist society, not the brand of communism the Soviets operated as. They wanted the Soviets out of their country and out of their government, but they didn't want to return to the fascist capitalism they had before.

Fascism, such as Nazism in the Third Reich, shared a lot of similarities with Soviet communism, whether or not people would like to recognize that. They may have been opposites on the political spectrum, but political scientists have devised a theory to explain why they were so similar: the horseshoe theory. The further one goes towards the left, they will eventually wind up on the right; and vice versa. That's why there's a phenomenon of holistic, socialist, hippies falling down the alt-right, white supremacy, QAnon, conspiracy theorist pipeline; they went too far towards the extreme left and ended up on the extreme right. Extremists share characteristics, so it's easier for a communist to become a fascist than it would be for a libertarian.

If one were to objectively look at communism as it is compared to fascism, particularly Nazism, which is steroid-injected fascism and the counterpart to Soviet communism, they'd find a plethora of similarities that would require its own publication to fully flesh out.

To summarize, both were colonizing empires that carried out mass murder, ethnic cleansing, and genocides. Both were anti-democratic, operated under a one-party system, and solved political disputes by purging hundreds of thousands of their rivals and imprisoning them in labor camps if they didn't just kill them outright. In each empire there was a system of camps for political prisoners and people whom they considered undesirable. Both were highly nationalistic and held rallies to express their pride in their evil campaigns. They each had a hierarchy of power with one man at the top and the next most powerful man as the head of the secret police, and both used many paid informants who weren't necessarily part of the secret police.

In order to completely brainwash the youth, they began with indoctrination in school and in the official youth organizations, the Hitler Youth in Germany and the Pioneers in the USSR, and both taught the children to report and denounce their family if they spoke ill about the government. Within the countries they invaded to create their empires they installed "puppet governments" in order to control the country. They each had a manifesto that they held in high esteem, and both burned books of which they didn't approve. They both promoted the most elaborate propaganda and suppressed freedom of speech and freedom of press unless it supported the narrative they wished to push. Each regime targeted and murdered journalists, writers and intellectuals.

The Soviets actually created the mobile gas units—trucks with a hose attached to the exhaust to funnel it into an enclosed area in order to gas prisoners inside—first in 1937, and then the Nazis adopted the idea a few years later. The Soviets also began relocating mass amounts of people via cattle cars on trains when they started forcibly displacing millions of peasants in the 1930s; by some estimates, they had deported or displaced upwards of 10 million people, mostly via train, before the Nazis even started doing the same. And finally, both regimes were largely antisemitic and sought to displace and kill Jewish people.

Just like the regimes themselves, the infamous leaders had more in common than not. Hitler betrayed a pact with the USSR, but if he hadn't done that and instead had teamed up with Stalin, they would have been great partners in war crimes. The shortest explanation is that, just like Hitler, Stalin was also pathologically and physically unwell. They were both severely paranoid, sadists, previously imprisoned criminals, antisemites, and both suffered from a plethora of physical impairments and diseases. Stalin had been run over by a carriage *twice* in his childhood and was left with an atrophied left arm, a lame left hand, and a limp, he survived numerous childhood diseases including smallpox, and he developed arthritis, insomnia, and hypertension, and strokes which would eventually kill him. While Stalin couldn't have completely avoided those ailments, Hitler's were partially his fault. Hitler had contracted syphilis which developed into psychosis later in life and caused him much pain, for which he took a lot of drugs. Side effects of the constant painkillers he took such as morphine, cocaine, and methamphetamines, caused other health concerns like stomach ulcers, insomnia, and constipation, for which he took more medication. It's speculated that he had Parkinson's, Huntington's, hypochondria, and schizoaffective disorder, which he couldn't have controlled but his lifestyle exacerbated the symptoms. The most comical way that their health compares is that they both had severe bowel issues; Hitler had chronic constipation, sometimes he had diarrhea, *and* he had uncontrollable flatulence, and Stalin had symptoms of irritable bowel syndrome and had at least a few accidents. In any case, neither of them was physically well.

Even though they were both antisemitic, they did still use a few Jewish people if they could serve the regime loyally. Not to mention, they were both abandoned by their fathers and abused as children, which, as we all know from every super villain's backstory, never creates a well-rounded person.[33]

As far as their differences go, Stalin smoked tobacco, drank, and ate meat, but Hitler did not. Stalin was married twice, but Hitler was

---

[33] Recommended reading: *Stalin and His Hangmen* by Donald Rayfield, *Stalin: The Court of the Red Tsar* by Simon Sebag Montefiore, *Blitzed: Drugs in the Third Reich* by Norman Ohler, *A Concise Biography of Adolf Hitler* by Thomas Fuchs, *Hitler's Vienna* by Brigitte Hamann.

only married once (the day before his suicide). Stalin had five biological children and one adopted child, but Hitler never had any recorded children; if he had, he might have also abandoned his own first-born son as an infant, then let the enemy kill him as a prisoner of war during WWII, like Stalin did to his son, Iakob.

One of the benefits of communism that people always point to is that it is a "classless" system without a societal hierarchy, meaning all of the citizens were equal. In the USSR, all of the peasants at the bottom were indeed equal while the oligarchs at the top hoarded the wealth and the power. Under communism private businesses and private land ownership were not allowed because everything was technically owned by the state so the ones at the top could control everything.

To be perfectly honest, several things about a society that follows what Marx and Lenin intended communism to look like sound nice, but those features aren't usually seen when put into practice. In most communist countries, the practice looks like fascism, which is why many political scientists believe it has never been achieved. When everybody is "equal," as they are supposed to be in a communist society, it allows room for a dictator to seize control through violence or rigged elections. And the oligarchs at the top always receive more than their fair share of food, housing, and money.

There is a discernible difference in the sheer brutality of the authoritarian dictatorship in the USSR during Stalin's reign compared to both before and after his death, which is why "Stalinism" is often the type of communism that is criticized as most resembling fascism. It's true that the atmosphere in the Soviet Union changed after 1953, but not enough to definitively prove that it was no longer similar to fascism. Still, it should be noted that Stalinism was the USSR's most egregiously flawed version of a communist society.

Education was one of the most useful weapons the communists fought with, and they knew that by indoctrinating children in schools they'd be able to create loyal servants to the state. They did this in the USSR and in their satellite states when they were able to. Education in their schools boils down to spying and brainwashing.

The secret police would have spies planted in schools to report any of the teachers who didn't fall in line. In Hungary, at least, the monthly stipend for some of the AVH's informants would rival or beat the salary that teachers received, so it could be a lucrative activity to report fellow teachers for anti-communist activities. Teachers who didn't sing their praises to Stalin and the Soviet Union or those who may have looked annoyed during a meeting could be taken by the secret police in the middle of the night. These informers would also spy on the school children by asking probing questions to young ones such as, "Do you have a picture of Stalin in your home?"—which was a requirement—or, "What radio stations do your parents listen to?" If the child admitted that their parents did not have the required portrait of Stalin or listened to any station other than the approved communist broadcast, such as the Radio Free Europe broadcast, then the police would take one or both parents.

It should go without saying that school textbooks and curriculum in Soviet-occupied countries favored the Soviet perspective, but brainwashing goes beyond educational material. Much like students in the Third Reich, students in Hungary and other satellite states had a photograph of their revered leaders in every classroom. The communists were anti-religion, but they did like the term "Holy Trinity," which they called the trio of portraits of Stalin, Lenin, and Marx. Some Hungarians would use a portrait of Rákosi instead of Marx, though, to display their nationalism.

Students were routinely taught of the evils of capitalism and the western nations, so they'd be more grateful for the benefits communism brought them. There was an obsession with waste reduction in communist societies that was, in part, influenced by simply being against the throwaway culture of western countries. The Soviet Union renounced anything from or related to the west, capitalism, and consumerism, and they strived to oppose it.

The people generally assisted with the collection of trash and recycling, and children weren't exempt. Young students in primary school were required to collect recyclables to turn over to the state to reduce waste for their industrial recycling program. My grandfather remembered that on Sundays young students had to perform mandatory service to the state by participating in collecting the recyclables, if students didn't show up it could count against their grades. That was another way that students were indoctrinated from a young age to participate in state-sponsored activities and praise communism.

Raw materials were often hard to come by, so entire industries were created to collect and repurpose industrial and consumer waste such as bone, fat, feathers, cardboard, glasses, clothing, metal, paper, and a laundry list of other materials. Those were "secondary materials," and if they didn't have a use at the time, they were saved in case they could be used later on. This system sought to prove to the west that communism was more economically sustainable and "thrifty" than capitalism.[34]

Young students were also coached to report their classmates' behavior and conversations that might be harmful to the communist state. Although many Hungarian children were opposed to spying and snitching on their classmates, there were always some that were already corrupted by the regime and willing to do so. Students who sought approval and recognition from their teachers were rewarded for reporting their own parents because they were conditioned to believe that it was righteous to report any anti-communist activities. Students in the Soviet Union were also conditioned to report their friends and families, more so than in the satellite states. Soviet leaders knew that they must destroy all loyalty to family in order for loyalty to the state to prevail. Not only were children trained to mistrust their families and place blind faith in the communist state, but many millions of families were also physically ripped apart when parents were killed, imprisoned or deported, which orphaned many thousands of children who would then grow up in an orphanage that indoctrinated them further. Children of "enemies of the state" were often ostracized in their orphanages as well, and the "crimes" of their parents would haunt them for the rest of their lives.

In addition to destroying allegiance to one's own family, the Soviets also needed to demonize religious leaders as anti-state to eliminate loyalty to religion. The USSR had an ideological goal to eliminate religion and became completely atheistic, but religion was never officially outlawed, and it persisted even through intense discrimination. Church leaders were persecuted, church property was confiscated if not destroyed outright, and believers were targeted and harassed by the League of Militant Atheism, which was established with about 3.5 million members whose goal was to stamp out religion

---

[34] A few of the countries which currently operate incredible recycling programs to reduce waste were formerly occupied by the Soviets: Germany, Austria and Slovenia.

entirely.

Students whose parents wished for them to continue having religious instruction in Hungarian schools were allowed to request such instruction by writing a letter to the school; those children got a heavily propagandized version of religious education, and their parents' letters were sent to the local AVH and even the parents' employers. Any parent who worked for the government or in a "sensitive position" could be taken to a labor camp for making that request. The retaliation became known, and parents stopped making that request.

Parents began talking to their children about the evils of communism generally between the ages of 8 and 10. Families had to correctly judge when their children were ready; too young and they might accidentally tell somebody at school, too old and they might already be too indoctrinated and report their parents. They would get their kids out of bed late at night and tell them that everything they'd learned in school was a lie. Parents pressed the importance of keeping silent about their conversation or else the AVH would arrest their parents and possibly kill them. They had to take the risk that their children could blurt something out that would lead to the family's destruction to save them from further brainwashing before it was too late.

Many, especially within the Hungarian government, would disavow the freedom fighters for lynching AVH officers, but there were still voices there to support and excuse the murders because the AVH was so widely hated. Later, the narrative that the revolution was actually an antisemitic witch-hunt committed by fascists began spreading and has permeated throughout the years, and it isn't far-fetched to assume that it only created more, and real, antisemitism in people who hated the communists.

After all, the Nazis, who were adamantly opposed to the Soviets, spread the narrative that Soviet Communism was actually a Jewish plot to take over the world. The Nazis often referred to the Soviets as "Bolsheviks," which was the far-left faction in Russia that seized control in the October Revolution of 1917, and in 1907 only about 10% of their party membership was Jewish. Historically, countries in Europe have been overwhelmingly antisemitic, so the idea that yet another country was on an antisemitic rampage wasn't far-fetched.

However, looking at the revolution with logic and objectivity, it's clear that the Hungarians weren't seeking out Jewish people to lynch *because* they were Jewish; they sought out the AVH to lynch because they were the secret police and had been actively working to destroy and betray Hungarians for years, some just so happened to be Jewish.

Leaving the slain secret police on piles of money, or with money in their mouths, wasn't a dog whistle to other antisemites, it represented the blood money that the AVH were paid for betraying their fellow Hungarians. This doesn't dismiss the fact that Hungarians could be extremely antisemitic, including the revolutionaries, but to reiterate, they weren't attacking Jews on the basis of being Jewish.

Hungary, like most of Europe, had a history of antisemitism, and they'd been aligned with the Axis powers during WWII. Even though some government officials didn't want to join forces with Hitler, the ones who did overpowered the others. But not all Hungarians were bigoted, the Prime Minister in 1941, Pál Teleki, had attempted to keep Hungary neutral, but on April 3, 1945, when he learned that would be impossible after the Nazis entered Hungary on their way to invade Yugoslavia, he committed suicide in despair. Then, the Hungarian military and police actively participated in the Final Solution; public massacres and deportations of Jewish people were executed by the hands of Hungarians on the orders of Nazis. Hungary had antisemitic pogroms of their own before and after WWII, and unfavorable opinions of Jewish people still permeated society. They spread rumors of blood libel and conflated Jewish people with communists, just as the Nazis had, which made the rumor that the freedom fighters were antisemitic plausible.

Another thing that made the freedom fighters look antisemitic was the fact that many of the high-ranking officials whom they despised were Jewish, but again, they didn't hate the AVH and government *because* there were Jewish people in it.

Rákosi, former First Secretary of the Hungarian Communist Party, a tyrannical dictator whom the citizens hated, was born Jewish but later repudiated religion because being religious is anti-state to the communists. Religious suppression is one of the cornerstones of communism and their leaders couldn't be openly religious.

Gábor Péter, the absolute leader of the secret police from 1945 to 1952, was also Jewish, and he was despised by Hungarians because he was an evil man.

Ernő Gerő, who *briefly* took over as First Secretary after Rákosi, and was a KGB agent, was also born Jewish, and was also despised.

Mihály Farkas, Minister of National Defense, and József Revai, the chief cultural commissar and a founder of the Communist Party of Hungary, were also both born Jewish and later abandoned their religion.

In fact, nine out of the twenty-five of the first central committee of the Hungarian Communist Party were born Jewish. Many had spent years in the USSR, some because they were exiled there and others because they wanted to be there, and only returned to Hungary after the Soviet Union occupied the country after WWII. There were also many Jews within the AVH, arguably the most vicious of all Eastern Bloc secret police forces, but the officers' religions didn't quantifiably contribute to their brutality.

There were, of course, Jewish people on both sides of the revolution. Several of the leaders of the freedom fighters were Jewish, and many other Jews participated in the revolution and despised the AVH and communism as much as the next Hungarian.

There is a great irony in the claim that the Hungarian Revolution was fascist and antisemitic. Firstly, many prominent communists in Hungary were Jews who rejected their own religion and even promoted antisemitic propaganda that harmed the Jewish community. Secondly, the Soviets were extremely antisemitic and committed some of the worst pogroms against Jewish people outside of what the Nazis committed, so for them to claim the freedom fighters were just antisemitic was hypocritical to say the least.

Despite Vladmir Lenin (the founding head of the Soviet Union from 1917 until his death in 1924) and the Bolshevik Party's condemnation of antisemitism, violence against Jews continued to happen in the USSR, and most often was committed by members of the Red Guard and the League of Militant Atheism to suppress religion.

Judaism is an ethno-religion, meaning that people who are born Jewish are forever Jewish, like an ethnicity. Judaism is more than a religion, it's a culture, it's an ancestry, and it's sometimes confused with a race. Therefore, even if Jews in the communist party renounced their religion and became atheists, they were still Jews, and people were still antisemitic. Jewish people could never escape their identity or completely blend in with the Party.

Before communism, during the Russian Empire, millions of Jewish people in Russia were often persecuted and harassed. Antisemitism was endorsed by the government, pogroms were sometimes organized or approved of by the Tsarist authorities, and due to the constant persecution, they sometimes joined radical political groups like the Bolsheviks or the Jewish Bund, a secular socialist labor party. Antisemitic laws were passed in 1919, even with the Bolsheviks in power after their successful coup d'etat, and persecution continued throughout the 1920s and 30s.

After WWII, Stalin initiated more severe antisemitic policies and purges, and Jewish people were executed and deported to gulags. In his final years, Stalin became even more antisemitic because he was increasingly more paranoid that there was a Jewish conspiracy to kill him and other communist leaders in what he called the "Doctor's Plot." He thought that Jewish doctors in the Soviet Union were planning to kill him, so he purged them in his last Jewish pogrom before his death on March 5, 1953. Antisemitism in the USSR under Stalin shared many similar characteristics with antisemitism in Nazi-Germany, including the belief that there was a "Jewish conspiracy" to take over.

In the years after Stalin's death, Jewish people weren't as intentionally persecuted, some even thought that Jews were safer in the USSR, but antisemitism ran so deeply in society and Jews were still sometimes barred from enrolling in university, participating in government, and certain professions.

Mátyás Rákosi, the First Secretary of the Hungarian Communist Party and de facto leader of Hungary from 1947 to 1956, was a loyal Stalinist. He was bald and rather rotund; his gentle appearance was entirely mismatched with his depravity. Despite his complete devotion, Stalin didn't like or trust him; Stalin was an antisemite, and Rákosi was a Jew first and foremost.

Rákosi was born in 1892 and he traveled a lot in his prime. He worked in London and Hamburg, joined the military at the outbreak of WWI, was taken as a prisoner of war to the USSR, returned to Hungary and helped found the Hungarian Communist Party, escaped per-secution when Horthy took control by fleeing to Austria where he was interned, and then he ended up back in the USSR all by 1920.

Upon realizing Rákosi's charm and his ability to speak 10

languages, the Soviets appointed him as Secretary of the Comintern—the Communist International. His job was to travel around Europe setting up Communist Parties that would be loyal to the USSR. He returned to Hungary in 1925 and a year later was arrested on charges of sedition, imprisoned for 8 years. He was released in 1935 and he was almost immediately put on trial again for different charges and jailed for 5 more years. In 1940, after his second stint in prison, he was allowed to return to the USSR in exchange for two Hungarian battle flags that were symbolic to the Hungarian revolution of 1848. Those flags had been stolen by the Russians and held in Russia for nearly 100 years after the tsarist army defeated the Hungarians.

Rákosi was given a warm welcome as a hero when he returned to Moscow, even though when he was arrested and interrogated in 1925, he gave away secrets about the Comintern. He compromised the mission and their agents, but he was merely given a slap on the wrist instead of being "purged,"—imprisoned or executed. Other communists died for lesser offenses,[35] but Stalin felt uncharacteristically forgiving because he saw use in Rákosi. He returned again to Hungary in 1945 after the USSR defeated the Nazis and captured Hungary with the order to transform Hungary into a model communist state.

The Soviets had purged about 1.5 million politicians during the Great Purge from 1936 to 1938, but primarily during 1937, and primarily in Russia. Their political trials weren't contained within the USSR, nor did they end after the Great Purge was over, they just lessened. They imprisoned people for whatever reason they wanted, especially when no evidence was present, but the fact that there *was* evidence of Rákosi's crime and he wasn't punished for it is odd.

Stalin's final antisemitic pogrom before his death was to purge the Jewish doctors because he feared that they were plotting to kill high ranking communists, including himself. The Doctors' Plot frightened Rákosi, a Jew, into thinking that it was only a matter of time before he and other Jewish communists—no matter how loyal—would be

---

[35] For context, they would imprison people for something as simple as writing poetry. In Russia, a 23-year-old student, Semyon Samuilovich Vilensky, was sentenced to 10 years of hard labor in a Russian gulag for writing the following poem: "Educated people, you must be harder than steel! There are spies all around, and the worst is Stalin!" Vilensky started a publishing company later in life and co-wrote the book *Children of the Gulag.*

purged. To save himself, he needed to prove that he was loyal through flattery and imitation, he needed to prove that he was just as anti-semitic as Stalin.

In Hungary, the secret police made lists of the Jewish doctors to purge just like in the Soviet Union, and Rákosi repeated communist rhetoric against the "rootless cosmopolitans,"[36] Soviet slang for Jews. At his core, Rákosi was a sycophant, and he was clearly afraid of Stalin, as were many people. He knew that Stalin wasn't fond of him and tried his best to foster a relationship with him still, supposedly going on holidays with Stalin in Crimea (records of that don't exist, but it was rumored), and writing Stalin constant letters in which he asked for advice and sung Stalin's praises.

There was one instance when Rákosi met with President Truman in 1947 and he seemed very comfortable around him, whereas other Communist Party members there were uncomfortable, nervous, and embarrassed. To many, this looked like Rákosi was too friendly with the President of the United States, a western enemy, and was possibly a spy. A simple explanation would be that Rákosi spoke English fluently, making it easier for him to communicate and joke around, but the rest of the communists on that trip knew little to no English.

---

[36] Derogatory terms for Jewish people allude to the idea that Jewish people have been wanderers, without a home, nomadic, or had betrayed their country and moved away, therefore "rootless." The Soviets often made reference to the "cosmopolitans" who had connections with the "bourgeois westerners" and lacked loyalty to the USSR. In 1952, 13 Jewish intellectuals, whom they also called cosmopolitans, were convicted of espionage and treason and were executed in the "Night of the Murdered Poets."

Left: **Pál Maléter Hungarian Soldier, Minister of Defense**
(Maléter Pál magyar katona, honvédelmi minister, Anefo, Dutch National
Archives, CC0)
Right: **Imre Nagy, Hungarian Prime Minister**
(Nagy Imre igazolvanykep, by Jánosi Katalin adományozó CC BY-SA 3.0)
Bottom: **A tank at the crossroads of Pozsonyi and József Katona street**
(Pozsonyi út - Katona József utca sarok, by Pesti Srác, CC BY-SA 3.0)

Left: **Nikita Khrushchev, Soviet Prime Minister**
(Nikita Khrushchev, Dutch National Archives, The Hague, Fotocollectie Algemeen Nederlands Persbureau 1945-1989, CC BY-SA 3.0 NL)
Right: **Mátyás Rákosi, Hungarian Prime Minister**
(Mátyás Rákosi, General Secretary of the Hungarian Communist Party, National Archives of Hungary via Google Arts & Culture, public domain)
Bottom: **The head of the Stalin statue torn down by protesters on October 23** (1956 Hungarian Revolution Gabor B. Racz, CC BY-SA 4.0)

Top: **Lajos Kossuth square, the building of the Labor Movement Institute (once a mansion, now an Ethnographic Museum). Kossuth square is the site of the Bloody Thursday massacre.**
(Kossuth Lajos tér, a Munkásmozgalmi Intézet (egykor Kúria, ma Néprajzi Múzeum) épülete, by Nagy Gyula, CC BY-SA 3.0)
Bottom: **Teenaged Freedom Fighters**
(Ungarischer Freiheitskampf,1956 by Jack Metzger, CC BY-SA 4.0)

Top: **Freedom Fighters atop a tank where Lajos Kossuth Street and Magyar Street cross**
(Kossuth Lajos utca, balra a Magyar utca torkolata, by Nagy Gyula, CC BY-SA 3.0)
Bottom: **Dead bodies on streets next to trucks**
(József körút, holttestek a Pál utca torkolata előtt, by Nagy Gyula, CC BY-SA 3.0)

Top: **A completely destroyed building on Móricz Zsigmond boulevard**
(Móricz Zsigmond körtér, by Nagy Gyula, CC BY-SA 3.0)
Bottom: **The ruins of the Magyar Divatcsarnok, a fashion hall**
(Rákóczi út 70., a Magyar Divatcsarnok romjai, by Nagy Gyula, CC BY-SA
3.0)

Top: **Üllői street seen from Nagykörútról, the Kilian barracks to the right with the wreckage of an ISZ-3 tank in the foreground**
(Üllői út a Nagykörútról nézve, jobbra a Kilián laktanya. Előtérben egy ISZ-3 harckocsi roncsa, by Gyula Nagy, CC BY-SA 3.0)
Bottom: Right to left: **Joseph, Károly a.k.a. Charles, and László, circa 1955**

Left: **Edit, Joseph's little sister, approximately 2 years old, 1954**
Right: **Ilona, no date given**
Bottom: **On my grandparents' first trip back to Hungary in 1988 before his mother died. Right to left: Károly, Joseph, Edit (junior), Linda, Edit**

Charles, Dee, and their daughters, Robin (left) and Daneen (right), at Robin's first Communion, circa 1967

Top: **Christmas at sea on board USS General LeRoy Eltinge, the voyage Joseph was on. Lieutenant Commander T. F. Crane is surrounded by children at the Christmas Party in the ship's dining room**
(330-PS-8155 (USN 1003750) National Museum of the U.S. Navy, public domain)
Bottom: **Joseph as Santa Claus, he did the Santa gig for about 15 seasons, circa 2015**

Linda and Joseph on their wedding day, July 16th, 1960

PART THREE:
THE ESCAPE

"Can a nation be free if it oppresses other nations?
It cannot."

—*Vladimir Lenin*

CHAPTER 28

CAUGHT

"*Stoy!*" the voices demanded again, as they flashed their lights through the trees.

"Run!" somebody shouted and the hoard of more than 40 people fractured. They were cursing, screaming, running, and shoving past each other to flee. A band of people that once worked together fell apart; it was every man for himself. József was in shock, he had never seen such an instant dismantling of comradery.

"*Stoy! Stoy!*" more Soviets shouted at them.

József and Károly gripped each other's hands, they felt like little kids again, running so the Soviets didn't catch them out late at night. But there was nowhere to run, the Soviets had surrounded them.

Emil was shouting and spitting in a soldier's face, not ready to give in after the Soviet seized his arm. The wealthiest man among them was long gone, he had taken off with his young son into the woods. Amós let himself be seized, running or resisting meant certain death, but capture meant the possibility of survival. Someone rammed into Károly and sent him to the ground, breaking the grip he had on József.

At the same moment, József noticed that the little girl, Isla, had been separated from her mother. She was alone and crying, József didn't even think before he sprinted to get her, his only concern was protecting her. József grabbed her hand and started to run, but she kept her feet firm on the ground and cried louder. Her mother suddenly appeared and yanked Isla up by her arm and started to run, József hadn't even had time to react before the Soviets seized both mother and daughter.

The Soviets had formed a semi-circle around the few stragglers, including József, and they were closing in, capturing the Hungarians as they tried to run. József couldn't run, they'd catch him or shoot him, so he thought on his feet and dove into a snowbank to hide. He buried himself in snow and tried to take up the least amount of space possible. He could still look out from a small hole in the snow, but his line of sight was limited. But he could still hear everything, so he heard when Károly started calling out for him.

"Dodi! Dodi!" Károly screamed as the Soviets dragged him towards the wall.

József listened to his brother call for him, *cry* for him, but he couldn't see him and was too afraid to come out. "Károly," he whimpered, barely even audible to himself. He felt selfish for hiding but was so paralyzed with fear that he couldn't move.

All around him people screamed; kids cried, and parents begged for their children's lives to be spared, soldiers barked orders and bold teenagers spit in their faces. Several Soviets guarded the Hungarians they'd caught, they had them lined up on a wall and kept them there with the threat of a bullet in the chest, some soldiers had even smacked people to the ground and kicked them for their disobedience. One of them began firing a submachine gun into the air and the forest. They all stopped in their tracks, afraid to move or fight anymore, expecting the next bullet to hit them. The Soviets laughed, enjoying the fear they caused. The Soviets outnumbered them two to one and nobody dared fight back. What would they have fought with, anyways?

A blood-curdling scream ripped through the forest, then everybody was silent. It was a woman in her mid-thirties, she was fleeing Hungary with her husband and two young children, and her husband had been shot three times in the back. Their children started screaming when they saw their father face down in the snow with blood pooling around him. A Soviet dragged her away by her shirt collar and commanded the children to follow, they were hysterical and afraid to lose another parent, so they obeyed.

József sat, crouched in his hole, and listened to the commotion. He knew that if his father could have seen him, he'd have been so disappointed in the cowardice. His mother's voice rang in his head: *Keep each other safe.* He felt that he had failed her already.

Then, from his little peephole, he saw a soldier approaching his hiding spot. He didn't know what else to do so he held his breath, but he feared that his thumping heartbeat would give him away. The soldier began jabbing at the snow with the muzzle of his gun, poking around for anybody who could be in there. József only had seconds before the soldier inevitably found him, so he did the only thing he could and gave himself up. He stuck his hands through the snow and rose slowly.

"Don't shoot! Don't shoot!" he pleaded.

The soldier grabbed him by the arm and forced his gun into József's back, they walked like that towards the wall, it was extremely uncomfortable. As József stumbled through the snow he caught sight of a boy, no older than five, who took off running. His flight response was apparently triggered, and he knew to run in such a way to avoid stumps in the snow, which made him a difficult target.

His father realized he'd run off just as a soldier fired the first bullet. The boy continued to run because he knew, even at his young age, that he would be dead if he stopped. His father, realizing the gun was aimed at his boy, tried to rush the soldier in an attempt to knock the gun out of his hands. It worked, but he was knocked to the ground by another soldier; he wasn't even given a chance to plead for his life before they shot him in the forehead. The boy was well out of sight, but it wouldn't be long before he would also be dead. If the Soviets didn't get to him first, the cold would if he couldn't make it out of the forest to find help.

József flinched watching the execution. They had almost made it to the wall when the soldier threw him to the ground in front of their captain. József didn't have the courage to look him in the eye, but the captain glared at him.

He stuck out his hand and demanded, "Book."

He was a considerable man with a surly face, and he towered above József which made him appear even more sinister. His hands could have crushed József's skull like a balloon, and his arms would have surely bested a boa constrictor.

On his knees, József shrugged his bag off his shoulder and brought it to his lap to find his identification booklet. He tried to flip through the pages quickly to retrieve the photograph he stuck inside before he had to hand it over, but the captain snatched the passport from his hands impatiently. József made brief eye contact with the soldiers before he carefully stood up; they watched him suspiciously, as if daring him to make the wrong move.

The captain flipped angrily through József's passport to the identification page that listed József's name, his father's name, his birth year and nationality, and other information like his occupation, which said "none" at the time.

The captain wanted to know a little bit about his victims before he could decide what to do with them. His options were to kill him, send him home, or send him to a gulag. He was clearly having a hard time deciphering the information because the Soviets didn't usually try to learn to read the language of the country they occupied, they hardly learned to speak it, instead they forced the Russian language on their satellite states.

He saw the "B" in Baranya County, where József was born, but he couldn't read Hungarian so guessed and asked, "Budapest?" He lowered his eyes to scowl at József. Anybody who escaped from Budapest must have gotten past the Soviet army's blockade.

József, who was not from Budapest, didn't know how to respond without angering the Soviet. "No," he hesitated, "I'm from Pécs, I was born in Baranya." Pécs was about 200 kilometers from Budapest.

The soldiers behind József tensed up and the captain huffed and lifted his chin. He beckoned the soldiers to get closer and he showed József's passport to them both. They muttered to each other, they sounded angry and disgusted as they spoke. While they were otherwise occupied, József took the chance to scan the captives in search of Károly and their friends.

He scanned over the forty-plus people quickly, but he didn't notice that the children had already been separated from the rest. The children weren't of much use to them alive; the physically fit men could always be of use in a labor camp, and the women were of a special, more sinister use to the Soviets. József finally saw Károly in line against the wall and sighed with relief that he was at least still alive.

The captain refocused on József and cleared his throat haughtily. József snapped his attention back to him and made his best impression of an innocent child. He opened József's book and pointed to the word "Baranya" with his finger.

"Budapest," the Soviet emphasized, as if József was too dense to know where he was from. József was not sure what the captain was playing at, so he stared blankly until the captain continued.

"Your book goes to Budapest police station. You leave. You get book there." He nodded decisively and snapped the passport closed before handing it to a soldier who kept a stash of the passports in his pocket.

The Soviets may have thought that by sending people's passports to a police station in a city, especially Budapest, that the refugees would have no choice but to return from the border and go get their passport, thereby stopping them from leaving and even perhaps trapping them in the city that was under a complete military occupation and blockade. The captain grabbed his gun threateningly and said, "Go."

József was astonished. "No, I don't live in Budapest! I live in Pécs," he raised his voice, which the Soviets did not appreciate. "I was born in Baranya County, that says Baranya. B-A-R-A—" but he could not finish, as he had been kicked swiftly in the leg by a soldier. Apparently, József had angered him by shouting at his captain.

"No, I send book to Budapest. You will go there." He towered above József so that he had undoubtedly the ugliest view of him.

He was completely vulnerable and confused. Why would the captain let him go, but nobody else? It just didn't make sense, and it seemed like a trap. József could have obeyed the captain's orders and left immediately, and that thought had occurred to him, but he couldn't just leave.

He pointed defiantly, though the shiver of his finger showed his fear, "That's my brother over there, I have to stay with him, if I leave then he leaves, too."

"No, just you," the captain said each word slowly and clearly. His eyes were hard and cruel.

He put on his kindest voice, "Captain, sir, I can't leave without him. We came here together, so we need to go home together. I'll go to Budapest, just let my brother come with me."

The captain took a few seconds to consider it, but he yanked his gun up, cocked it, and pointed it at József's chest.

"You want to go with your brother? Go," he jerked his head in the direction of the others and smiled.

He wasn't sure if the captain was trying to trick him or not, and if he made any sudden moves, he knew the Soviets wouldn't hesitate to shoot. Cautiously, he leaned to pick his knapsack up, but the captain told him not to grab it. József obliged and raised his hands as he stood. The others on the wall were being searched violently, and their belongings were confiscated. The Soviets were searching for any kind of weapons, money, or food, all of which were valuable resources. The soldiers started yelling and forcing their prisoners to walk and without thinking József started jogging towards his brother. Before he got too far, a soldier jammed the butt of his gun onto the side of his head, a punishment for running without an order.

CHAPTER 29
CAPTIVE

The steady sound of water hitting concrete was the first thing he heard when he came to. For a moment, József listened to the repetitive droplets, too groggy to lift his head. He opened his eyes, but he couldn't see, his head throbbed, he was wet and cold and then he realized that they'd been imprisoned. He lifted his pounding head from the concrete, he instinctively reached up and felt something dried and crusty on his temple and tried to wipe it off with his sleeve, but it was no use.

Nobody could be certain exactly how long József had been unconscious, but they guessed it was only a few hours. Humans are remarkably good at guessing the time since it stays the same, but eventually they'd lose track of time while in captivity. They could assume that it had been about an hour in between each time the Soviets barged in to retrieve a prisoner for interrogation, and four people had been taken so far.

"Dodi?" Károly noticed József get up, he'd stayed right next to him the whole time he was unconscious. He'd even had to carry József's body inside the prison cell, the Soviets didn't want to waste their energy on him.

"Thank God, I didn't know if you were going to make it!" He was happy to see his brother awake, but he was also visibly exhausted, he barely even leaned over to hug József.

"Károly, where are we?" he asked, but he already knew the answer.

Someone to their left spat out the words, "We're prisoners."

"Is that you, Emil?" József recognized the voice. He turned to see what he thought was Emil's shadow sulking in the corner.

He tried to look at all the sullen faces surrounding him, but everybody's shadow blended in with the next person's from more than two feet away. They were so cramped that each person had just about two inches of space on either side of their shoulders and everybody's legs were pointed towards the center of the square room. When József had finally sat up after lying unconscious on the ground people shifted so they had a little more room.

"Yeah, it's me," Emil answered.

"Where's Iren? And the other girls, the kids? Where's Isla?" József asked, but nobody answered him. He knew the answer, but he hoped he was wrong.

"They took them all," somebody said quietly.

It was the husband of one of the women who had been taken; he looked blankly up at the low ceiling which looked like it could have caved in on them at any moment. There were less than ten women and children and they'd been locked in an adjacent cell.

They knew that nothing they could have done would have prevented the events from taking place, but József felt that he should've mentioned the unease he felt before, that maybe he was at fault for not saying, "Hey guys, I don't have a good feeling about this." Perhaps, he thought, that may have saved them.

József noticed his friend Gellért, who was usually quite boisterous, was weeping quietly against a wall, he looked scared for the first time in his life. The gray concrete door wall behind him blended perfectly into the gray concrete door, without even so much as a handle on the prisoner's side; the only indication that a door existed was the small window for the guards to peer in through. That was also the only source of light in the prison cell.

József knew that they were going to die there.

Ten minutes, twenty minutes, then an hour went by in near silence. The only sound was an occasional cough, though the men tried their best to suppress even that.

The peace was broken by the commotion on the other side of the wall.

"Not again, please God, not again," one man lamented.

They listened to the cacophony of shrieks and moans coming from the other side of the wall. Some began praying or crying, others covered their ears as best as they could, and József was confused at first, but when he heard the women screaming, he knew; he'd heard that noise before. The cries of a woman who couldn't fight the monster atop her. He closed his eyes and pictured the baseless Soviets burning in hell.

Later on, the distinct sound of keys jingling against the door made everybody stiffen up. József leaned back against the wall, trying to blend in. They all watched as two soldiers entered and a third stayed behind to guard the open door. Everyone looked down at their knees, Károly nudged József and he followed suit. Two guards stood in the middle of the small open space to look at everyone, trying to sniff out who would be the best victim to choose next.

József was only brave enough to look at their boots: black, chunky, and covered in dried mud. He watched as the boots shuffled in a small circle slowly, savoring their fear. He stopped and stared at Markos, the nice old man from the train, who was obviously too weak to try anything smart with the Soviets.

"You, up," he commanded.

Markos obeyed, it was easier. He struggled to get to his feet because his knees and hips had grown stiff—he was old, but everybody was feeling the pain after sitting on the concrete for several hours. The soldier shoved him toward the door, he stumbled but he did not curse or complain. He looked at the men who sat closest to the door as he exited and gave them a heavyhearted sigh and a nod. The knowing look in his eyes indicated that he had already given up, that it didn't matter what they were going to do to him, Markos knew he'd come to the end of his rope, and he wasn't going to fight it. The soldiers closed and locked the door again and four sets of footsteps faded down the hallway.

"Bastards," someone muttered.

A young teenager asked, "Are they going to take all of us?"

"They'll take us all eventually, that's how it works," Emil answered.

They looked over to Emil, who was still brooding in the corner. József looked around the faces trying to find Elias, Emil's twin brother, but Elias wasn't in the prison cell. He knew what had happened. Emil had blamed himself for his father's death during the revolution, and then he blamed himself for the loss of both of his siblings in their attempted escape. Nothing that anybody could say would change the situation or bring back those who'd been taken by the Soviets, so they returned to silence. Within minutes, pained cries echoed through the little concrete building. Long, helpless yells bounced around the room like a wayward tennis ball.

The screaming turned to begging, "*Stoy! Stoy!* Stop! Stop!" Markos cried in any language they might hear him.

The Soviets yelled, demanded that he answer their questions, "*Otvet mne!*"

And when he couldn't give them the answer they wanted to their ridiculous questions, they beat him until he begged for mercy.

The questioning and beatings went on for a while, nearly another hour, nobody thought that Markos would survive the torture. To the Soviets, he was disposable, and they let prisoners bleed out in their interrogation cells if their torture went too far. Later, they disposed of the bodies in a shallow grave just outside of the barracks.

It was not long before someone noticed that one person was missing, but they knew he hadn't been taken by the Soviets for interrogation.

"Did anybody see where Cain went?"

"The last time I saw him was before the Soviets ambushed us," one said.

"Ambushed? I hardly think it was an ambush. We walked right into them," another refuted with a bitter tone.

"No need to argue," a voice of reason offered.

"No, he's right! And Cain was the one with the map, he led us through the forest to this spot."

"You're not saying. . ."

They were suggesting that Cain may have purposefully led them through the forest and to the Soviet camp. It wasn't uncommon for Hungarians to double-cross one another and turn in their own friends and family. Interrogations and being spied on by the secret police were common, and often the only way to save yourself from some of the punishment was to rat somebody else out to the AVH or begin working for them. It wasn't too far-fetched to think that somebody had led them straight to the Soviets on purpose, perhaps with the promise of money or a lighter punishment. But this felt lower than the average disloyalty. Cain led as many Hungarians as he could to the Soviets. And a handful of AVH spies or informants had posed as a guide to help Hungarians cross the border into Austria, but instead led them to capture.

Amid the arguing, someone started to panic. He shivered, gasped for breath, clutched his knees and closed his eyes tightly to dissociate from his surroundings. Everyone watched the poor kid spiral, unable to do anything that would really matter. A middle-aged man calmly asked him what his name was, to try to distract him.

He tried to catch his breath and asked, "Huh?"

They looked at each other through the shadowy cell.

"We're gonna get out of here," he tried reassuring him in a strong voice. "What's your name?"

He sniffled and stammered, "Tamás."

"Tamás? I'm Jakob. We're not dying here." He gave the best smile he could manage.

Tamás was pessimistic, he dismissed Jakob, "Yes we are, they're gonna kill us all."

Before he could begin crying again, before Jakob could even say anything to counter his argument, a soldier burst through the door.

Once more, everyone stiffened and looked anywhere but up to avoid catching the Soviets' eyes. Several guards stood outside the door as the gargantuan soldier stalked in to pick his next prey. For a second József was afraid that the Ogre was going to pick him when those boots stopped in front of his own. József tensed in preparation for the worst, but when he heard the sniffles on the other side of the room, the soldier spun around.

Tamás' sobs turned to screams when the Ogre reached down and snatched him up by the collar of his coat. Everybody sat idly by, looking away while Tamás shrieked and begged to be let go. The Ogre heaved Tamás up by his collar and dragged him out of the room. Tamás didn't have the energy or the strength to physically fight against the Ogre, but he cried out in protest as the Ogre dragged him down the hall.

He's not coming back, József thought.

Chapter 30

The Ogre

He came in every hour to take another victim to an interrogation. Daylight was breaking and their prison cell was emptying out quickly, but nobody had yet returned. The Soviets' small building couldn't possibly have dozens of individual interrogation rooms, they wondered where everyone had been put, or if prisoners were being murdered to make room for more interrogations. Occasionally, the men would scream out from their interrogation cells where they were being tortured, but eventually all of their screams sounded the same so the others couldn't tell who was who.

The guards still paced outside the door, peering into the cell every now and again to see that the prisoners were still not up to anything. It was extremely uncomfortable, but most of them tried to sleep because they were exhausted from the previous day and the entire night of horror. Károly rested his head on the concrete wall behind him, too tired to move but too afraid to sleep. József stared blankly ahead, thinking and praying.

God? If you're listening, then just please get us out of here. If this is punishment for what I did, then I'm sorry. I'll repent, I promise I'll do it!

József believed that his silent prayers went to God, and as a child, he'd often wonder if all of his thoughts could be heard by God, or if he could hide some thoughts. Eventually, he began to wonder if God was even listening at all. After all, there were plenty of people on Earth, all trying to talk to God at the same time. József knew that he didn't regret what he had done, but he didn't want God to know that. He didn't regret it, even though he knew that murder was wrong, but he knew that righteous revenge was sometimes permissible, and he felt that the Soviets deserved far worse.

The Ogre barged through the door again, he was the one who picked. He thrived on the smell of fear, so he took his time choosing his victims. József never looked up so that he didn't have to see the Ogre's face, but he did see the clunky boots stop right in front of him. He'd made his choice; he reached down and yanked József up by his coat. The skinny sixteen-year-old struggled, but it was no use, the Ogre was massive and extraordinarily strong, he held him above the ground effortlessly. Károly gasped as soon as József was plucked up, but he was too paralyzed to protest in any way. He watched helplessly as the Ogre turned to leave, József kicked his legs and he caught Károly's eye for a split second before the door closed, he didn't understand why his brother hadn't even reacted or tried to help.

The Soviets took him to a room down the hall and restrained his hands behind him and tied them to the rear legs of the chair and tied his ankles to the front legs of the chair. The Ogre watched with pleasure as József struggled in vain against the restraints. József stared back at the Ogre defiantly, trying to give the illusion that he wasn't scared. The Ogre commanded the two other soldiers to leave, they obeyed and stood guard outside, waiting for their next orders. The Ogre asked József if he spoke Russian. József cursed at him in Hungarian, which made him grin wickedly; József knew that wasn't a wise choice. He chuckled, getting within an inch of József's face, close enough to hear József's heartbeat.

He spoke in broken Hungarian, "You think this funny?"

He scoffed and took József's head in his massive hand, squeezed tightly, then threw him and the chair to the ground. József's head hit the concrete with a thud, his body radiated with pain.

"Cooperate now, huh?" His tone was airy.

He yanked József and the chair back upright with one hand, and with the other, he pulled another chair up for himself to sit in front of József.

"OK. What your name?" he asked, a little bit more pleasantly.

No answer.

The Ogre sighed heavily, he seemed irritated that he would have to do this the hard way. Effortlessly, and without warning, he punched József in the jaw with a quick uppercut. József felt the warm metallic taste of blood filling his mouth and tried to hold back his cries.

Pleased with himself, he asked again, "What your name?"

With his bloody mouth he mumbled, "József Kutnyak."

"Good," he cooed, "City?"

"Pécs," József answered quietly. He swallowed the blood, afraid to spit it out and anger the soldier.

"That boy, your brother?"

"Yes."

"You two escape? With all the people? Where?" he probed.

"We were only going to visit family."

"Ah," he said uninterestedly, he knew very well that József was lying through his bloodied teeth. He stared at the frightened and beaten boy with a strange smile for several moments, then he threw a punch at József's chest.

That knocked the wind out of him, he gasped for air as the Ogre watched amusedly.

When József could finally breathe again, the Ogre looked at him with apathy, "You escape," he said, he didn't ask.

"Yes," József sputtered.

"Good. You a rebel?"

"No. . . No, we're not with any rebels, I swear, I'm not one of them!"

The Ogre took a second to consider this, but he figured József was still lying, so he asked again, "You work with the rebels, no?"

"No, I don't, I'm not working with them!"

He nodded affirmatively and tutted. József feared that he was going to be punched again, so he tensed up in preparation, but the Ogre did not move.

József wished very much that he had stayed at home because at least he might've been able to evade capture by hiding. And, if he was found out by the Soviets somehow and forced to join their army or sent to a gulag, at least he could still make it out alive. There, on the other hand, he was positive he would die because he'd tried to escape and that was punishable by death.

The Ogre presented József with a metal crowbar and smiled. He held it in one hand while he caressed its cold, shiny shaft with the other. He asked, "You know what I do with this?"

"Please," József began to beg.

"I get information."

"No, no, please," his voice was breaking.

"Tell me, where are the rebels?"

"I told you, I don't know!"

The Ogre took a step back and prepared to swing the crowbar. József closed his eyes, expecting it to collide with his face or stomach, but the Ogre hit his shins instead. Breaking and splintering bones was an easy and effective method of torture. Shockwaves of pain reverberated throughout his body, he had no way to protect himself or prepare for the blows as the Ogre lifted the bar again, all he did was scream.

"Stop!" he cried.

But the bar smashed his shin again, sending a prickling pain throughout his whole body. He grimaced and grunted to stifle his cries, he hated giving the Ogre the satisfaction of him screaming and crying, but he couldn't help it.

The Ogre leaned in so their faces were only inches apart and screamed, "Tell me what you know!"

József flinched when he felt the warm spittle cover his face, and smelled the hot, oniony breath.

"Tell me!"

József began to panic, "I don't know anything! None of us do, we weren't part of the resistance!" But he knew that he'd lied, he knew at least Elias, Emil, and Iren were freedom fighters, he couldn't be sure about the rest, though.

Veins in the Ogre's neck bulged, he was frustrated. "You think, I'll come back," he warned, and he smacked József across the face before he left. All things considered, he was lucky that his shins and face were all the Soviet beat.

When the Soviets tortured somebody for information they didn't stop until they got a confession, even if it were a false confession. They were giving him time to think, time to become more afraid. He tried adjusting his wrists against the rope to relieve some of the pressure, but it was of little use. He couldn't help but think of all the ways they could torture and kill him, exactly as the Soviets wanted intended for their victims to do when left alone.

His adrenaline was running high so he didn't feel all of the pain he was in, and he tried to think about anything else to distract himself. The lightbulb above his head flickered softly as it swung slightly on its chain. A fly was bouncing off of it, attracted to the brightness. He watched the fly buzz from the lightbulb to the ceiling, back to the light, then to the wall again, over and over. The fly was searching for the escape József could not have; he envied the fly.

Soon he was bored with the fly's tediousness so he started trying to free himself from his restraints. Unfortunately, he found no slack in the ropes; and try as he might, he could not loosen them enough to slip his hands through. The Ogre had left his chair with its back facing József and he got an idea. He jerked his body so hard to move his chair, which scraped noisily on the floor, and he thought he'd get caught making all that noise. He did his best to propel his weight up while thrusting his hips to one side, he did that again and again, nearly tipping over, until he had successfully turned his chair in a half circle. It was physically exhausting, but he did it.

Once turned around, he looked around his shoulder at the Ogre's chair, and began pushing himself backwards towards it. It was difficult, not being able to see, but he fumbled around under the seat and eventually found where the screws on the chair were placed. He stuck his thumb nail in one of the screw heads and began to turn. It hurt like hell, and he could only twist his thumb about 30 degrees, but he repeated that motion adamantly to retrieve the screw. When he unscrewed it enough, he could twist it out the rest of the way by gripping the threads of the screw which hurt his fingers more. He began to lose feeling in his hands, he feared he would drop the screw so he stopped until he could feel the blood flow in his fingers again. Finally, when he pulled the screw out of the wood, he rejoiced quietly, then he listened for the Soviets.

Between his thumb and forefinger, he laid the screw against his palm and tried to reach the ropes on his wrist, but he couldn't manage it. He carefully passed the screw to the other hand, and he was able to scratch at the rope where it lay between his wrists with the grooves of the screw. He scratched away at the rope for minutes until his fingers felt numb and he had to stop, it didn't feel like any progress had been made on the ropes either. When he was ready to begin again, he tried to adjust the screw, but it fell from his hands. It rolled between the legs of the chair and stopped at the edge of the floor in front of him. Even if he could throw himself on the ground to retrieve it, he wouldn't be able to reach.

His clumsiness had foiled him, he felt stupid and hopeless; he slammed his back into the chair and cursed himself. The soldiers in the hallway noticed the racket and yelled at him to stop, he stiffened, but they didn't enter the cell. To avoid further suspicion, he stopped trying to free his wrists for the moment and stayed as still as he could.

He jerked his head back up each time it drooped, trying to fight the drowsiness, but eventually he drifted to sleep. It wasn't a comfortable or restful nap, and when the Soviets in the hallway realized he'd fallen asleep they sent in a soldier with a bucket of ice water to wake him. The henchmen entered the room quietly so as not to wake József before he turned the bucket over his head and drenched him with ice cold water. The soldiers laughed cruelly.

After being startled awake, József was so angry that he cursed the soldiers out loud, they only laughed more. He knew the torture was just beginning. József was angry at them, and angry that they got caught.

CHAPTER 31

AGONY

József's anger turned to grief and then to fear the longer he dwelled. The Soviets had taken everything from him; his country, his home, his childhood, his freedom, and next they'd take his life. They'd taken his bag as well, which had his Bible and the photo of his family he kept, he'd never see those again. He felt hopeless, he couldn't even think, the only positive thing about his situation was that he'd lost the feeling in his beaten body because he was wet and freezing.

It wasn't long before the Ogre came again. "I have surprise for you," he growled, "Hold out your hand." He moved to József's backside where his hands were still tied up. Luckily, he hadn't noticed the stray screw in the corner, or that József wasn't in the same position he'd left him in.

József was reluctant to stick out his hands but he obliged, fearing what would happen if he did not. The Ogre didn't place anything in his hand, as he expected, instead he snatched one finger and held it tightly. He didn't waste any time before he jammed a tweezer-like pair of pliers underneath József's forefinger nail and ripped the nail off a little at a time.

He didn't do it quickly; his goal was to do it agonizingly slow to cause the most pain possible. József screamed and began to cry out in protest. He struggled to free his hand but that only made the pain worse as the Ogre had to tighten his grip and yank the pliers harder. József had never felt such an intense pain in his finger before, he had not even thought it was possible to hurt a finger that badly; after all, he used his hands quite often for work and they had taken a lot of abuse, but this pain was beyond that. The Ogre had ripped the nail completely off, dropped it, and let the blood trickle out while József wailed.

Smirking, the Ogre asked, "Again?"

József screamed, "No! What do you want from me?"

"Tell me where the rebels are!" he demanded.

"There's some in the forest, outside of Pécs! That's where I'm from, but I was never a freedom fighter, I swear! That's all I know!"

"Where are the others?" he asked again, as he bent another finger unnaturally.

József cried, "I don't know!"

"You know something," the Ogre shrugged.

"I swear, I don't!"

József had never rehearsed what he would say in the event of an interrogation, he was naïve to think he'd never need to. He certainly knew what they were capable of, but he didn't think he'd get caught.

The Ogre gripped another fingernail with the thin pliers and began lifting. József cried out and struggled against his grip, but the Ogre was already done, he let the nail fall, and the blood began to drip from the second finger. He could have left it at that and left József to suffer in peace, but he could not resist inflicting more pain; it was in his nature. He stood up, placed the tool into his pocket, and placed his hands around József's throat. They were so massive that the thumbs could hook in the back and all eight fingers could lace together in the front.

"Please, don't," he gulped and his Adam's apple bobbed against the Ogre's fingers.

The Ogre breathed deeply and closed his eyes, feeling for the tender spots under József's jaw. He applied the tiniest bit of pressure and József gasped for air, he tightened his grip and relaxed it repeatedly, playing with József's life. Like many Soviets and secret police officers, he enjoyed having the power to take somebody's life. József expected to suffocate and die, but before he ran out of air completely, the Ogre let go and left the room again.

His parting words were simple and purposefully ominous, "Next time."

József sucked in as much air as he could before he bawled uncontrollably. He was terrified and angry that the Ogre didn't just kill him and get it over with. He cried and yelled loudly enough for the Soviets to hear, but they didn't try to stop him, they only mocked him from their post outside the door. His throat ached but the crying gave him a welcome release of emotional tension; he was so exhausted afterwards that he could do nothing except sit quietly and miserably.

The following day, the Ogre tortured his other victims and left József alone. Though he was not completely unbothered, he was woken several more times by the guards. Each time he fell asleep, a henchman was sent in with a bucket of ice water to pour over his head. Not only did they not allow their victims to sleep, they also didn't allow them food or water. They often starved their victims completely, sometimes for weeks at a time. Sometimes, they fed the poor prisoners a ton of greasy, nasty, food so that they'd get sick from it after being starved for so long. Or they'd feed a very dehydrated prisoner a lot of salty food so that they'd be dying of thirst from it. The Soviets and secret police often devised small ways to torture people like that, in addition to the physical beatings.

Without water, József had resorted to sucking the residual water from the chest of his wool coat which retained much of the water poured on him, keeping him cold. The technique of sucking water from the lapel of his coat worked well for him until he couldn't stretch his neck any further.

There was no window in his room, so he had completely lost track of time—the Soviets preferred it that way; their victims tended to break after several days without sunlight or a sense of time. They knew they could drive their victims insane by depriving them of light, food, and water, it was just a matter of time. They called it the "softening up" period, the first few days were supposed to break the prisoner's spirit, making them more likely to cooperate during interrogation. Sometimes, rather than depriving prisoners of light, they flood their cell with inescapable fluorescent lights that never turn off, this period could last for weeks.

József passed his time worrying that the Soviets would find out that he'd lied to them about working with the freedom fighters. He wasn't a soldier or a fighter, but he'd helped them by standing guard in the woods or running messages between groups. If the Soviets found that out, they'd surely kill him.

Eventually, he started humming a tune he had heard often growing up, something his mother would sing while she cooked or cleaned. The song made him think of how much he missed his family already, and how they'd never find out what happened to him or where the Soviets would bury him. But when he thought of his little sister, he got the urge to keep fighting, not to give into torture, so that he would survive to see her again. It was his love for Edit that got him through the silent hours alone and kept him strong enough to endure the pain. When he got tired, he found things to keep him awake, he hummed, he talked to himself, he wiggled his legs or shook his head, anything he could do to keep himself awake so they wouldn't pour more water on him.

At least he was able to sit in a chair during his torture, the secret police had been known to force prisoners to stand on one foot or kneel on gravel or something equally uncomfortable, which could last days. Standing on one foot isn't hard to do for a few seconds or minutes, but it's nearly impossible to do for hours or days, and if they lost their balance or wavered, they'd be punished or shot at.

Prisoners who were allowed a bed weren't always given a blanket or pillow, and the bright lights were kept on all the time, but that was the least of their worries. They had to lay on their backs with their hands on their chest in full view of the guards, if they rolled or moved at all they'd be shot at.

Sometimes, prisoners were put in cells that were so small they couldn't even sit and stretch their legs out, let alone lie down in them, and they were forced to stand for however long pleased the torturers. People told about their experiences of being forced to stand in several inches of freezing water, or of having to stand in human waste, or even forced to use the bowl they used for food as the bowl they would catch their own excrement in.

A favorite technique used by the Soviets, the AVH, the KGB, and many other secret police organizations was making the prisoners choose the weapon they would be beaten with. They would display an arrangement of belts, whips, switches, tools, whatever was at the ready, and tell prisoners to choose what they wanted to be beaten with. Avoiding the beating was not an option. They'd mercilessly whip or bludgeon a person, sparing nothing; people's bones were shattered, genitals were whipped, vital organs were pierced, nothing was off limits for the torturers. And on Sundays, the AVH liked to torture their prisoners with extra gusto in order to defile the holy day for those who still practiced religion.

All sorts of methods were used to beat and torture prisoners, including, but not limited to: carving people's bodies with knives, crushing or shattering bones with metal rods, using pliers to crush extremities, jamming a knife underneath fingernails or ripping them off completely, punching while wearing metal gloves with nails on them, pinching or burning genitals, whipping the soles of feet, depriving people of sleep, forcing them to sit on a metal pole for hours, forcing physical exercises such as squats for hours, burning, and of course sexual violence such as rape, sodomy, and genital mutilation.

They'd often send prisoners to gulags, sometimes outside of Hungary's borders, after they were done torturing them. Some of the forced labor camps were secret, like the Recsk [Rechk] prison camp outside of the village of Recsk, a notoriously brutal camp that (officially) operated from 1950 to 1953. There, prisoners were forced to endure hard labor as punishment, but they had had no trial or official sentencing, but legalities didn't matter when they usually arrested and imprisoned people who were completely innocent. Everybody in Hungary had known somebody who'd disappeared one day without a trace, sometimes they came back weeks or months later, but other times they were never seen again. Sometimes they were sent to a gulag within the country, but other times they were sent to Russia, Siberia, or a central Asian country to perform hard labor.

Cattle cars were used to deport mass amounts of people to the labor camps, or the "relocation camps" for the kulaks from all of the satellite states and the republics of the USSR. The Soviet Union started deporting minorities from every country they invaded to concentration camps via cattle cars in the 1920s.

József heard a train screech to a halt nearby—they had not been far off from the tracks, since they used the tracks as a guide into Austria. He listened carefully to the hustle in the Soviet camp, trying to figure out if people were coming or going. József assumed that they'd loaded up prisoners to take them to a gulag in Russia, it was not uncommon for people in the Eastern Bloc to be carted off to perform forced labor. József worried that he'd never see his brother again.

CHAPTER 32

RELEASE

József had no idea how much time had passed when he heard keys jingling outside of the door again. He didn't know if it was night or day and hadn't heard much more commotion from the Soviets after he heard the train earlier, he'd been in a daze since. His neck was so stiff that he could barely look to see who was coming into his cell.

"Don't say anything," the guard whispered.

It wasn't the Ogre, and he didn't think it was any of the other Soviets he'd met so far. The soldier pulled out a small knife and bent down to József's hands, he jerked away, his heart racing, but afraid to speak. He shushed József again so he didn't yell out or protest while he cut the ropes that bound his hands. József's mind swarmed with possibilities, but the foremost thought was that it was a test, a trap, so he didn't move. He watched curiously as the young soldier moved to cut the ropes at his ankles.

"We have to go," he urged József out of the chair. He had a small voice but József realized that he spoke without an accent, he was Hungarian.

The young soldier was scrawny, he barely fit in his Red Army uniform, and he couldn't have been older than József was. When they saw each other's faces, József saw a fellow Hungarian teenager and he realized what was happening. His feet were numb, and his body was weak, but he got up as quickly as possible; the young soldier was making sure the hallway was clear.

"Come on," he whispered.

József followed close behind through the musty corridor, hunching over to stay below the view of the windows to the other prison cells. There was one hallway intersection and a corner they had to get through without being seen, but they made it to the exit quickly and invisibly. The young soldier fumbled for his keys as quietly as possible, but it still seemed to echo in the concrete hallway. József tried to keep an eye out for any Soviets who could pop out at any time, and luckily, he didn't see any. The right key was found but when he inserted it into the lock it got jammed, the young soldier was getting frustrated and that's when they heard footsteps in the distance; an actual Soviet soldier had heard the keys jingling and was going to investigate. The young soldier got the door open in the nick of time and started pushing József through.

"Go!" he shouted.

József went but he hesitated on the outside of the doorway, the brightness of day burned his eyes, he looked back, "Come with me."

The look in the young soldier's eyes was pure horror, "They'll kill my family."

The Soviet behind them rounded the corner, József caught a glimpse of him before the door started closing.

"Go!"

He pushed József out of the threshold and shut the door just as the Soviet closed in on him. József heard the Soviet slam the young soldier against the door, he didn't wait for the Soviets to come after him, he turned tail and ran. He hadn't the faintest idea which way he was running, but he would figure it out when he got there. He wasn't far away when he heard a gunshot from within the barracks. József felt guilty for leaving the young soldier behind and being the reason that he was probably killed, but there was nothing else he could do so he sprinted away.

It wasn't uncommon for the Soviets to conscript young men into their armed services by force—threats against their life or their family members' lives. They'd train the soldiers to be ruthless killers and serve the tyrannical dictatorship and eventually force them to turn on their own people. It wasn't just Hungarians; it was every satellite state and republic within the USSR. The threat of the torture or death of a loved one would stop many headstrong young boys from rebelling against the Soviets, but occasionally integrity outweighed self-preservation, or they thought they could get away with it. The moral obligation that young soldier felt to save József's life cost him his own, and that's the purest definition of a hero.

Refugees who crossed the bridge at Andau recalled one Hungarian AVH guard who was assigned to the guard tower nearest to the bridge; but instead of preventing refugees from escaping, he helped them through. Reportedly, he told his comrades that he would deal with a group of Hungarians they caught, he led them away, fired shots into the air to fool the other guards, and let the Hungarians escape.

József's shin bones were splintered, but he couldn't feel it yet, his adrenaline pushed him to keep running. It felt good to run, it felt free; he didn't have to think or worry, he just had to focus on where his feet landed because large rocks and branches were hidden under the snow and mud. Luckily, he'd spent many years tramping through the forest helping the partisans, so he'd had practice. He ducked under low-hanging branches, jumped over small creeks, weaved between rocks, and he cleared the forest nearly twenty minutes later.

He slowed to a stop, feet pounding on the narrow gravel road, he could hear his blood pumping and feel his heart in his throat. Running on an empty stomach, with broken bones, and such high anxiety, made him nauseous. József hated throwing up, but he knew the feeling when his dry mouth began to salivate; he doubled over, holding onto his knees for balance, and tried breathing through the queasiness. His breathing was closer to dry heaving, but he recovered and the feeling subsided. There was fresh clean snow on the side of the road, he bent down to shovel snow into his mouth. It was so cold it burned his mouth, but he was dying of thirst, he closed his eyes and let the snow melt in his mouth, it was wonderful.

The last time he'd eaten or had a proper drink was on the train from Pécs, he had no idea how long ago that was. It was at least two days, but time doesn't feel normal in prison while being beaten so it may have been more. He was starving, and as he knelt on the ground, he became aware of how empty his whole body felt.

He wished that he could open his eyes and see his bedroom ceiling and his brother on the bed next to him; but he knew that when he opened his eyes, he would still be lost and alone on the edge of a strange forest. He examined his missing fingernails, the dried blood, the scratches and bruises on his wrists. Although it pained him to touch his fingers, he tried to clean the dried blood off with snow. It worked well enough in a pinch, but it made a pink watery mess. He didn't try to clean the blood and grime off his forehead, simply because he forgot it was there.

The road was deserted, and he didn't see any houses or anybody, which both relieved and scared him. He noticed a low fence beyond the ditch and decided to test its strength; it seemed sturdy enough to hold his weight, so he sat to relieve his tired legs. The fence looked like a border to a farm, but he couldn't be too certain because in November everything looked like a frozen wasteland. The sky was growing cloudy, he was freezing, and he began to worry that he was in danger out in the open, he never knew who could be watching and listening.

József's heart rate increased as he looked up and down the road, behind him, and peered into the woods from which he came, looking out for anything that moved—nothing moved. For the first time, he had the profound feeling that he was alone. He tried to hold back tears, not wanting to let his emotions and worries get the better of him, he still had ground to cover, and he couldn't give up hope yet, but it was feeling more and more hopeless each day. Tears fell, leaving a hot streak on his cold cheeks, and he choked back his sobs. He mourned for those the Soviets killed, for his brother, whom he thought had been carted off to a gulag, and for himself.

There was always a chance that they wouldn't make it out of Hungary alive, they knew that when they left, but he didn't know if he could continue without Károly. Frankly, they hadn't really thought about what they would do once they made it to Austria, *if* they made it, because first and foremost they had to make it out of Hungary alive. He thought that everything would fall into place once they made it into Austria, but his prospects seemed so grim.

József dreaded the day he would have to write home to his parents about how he left Károly behind, he'd promised his mother that they'd stick together. But when the young soldier gave him the opportunity to run, he had to take it. Although, he wondered why, out of all those people, he was freed while the rest had to remain.

He noticed the sun drifting towards the west, so knew which direction to follow when the time came. But still, he waited, he didn't know why, but he knew he had to wait. József foolishly hoped that he might be reunited with Károly, and as if right on cue, he noticed someone coming from the woods. His eyes went in and out of focus trying to see who it could be; whoever it was, he started waving at József. It wasn't his brother or his friends, but it wasn't a Soviet.

"Hey!" József called out as he waved.

"Hello?" asked the average looking man, József recognized him as Tamás, from the prison cell. "They let you go, too?" He was surprised.

"Oh, my God." József made a quick cross over his chest out of habit, the way his mother used to do. "You're alive! I thought they killed you," he said in a breathy sort of laugh.

They hardly knew each other, but they were excited to find each other. Tamás looked rough, as if he had been tied to a hitch and dragged through the dirt. His face was bruised and bloody, one eye was swollen near shut, and he had several fractured bones which made it hard for him to walk.

"*I* thought I was dead, but he took me to the interrogation room and just beat me until I went unconscious. He came in again and again to question me and beat me, but he never killed me. I wanted him to kill me, it would have been a relief not to be beat! Then today that kid came in and let me go. At first, I thought it was a trap, but I didn't ask questions, I didn't look back, nothing. I've been walking for a while, I think I'm going in circles, I'm completely lost." He was winded and panicked, he ran his hands through his matted bloodied hair.

It turned out that Tamás had been let go before József, he'd started to make his way through the forest when József was let out. József had not seen Tamás at all, but then again, he hadn't been looking. Tamás had actually heard József gaining speed behind him, so he hid behind some boulders, thinking it was a guard who saw him wandering in the woods. He watched and waited until József was out of sight before continuing.

"But why were you let go, did he tell you?"

Tamás shrugged, "No idea."

They wondered what made them special. Why did they get to live while the others were probably forced into slave labor or killed? Nothing made them different or special, it was merely a lucky draw that they were spared.

The silence grew between them and József felt the need to break it. "Should we wait here to see if any more people are let go? That way they can come to Austria with us."

"Me? What, oh no, I'm not coming. I'm going home. I've had enough! If I don't go home then they will know, they have my identification!" Tamás was distraught, waving his hands in front of him to bat away the absurd idea of leaving Hungary.

József thought that was odd, just the other day Tamás had been trying to escape but getting caught scared him into not wanting to leave anymore.

"But if you *do* go home, they have your identification! They'll know where you are!" he was almost shouting. "I'm not staying, we're so close to the border, if we just keep walking west then we will be in Austria!" He hoped his excitement would entice Tamás to join, if only for his own sake so he had a companion.

"There will be more Russians at the border—there's always more Russians! I'm going home," he proclaimed.

"Look, Tamás, why would you go home now? We're not that far away, all we have to do is get in, and then the Russians can't touch us." József tried to reason with him, "If you go home, then the Russians will know where you are, and they will take you in the middle of the night and kill you. I know, because it happened to people in my village a few days ago. When we get into Austria they will help us."

Tamás knew that people disappeared all the time, he knew what the Soviets were capable of. "Yeah, I guess," he mumbled.

"They can't hurt us if we're not here." József was thinking logically, he knew Tamás would be in danger if he stayed and he selfishly wanted a companion to escape with, he was afraid to be alone.

Generally speaking, Tamás was not the kind of man who got back up when he was knocked down, but he had already made it that far, and József was persuasive, and his argument was reasonable. They bantered back and forth for a while until Tamás arrived at the conclusion that leaving Hungary was his safest option. They were going to continue into Austria together, but first they decided to wait where they were for a little while longer on the off chance that any of the other prisoners would be let free and appear out of the woods. That gave Tamás the chance to rest his weary legs, as well.

"Say, József, where are you from?" Tamás asked.

"Pécs. What about you, where is your home?"

"A village near Debrecen."

"Debrecen? And you wanted to go all the way back home? You wouldn't have even made it halfway before they found you!" József said, rather snidely.

Tamás was a little offended, he reasoned, "To me it seems safer than going west. We don't know what's over there. At least I know what's at home," he shrugged.

"Yeah, I guess I understand that." József felt a little guilty for his rude retort. "Did you come with anybody, before, you know?"

"No. I was alone."

"You're alone?"

"Yeah. My village was raided a few days after the protest in Budapest. Lots of people started a protest in Debrecen but then the army came. I didn't stay at the march long enough to see much. When I heard about how the Russians attacked Budapest again, I knew it was time to leave. So, I packed a bag and left my apartment without telling anybody where I was going," Tamás admitted.

"Oh, I'm sorry," he offered sympathetically, then he waited quietly, hoping Tamás would say more, but that was all he was willing to share. József felt like he was hiding something, or not telling the complete truth, but he didn't probe.

He changed the subject, "It's getting dark, I think we should start walking. I don't think the Russians are letting anybody else go."

"Yeah, you're probably right."

With weariness, they stood up.

"You ready?"

Tamás nodded stiffly. They stretched their legs and looked into the forest from which they came for a moment. It was bittersweet; they wanted to escape and live but felt guilty that they had to leave others behind. They set out on their journey towards the free west, not knowing when, or if, they'd ever be able to return to Hungary.

CHAPTER 33
"I WAS A MODEL CITIZEN"

After we got to Portland, there were Hungarians I knew who went back home because they were home sick and all that and they says, "Oh, I'm gonna write you, I'm gonna write you," and we get one or two letters from them saying I made it home and all that, then the letters stopped. We sent more letters 'cause we thought well maybe they didn't get it, and not one of them was answered. But six people don't just disappear. So, there it was, a year or two after the revolution, anybody who went back to Hungary, chances were good that they disappeared.

One of my friends, he went to Sweden and the mindset was, "I don't wanna go too far from Hungary so I can go back," you know. And to go to America, that is far away.

I know my friend didn't want to go to America, he wanted to go to Sweden. But you had to learn to take care of yourself. You come first, you know. Whatever was best for you, was best for you. That was what most everybody was thinking. To stay close to Hungary was more of a priority than getting away from Russia. You know, I still have very bad feeling for Russia. Okay, maybe not Russia, communism, that would be a better way of saying it.

When in 1976 we wanted to bring my parents to the States to visit for the first time since I left, the Russians wouldn't let all of the family members come, one had to stay there for insurance that the others would come back. So, my little sister Edit stayed, and my mother and father came. I was really sad because I wanted to see my sister, but hey, what're you gonna do?

It was the first time I seen them in 20 years. We were waiting at the airport and Linda says, "You know, I don't know what they look like," and I says, "Neither do I!"

What I remember was my mother was short and plump, and my father was tall and thin, but when I saw them, I thought, "Wow, these aren't my parents, they must have switched or something 'cause they not like I remember them." My father grown this hump in his back, and he's wider now, and my mother was getting so thin, she was getting sick.

The first year we went back was in 1988. I was very, very nervous going back home. We got the letter from my father, "Your mother is sick, she won't last long, if you want to see her then come now."

She wanted to see her "Dodika," is what she called me. That's what you call kids, you add "ka" to the end of their name. But when you an adult, you don't do that, you call them Mr. or Sir, but not "ka."

Linda and I, we went back, and I tell you, I did not step on a crack, I did not spit on the sidewalk, I was a model citizen. I was scared. I was an American citizen, but even that wouldn't have stopped them if they wanted to do something. . . take me away, whatnot.

When we landed in Hungary, we had to check in at the police station to say, "Hey, we here," and they took our passports and held on to them until we left so they knew we were leaving.

We stayed at the Russian's hotel, that's what everybody says; they teased about it, you know. There was this big, fancy hotel at the top of the street in Pécs where the Russians stayed when I was a kid, and we stayed there at the hotel when we visited.

Well, my mother died the next year, and we went back yet again for the funeral. And that's when my sister was sick, she had stomach cancer—like my mother.

The Russians weren't as out in the open as they used to be, though. In the 40s and 50s it was bad; it was very bad to live in Hungary. In the early 80s though, things started to change. They weren't gone until '89, after my mother was gone. I remember we were watching the TV the night when the Berlin Wall came down; it didn't mean much to Linda, but to me it meant "We are finally free!"

One of those things that I remember from the early years, that people went back home, and we never heard from them again. They just, poof! Disappear, and you don't know what happened, or if they are alive, but one thing you do know, it was the Russians. So, to go home, I was scared as the Dickens. I made myself so sick I had stomach ulcers.

Edit turned twenty-four in 1976, and my grandfather hadn't seen her in twenty years, and they'd only see each other again two more times in the late 80s before she died.

My grandmother told me what she remembered from the 1976 visit when Edit couldn't make it; apparently, Ilona was very reserved and afraid of the new culture and sights, but that Károly was so excited about everything new. They didn't speak any English and my grandmother didn't speak Hungarian so they couldn't communicate very well, but when grandpa would go to work, she would take them sight-seeing.

When my grandfather would come back from work, his father would meet him in the driveway holding brochures from whatever sights grandmother took them to that day, asking his son to translate the brochure and explain what it was that he saw.

Chapter 34

Austria

The temperature dropped rapidly as the sun set, it wasn't long before it was well below freezing. Their boots and socks were wet, and they knew they'd be at risk of getting frostbite soon enough. Obviously, they only had the clothes on their backs, it wasn't much, but they knew they were lucky that the Soviets hadn't taken their boots and coats. They kept their hands tucked tightly under their arms and scrunched their shoulders to their ears to cover their necks, but they couldn't escape the cold.

The wind howled distantly, unsettlingly. They were acutely aware that they were extremely vulnerable, but there was nothing they could do but to keep walking. Even though it was unlikely that they'd be seen in the darkness, they walked in the ditches and took detours into the woods to avoid an open area. They tried to pay attention to not veer too far away from their path so they wouldn't get turned around. Neither one told the other how frightened they were, but their faces surely showed it.

Sometimes they'd hear something that made them jump, but they convinced themselves it was just the wind or an animal. The evergreens stood tall, and the moon cast shadows that played dangerous tricks on their eyes.

They didn't talk much outside of where to walk next. József was in his own world, thinking about all he hoped for and worried about, something better had to be waiting for him over that border. He daydreamed about getting a construction job and an apartment, learning to speak English and writing home to tell his parents of all the wonderful things about America. He even let himself fantasize about reuniting with Károly. In the perfect world, Károly would've escaped the Soviets' clutch and fought his way out, he'd get to America, and miraculously find József on a street corner one day (he wasn't aware how large America would be). Together, they would earn enough money, and bring the rest of their family to America. József knew his sister Edit would love that, and he would buy her as many dolls and toys as she wanted. In America, József thought, they would never have to worry, because the Soviets couldn't reach them there.

After tramping through the mud and snow for about an hour, Tamás said, "Hey, I think we made it, look over there!" He pointed towards a metal sign posted on a fence. József didn't know what he was so excited about, he couldn't even read the sign, it wasn't written in Hungarian.

Wait, it's not Hungarian, he thought, "It's German!" József almost shouted.

A German sign meant they had reached Austria. Aside from the sign there were no other indicators that they'd crossed a border—no gate, no bridge, no sign. Except for in the large cities or highways, borders weren't usually marked, so you could just walk right over without realizing it. They rejoiced together, they laughed and shook each other by their coat sleeves. They were officially refugees from Hungary, and they were free!

They continued walking, assuming they'd find a police station or stumble upon a refugee camp somehow. They didn't really know what the plan was, but they knew that the authorities would be able to help them if only they could get to them. Austrian citizens actually took on the responsibility of patrolling the borders to help any refugees they found, they'd sit and wait with a flashlight to use as a beacon to wave people over parts of the border that could be confusing, or they'd drive back and forth to pick up the weary Hungarians and take them to a shelter. József and Tamás weren't fortunate enough to be found by any good Samaritans trying to help, and they wished they'd have known that people had been rescuing the refugees at night.

A spark of optimism was in the air, they walked with a pep in their step even though they barely felt their frozen toes. József was elated, he thanked God for having brought them to salvation. Their aching bodies and hearts momentarily lifted, but after only a few minutes and a few winding roads, József noticed something that made him stop in his tracks.

"Hang on a minute," József turned around, walked a few feet back and stared at a telephone pole. Tamás joined him, and they stood helplessly looking at a sign. Sure enough, it was written in Hungarian.

"Dammit!"

They had walked back into Hungary without realizing. There were no markers along the border, and the countries had been split so haphazardly that one wrong turn could lead you astray. Their whole journey was a crapshoot. Tamás hung his head in grief and József grumbled angrily before he walked away from the pole to scan their surroundings for any clues. He wasn't sure which way he was going anymore. They had been teetering on the border, probably crossing back and forth several times.

"Which way is west?" Tamás asked rhetorically, he was exacerbated.

"I think it's still that way," József pointed, but he couldn't be sure. "We need to go as far as we can without making any turns, no matter what."

"How can you be certain which way is which, anymore? We just walked right back into Hungary!"

Tamás was especially shaken up, he was afraid they had been completely turned around and began walking towards the east again. Stopping for the night wasn't an option, they had to keep moving to stay alive, the mood turned sour, and they walked in bitter silence.

It wasn't long before they saw another sign in German that confirmed they were back in Austria, thankfully they weren't far off from the border, but they still feared accidentally walking in the wrong direction again so they walked as straight as they could for as long as possible before they had to turn with the roads. They were walking behind a desolate little village when Tamás grabbed József's sleeve to stop him.

"I think someone's coming," he warned.

A truck with blinding headlights rumbled around a corner behind them. Tamás pulled on his sleeve, urging József to follow him, afraid that it was the Soviets. The truck crept closer to them as they ran towards an alley, they ducked out of sight just as the truck passed, but they didn't feel safe outside anymore, so József began trying the back doors of the abandoned townhomes that faced the back alley.

The door to the second home he tried was unlocked, he didn't want to break a window, even though it had clearly been unoccupied.

He and Tamás slipped into their temporary shelter, hoping they were unnoticed.

They began trying light switches and opening cabinets in search of food, but the house had been without electricity for quite a while, there was no refrigerator, but they found a few dusty jars of vegetables and some dried beans in the cupboards. They hastily opened the jars of pickled asparagus, string beans and cucumber, and ate ravenously. The vegetables weren't wonderful, but it was desperately needed food, but they quickly noted that the vinegar didn't sit right in an empty stomach. They also needed to quench their thirst and tried the taps in vain, knowing that if the home didn't have electricity or residents, it most likely didn't have water.

With a stroke of genius, József dug through the cupboards once more to find containers to use. He found a few dusty bowls, cups and jars, he told Tamás to take an armful and follow him outside. There, they gathered the cleanest snow they could find into the containers, their hands were cold before but scooping up the snow made their hands burn. József was quite pleased with himself as they took the jars of snow back into the house and lined them up on the counter to melt.

They scoped out the rest of the house, fumbling blindly through the hallways and up the stairs, trying not to make too much noise. It was cold, damp, and mostly empty, but they were safe for the remainder of the night. The family that had lived there had probably taken their most prized possessions when they evacuated, leaving the rest for the looters. All that remained in the house were a few sofas, a bedframe, a grandfather clock and a China cabinet all too heavy to steal. Tamás opened a creaky closet door in the first room they entered, searching for something to wear or to use as a blanket, but instead he found an intrusion of mice scurrying back into the wall.

József moved on to the other two rooms and the bathroom where he rifled through the cabinets searching for something to sanitize and wrap his fingers with. He found a small dropper of iodine and an old, used, strip of gauze, but it was better than nothing. There wasn't enough gauze to wrap each finger individually, but he did his best to wrap the most wounded looking fingers. He wasn't concerned with the pain, since his hands were numb anyways, it didn't bother him, but he did wonder if his fingernails would grow back.

Meanwhile, Tamás had investigated all the rooms upstairs, even the shallow attic, but his findings were scarce. Luckily, he did gather a worn blanket and a grimy box of children's clothing. He took the blanket and the entire box to the sitting room to inspect the contents in case there was something useful in the box.

"Hey, come here, look what I found," he called out. Tamás started removing the clothing from the box and placing it on the cushion beside him. Even in stressful situations, people could still become so interested in snooping through somebody else's old items.

"I found some medical supplies that we can use! What is all that stuff?" József asked as he entered.

"It's children's clothing" Tamás was nonchalant about it. It didn't make sense to József *why* he was rummaging through an old box of children's clothes, it seemed like an odd time to do that, but for Tamás it was a much needed distraction.

József sat down next to him and took out a pair of tiny pale socks with small flowers stitched on, they were clearly handmade. He placed them gingerly on his lap and stared. A stranger's old socks became a poignant reminder of the life he would never know again. Tamás was finding several things that could be of use to them such as a little blanket, a scarf, even some socks for an older child they could squeeze into.

"I have a little sister," József said, starting a conversation.

"Oh yeah?" Tamás was too indulged in his own thoughts to notice József's melancholy.

"Yeah, her name is Edit, she's only four."

Tamás realized József's somber mood. "Oh, I'm sorry. That's rough."

"Yeah," was all he could muster.

It was more than just 'rough' to József, he missed his sister and he feared for her safety, especially now that the Soviets had his passport and knew where to find his family. If the Soviets were to question his family about his and Károly's whereabouts, or if they were to raid the city, or force them from their home, she would be put in danger, and he couldn't be there. He knew what the Soviets did to women and girls, he nearly made himself sick at the thought. He wiped his eyes with the back of his hands and breathed sharply before reaching down to take off his boots. Tamás, remembering that his boots were also soaked, did the same. Their feet were tired and smelled foul from being in damp socks for too long. József groaned as he stood up and took their boots and socks to hang somewhere to dry, he placed the socks over cupboards and the boots upside down on the handles and pipes coming off of the woodburning stove so they could air out.

When he returned, Tamás had repacked the clothes they couldn't use and cleared the sofa, they desperately needed to sleep. They started to remove their damp clothes and placed them over furniture to dry out. They'd stripped down to their underwear and shirts; they were too tired to feel embarrassed or shy. Tamás handed József a pair of old socks, far too small but better than nothing, and they sat on the sofa with the little blanket.

"If we lay with our legs together, we can keep warm," Tamás said as he inched closer to the one end of the sofa to give József enough room to slide under the blanket.

As they settled in, their legs brushed each other's and József jerked away, "Your skin is freezing!" he cried.

"What did you expect? So is yours!" he retorted, and they both laughed.

It was quite cramped on the sofa, they laid with their legs spooned together to preserve body heat and save space, they giggled and twitched as they got used to each other's freezing skin. They tucked in the blanket under their legs in order to retain as much heat as possible, their icy feet burned from the sudden warmth, but they eventually adjusted enough to stop shivering, even if they weren't yet warm. They curled their arms up under their heads and settled in; it wasn't exactly comfortable, but it didn't take long to fall asleep since they were completely exhausted.

CHAPTER 35

THE WAR

They woke when the afternoon sun came through the west facing window. They groaned and stretched wearily, extremely stiff and sore; József struggled to rise from the sunken sofa, Tamás rolled off and went straight for the jars they'd filled with snow the night before which had melted into water. He drank greedily as József stretched and finally joined him to take a jar.

"We need to look for matches," Tamás said when he'd finished drinking, and he began searching the kitchen. He opened the sparse cupboards and drawers and in one he found a lidded pot, he looked at it thoughtfully, blew most of the dust from it, and showed József with a decisive nod. "We can try to light a fire in the stove, I saw some dried beans last night," he explained.

It was a brilliant idea; the cast iron wood burning stove sat in between the kitchen, the living room, and the stairway, strategically in the center of the house so that the heat would carry everywhere. He took the socks and boots from the stove where they'd been laid to dry out, they were still slightly damp but nothing like they were the night before. They put on their socks and fetched their pants from the living room to dress themselves.

While Tamás was filling the pot with snow, József searched through the kitchen until he found a book of matches, he hollered excitedly, "Found some!" He took the matches to the stove, but Tamás pointed out that they didn't have any wood.

"I have an idea," József exclaimed as he bounded up the stairs.

Tamás heard a loud crack upstairs, then a few quick rips. József returned with an armful of wood trim from the doorways and even a random broken chair leg. He had to break the pieces of trim even more to make them fit in the stove, so he cracked them over his leg and made the best pyramid he could manage in the tiny stove. Tamás skillfully lit a match, they both rejoiced as the fire caught on the wood and started smoking. Tamás blew on the fire gently so that it would come to life, it took longer than they expected and when the wood was finally engulfed in flames the varnish on it made the smoke quite smelly.

They sat in front of the stove to warm their bodies for quite a while, and when the water began to bubble, they added the beans to cook. Tamás placed the lid on the pot and said, "This will take a few hours to cook."

They had nothing better to do so they returned to the sofa and tucked their cold feet underneath themselves. Tamás started up a conversation, "Say, József, how old are you?"

"Sixteen," he answered, but he didn't get the chance to ask the same question before Tamás blurted out his disbelief.

"Really? Only?" Tamás was incredulous.

"Yeah, so?"

"Well, it's just, you're so young. I was never as brave as you, I never had the courage like you do. If I did then I would have left before the war," he admitted sheepishly.

"The war? Wait, how old are you?"

"I'm Twenty-six."

József never would have guessed that, either. Tamás also had a young face, he couldn't maintain a beard and he always passed for a teenager.

The age difference didn't prevent them from becoming friends. They mused on the good luck that they had found somebody to travel with, Tamás was especially grateful that József helped persuade him to continue the escape from Hungary, he knew that he wasn't brave enough and relied on József's courage during their journey. József was also glad to have a companion, he didn't want to be alone, but he kept thinking that he would have made the escape on his own if he had to.

They fell into mindless chatter about their lives, of their dreams that would not come to fruition—at least not in Hungary—and of their hopes for what they would find in America. Tamás hoped to go to college and become a teacher so that he could help teach the truth to the younger generations. He was deeply empathetic and was inspired to shed light on the truth after reading the press coverage of the Nuremberg trials, but he couldn't go to school to become a teacher in

Hungary. The communists controlled education, indoctrinated the students, and forced teachers to promote pro-communist propaganda; besides, they valued laborers more than teachers and it was easier and more accepted to become a laborer, so that's what he did.

József drilled him about what it was like to grow up during the Nazi occupation, since he had only been about 4 when the Nazis left Hungary, he didn't remember much. Tamás told him stories of the Nazis raiding cities and carting off the Jewish population. He recounted the humiliating march of Jews being forced to move into the Budapest Ghetto, the Nazi propaganda, and how the Hungarian Prime Minister, Pál Teleki, committed suicide in 1941 when he learned that the Nazis had invaded Hungary on the way to Yugoslavia—he knew that Hungary wouldn't be able to remain neutral once the Nazis had stepped food on their land, despite cooperating with the Nazis previously.

"But the Nazis knew they wouldn't be able to carry on like they were forever, they heard the rumors of the Red Army and the Allied invasion, so they were trying to round up every last Jew they could find in the end, and the Arrow Cross murdered thousands on the Danube River bank before they were run out of Hungary, they'd helped the Nazis relocate Jews to the ghettos and then helped kill them.[37] The Budapest ghetto was huge, too. The plan was to move all the Jews to a death camp as soon as possible, but then the Soviets won the Battle of Budapest and they took over. Thousands weren't lucky enough to survive to the end."

József listened in awe. His parents hadn't really talked about the war, trying instead to forget and move on. They hadn't spoken much about the politics behind the Soviet occupation either, so what József knew was only from underground anti-Soviet propaganda. Of course, he also knew the narrative that the Soviets pushed, but he knew that wasn't to be trusted. Tamás filled in some of the gaps of József's knowledge with his own, but it was clear that recounting those

---

[37] During December 1944 and January 1945, the fascist Arrow Cross party took as many as 20,000 Jewish people from the Budapest Ghetto and executed them on the bank of the Danube River. They were either shot along the river and fell in, already dead, or they were pushed in alive or jumped in hoping they could escape and survive, but the river's temperature usually killed them anyways. They were forced to take their shoes and coats off because those were valuable commodities during the war, and today there is a memorial of sixty pairs of bronze shoes along the riverwalk.

memories pained Tamás.

"How do you know so much about Budapest, I thought you said you came from Debrecen?"

"Oh, I do live there—did live there—after the war. I was from Budapest at first."

József nodded but didn't press further. If he had, perhaps Tamás would have told him the truth about how he knew so much about the Budapest Ghetto and the death camps. However, after not having revealed his truth for more than a decade, Tamás was too detached from his past life, it didn't feel right for him to talk about it.

One topic led to another and, as conversations sometimes go, they found themselves talking about God. Tamás was a devout skeptic, he told József about how he had heard a few sermons in a Catholic church as a young boy which was the first thing that soured him against organized religion. The pastor, who was vehemently antisemitic, often tried to finagle his fascist beliefs into the sermons, which only added to Tamás' distaste for it.

He didn't disclose this to József, but he was raised Jewish. His family didn't live in a demographically Jewish neighborhood, even though the Jewish population of Budapest was approximately 200,000 people. They had to walk a few miles to get to the synagogue and often they were harassed on the way, so most of the time they didn't go. They were close to a Catholic church, so he snuck in a few times before the war, it was his way of rebelling. Since then, Tamás never felt like he belonged, or was welcome, to religion. Without it, he felt that he had lived a decently ethical life, save for a few transgressions here and there. He never went back to his roots, even after the war.

József was uncertain how to feel about Tamás' revelation. He'd been raised in a zealously Catholic family where he learned, or perhaps was forced, to praise and trust in God. Like many others, he believed that anybody who had not let the Lord into their lives was ultimately damned. When his mother took a job at the local cinema in town and was required to work during the Sunday morning matinees, József took the responsibility of taking his younger siblings to church when she couldn't. He asked Tamás why he didn't believe in God, he tried not to be aggressive about it, but that question is usually contentious.

Tamás thought for a moment and then very calmly responded, "Because, I've been perfectly happy going about my life without thinking that there is some divine being judging my every move, and I don't see any reason to start believing in some greater purpose now. Especially after the war. I just could never believe that a world as cruel as ours is governed by an all-powerful God who is supposed to love us but lets such evil things happen." Tamás believed that if anybody were ever justified in losing faith in that way, the Jewish people certainly deserved that right.

"But," József started, he didn't know what to say so he paused for a moment, mouth agape. "Do you believe in *anything*?"

"Science, I guess," he shrugged.

"Science?" József practically scoffed.

"Yeah," he said, casually. József looked doubtful so Tamás continued, "I'm not a devil worshiper or a communist or anything, I just don't need to believe in God to live my life, I've never seen any concrete evidence that a God exists."

Tamás never understood why he always had to defend his beliefs by denying nefarious acts like blood libel or being a communist, but it was unfortunately necessary to clarify that for people. Communists were notorious for being atheistic and valuing science over religion, it was part of the state-centered rhetoric taught in schools across the USSR and satellite states, but most average citizens kept their religious beliefs, nonetheless.

József pondered that for a moment, he didn't want to start an argument, nor did he wish to insult Tamás, but he felt uneasy about the whole conversation. The longer he sat with it though, the more it made him begin to question his own belief, though. He racked his brain trying to find evidence in his life that God existed to prove it to Tamás, more or less for his own benefit.

"I have proof! When me and my brother were on the train the day we left, the train stopped at a station and I went out to pee, but the train took off early, and I had to run to catch the train. I ran so hard, I ran, and I ran, and Károly was there to take my hand but we could never reach. Then, I got this extra power or something and I was able to run fast enough to grab his hand and pull myself up. What do you call that, if not an intervention of God?"

"Adrenaline?" Tamás chuckled.

"What about when that boy let us go back there?" he pressed, he considered that a miracle.

"Well, it wasn't God, was it? It was a boy with a conscience, and we were the lucky ones he let go, pure chance," Tamás answered, the pitch in his voice raised a bit.

József began, "But," and then realized that argument was a little silly. He was obstinate still, he huffed in disagreement, he didn't want to admit that he was beginning to question his beliefs. He knew that in recent years he had put more distance between himself and God, but he still held fast to his faith that God was the omnipotent creator of the world. But József had never asked himself why he still believed God was ultimately behind everything happening on earth, he'd always just accepted that as truth.

József wondered if maybe he were being punished for his crime, or maybe even punished for losing blind faith in God. But maybe Tamás had been right, maybe there wasn't an all-powerful God in charge of anything, maybe it was all just science or luck—both good and bad. He was pensive for a long while.

Tamás left to check on the beans on the stove and József went to the bathroom to try to find more gauze to replace his bandages. He didn't find any more medical supplies he could use, but he looked at himself in the mirror for a while; he hardly recognized himself. His face was blue and purple with bruises, his temple still had some dried blood, and his long hair was dirty and disheveled. He tried to comb his hair back with his hands, it didn't help much but he couldn't do anything else. József had always been so proud of his rock-n-roll hairstyle, it was the popular way that most young Hungarians wore their hair at the time, and he hated seeing it so messy.

It was not long before night fell again, they'd agreed to stay another until the next morning because they were still exhausted, they needed to finish recuperating. They ate the beans they cooked and the rest of the pickled vegetables they found and filled their bellies with water to feel fuller. József pulled more wood from the walls and ripped up pages from a few stray books to keep fueling the fire. Using his hands to rip things apart relieved some of his anger, even though his fingers ached.

They'd woken up late in the afternoon, so they weren't at all tired when nightfall came, they sat up and talked for hours about life, their homes and families, and simple things like their favorite movies and songs, they found that they both liked Elvis Presley songs. They weren't allowed to listen to or watch western media, but songs from popular American artists could be heard on Radio Free Europe. Young men were so enamored with the American artist that they all cut and styled their hair like his and tried to imitate the unique way his voice wavered. They thoroughly enjoyed each other's company, which was a nice change of pace after their brief disagreement about religion.

Eventually, Tamás drifted off to sleep as József talked. Even though he was also physically exhausted, he couldn't quiet down his thoughts enough to rest. József felt bored and anxious sitting next to Tamás as he slept, so he got up to wander the house.

He went upstairs hoping to find something interesting. In one of the bedroom closets, he found a small box of books, magazines, and newspapers. József rifled through them even though he couldn't read German, but a tattered copy of Adolf Hitler's *Mein Kampf* caught his eye. He had once heard a rumor that the book was mandatory for all citizens of the Reich to own and read, and the thought of it chilled his spine. Nevertheless, he picked up the manifesto to marvel at it. The sixteen-year-old wondered how a country of civilized people could follow the orders of such a vile man without questioning the immorality of it all.

As he flipped the pages absentmindedly, he heard the familiar sound of an engine. His heart raced as he went to the window to try to see the vehicle; he recognized the truck as the one from the night before. When it passed directly in front of the house, he saw an insignia and recognized the word *Österreich;* he knew it was the Austrian police or military and figured that they were doing nightly patrols of the area.

He bolted from the room and raced down the stairs, grabbed his boots and shouted, "Tamás! Wake up, we gotta go! The Austrian Patrol is outside! We have to go!"

Tamás woke up, understandably startled, but he didn't ask any questions. József, having just frantically pulled his boots, tossed Tamás' boots at him; he caught them and fumbled to escape his blanket.

József continued explaining while tying his laces, "The truck from last night, it's back, it's making rounds, and from upstairs I saw on the side it's an *Österreich* Patrol truck!"

They grabbed their coats and sprinted out of the front door as they put them on. It was freezing in that tiny, deserted village that was just a shell of what it used to be after the Allied bombings during WWII.

"There it is!" József pointed down the street at the truck driving away from them.

The truck had been driving at such a slow speed that it hadn't even left the street by the time they got outside, they waved their arms and shouted, "Hey!"

They started running for the truck and luckily, the truck stopped. József and Tamás were excited, they ran faster but when they were just about thirty feet away, the Austrian police jumped out of the truck and lifted their guns to signal that they'd shoot if necessary. Tamás skidded to a stop and put his hands up, prompting József to do the same. At first, they froze, not knowing what to do but afraid to move or say anything. The Austrians were patrolling the streets, they knew that refugees had been coming into Austria and part of their mission was to look for Hungarians.

One demanded to know what József and Tamás were doing in that village, but he asked in German.

József and Tamás didn't understand, they started repeating, "We're from Hungary! We're from Hungary!"

The Austrians contemplated them for a second, assessing the situation before they lowered their weapons and waved them towards their truck. One of them spoke Hungarian, he said, "Come, we will give you a ride."

They almost ran to the truck but didn't want to make such a sudden movement that might accidentally make the Austrians jumpy and pull their triggers, some still had their guns slightly raised.

"Thank you, thank you," József and Tamás said as the Austrians gestured for them to get into the truck.

They ducked inside quietly, trying to remain calm, but the Austrians could probably hear their heartbeats through their chests. Two of the policemen climbed inside after József and Tamás in the back seat; it was cramped and intimidating but at least they were safe— they hoped. The other two policemen sat in the front, only the one spoke enough Hungarian to communicate, the rest just nodded at the young men and smiled tersely.

The ride was rough and cramped, and József wanted to believe that the police truck had appeared at the exact moment he looked out the window by means of divine intervention, but a little voice kept saying that it was just random happenstance.

They were taken to a small compound a few miles away where the police had set up cots in their barracks specifically for the Hungarian refugees they kept finding. Refugees were given a place to sleep and meals at the police station until they could be transferred to a refugee camp; camps had to appear all over Austria and in such a short amount of time that they just had to make do with what they had. Austria didn't know how many refugees they'd receive, it wasn't like they had advance warning, but they anticipated that the Hungarians needed help and they stepped up to the plate without turning anybody away.

József and Tamás were grateful for the rescue and the warm place to sleep, it wasn't long before they passed out from sheer exhaustion.

Chapter 36
"Well Dad, I Turned You In"

Now, during the war, Hungary was with the Axis powers, so was Austria, with the Nazi and the fascist parties. The Hungarians got into the war and helped the Germans but then the Germans decided that they were going to take our people to concentration camps. At the same time, the Russians were pushing back against the Germans, and they invaded Hungary to kind of help us, but then they never left after the war.

After the war, Austria didn't have a good government when the Nazis left so the Allies took over and divided little parts of it for them to control; Russia got the eastern part. So, after the war, the Russians were controlling Hungary and the eastern side of Austria. Some people liked them there, but most people didn't. And the people that liked the Russians were not your friends, and the police that used to be Hungarians was now Russians, and everywhere you looked you could see Russians. Everybody was two-faced; you could not trust your neighbor.

Much later on, I was spending summers with my grandparents, they lived in a small village. I was, oh, I dunno, 8, 10, 12, that age bracket. Every house had a speaker in it, and in the morning, they wake you up, then political speeches and whatnot, a little bit of music, then at night, "OK everybody go to bed." The music and the talking stopped until in the morning when it was time to wake up. That's how they done it in Russia; they wake you up and they put you to bed.

It did not happen all of a sudden, they only put the speakers in small villages where there were less houses and it was easier to do. They did not do it in big cities, too many houses, too many wires, too difficult to do. Being that we were living in the city we had resources other than in the country, we had radios and stuff. At night time, we listened to Radio Free Europe. Of course, that was illegal as the Dickens, but you just don't talk about it. I had friends that their parents got hauled away because their parents were listening to Radio Free Europe. That was broadcasted from England or from West Germany, but we had access to it.

If they were caught, the police came to the house and arrested the person and take them away and you could not find out where they go, then after a week or so they come back all bruised and beaten. . . They weren't beaten in public, they didn't do it out in the open. They done it on the sly because people wouldn't stand for that. If they do things where people didn't see it, then it's your word against the police.

One of our neighbors, János, he was listening to Radio Free Europe, and just about everybody was but you did not talk about it to anybody because you never knew who would turn you in. He was hauled away quite a few times, and after I left I was in the States for a number of years and I could write home,[38] my father wrote back, "Do you remember our neighbor, János, he's been hauled away for talking against the government, they took him away about a month ago and a couple weeks later he come home and a few days later he passed away." So basically, they beat him to death. I have no reason not to believe my father when he said that. You know who to believe and who not to believe.

There was one old man in our city, he would listen to Radio Free Europe, and he was caught two or three times and I remember one time he was caught and dragged out into the street and taken away. When he got back, I remember he was black and blue, they beat him pretty badly. The old man asks his son how the Russians found him, and his son says, "Well Dad, I turned you in."

There were a few Russian supporters, which just meant that you cannot trust anyone, even family.

---

[38] They could send letters to and from Hungary, but the police would read most letters going in and out of Hungary, both before and after the revolution. The Soviets did that in all of their satellite states and in the USSR. They had to talk in code in the letters and not say anything that might sound like it was negative about the government or else the police might arrest whoever had written it.

Chapter 37

Villach

József's sleep was restless, he had a terrible dream of being caught in a horrible storm on the open sea. He felt the waves crashing into the ship so hard that it rolled sideways, and the harsh spray of the ocean soaked his clothes. He could have sworn he really did look out over a ship's railing to stare into the dark pit of the ocean opening up to swallow him. But when he woke, he felt the steady drip of water on his arm from a crack in the ceiling and he rationalized that the water must have spawned that phantasmal dream. He'd never even been on a boat before, why would he have dreamt of it?

It was still dark and nobody else was awake so József rolled over on his cot and tried to sleep again. Not long after closing his eyes, the door was thrown open and the lights flicked on, an officer barged in and announced in Hungarian, "The Russians are coming. Get up! Now! There is a bus waiting outside."

The policemen sprang from their own cots already dressed, boots and all. József, Tamás, and several other refugees who'd been picked up earlier than they had scrambled out of bed in a panic.

"Did he say the Russians?" one asked of nobody in particular.

"Yes! The Russians are coming!" another screamed.

"What's happening?" Tamás asked.

"The Russians!" József yelled.

"Are they here?" the first guy asked again.

"I don't know, just go!" somebody screamed.

It was chaos, nobody knew exactly what was happening, but they were certain about one thing, they were not getting caught again. The Austrians were running around madly, barking orders and carrying loads of their weapons and ammunition to the bus they'd acquired to use recently. Austrians quickly allocated city buses to transport refugees around the country when they realized how large the refugee crisis was going to become, that police station just so happened to have a bus ready. One man jumped into the driver's seat and turned the engine so it could warm up as the refugees boarded the shabby old bus.

Among them was a gentle, elderly man; a dour woman with two young children; two young boys, much too young to make such a treacherous journey alone; and five other young men in their late teens or twenties. When everybody had boarded, including some of the police officers, they took off.

József counted the number of refugees, with Tamás and himself there were thirteen of them and he felt a tinge of guilt, believing that they'd brought bad luck with him. He still had superstitions, even though he knew it might be a little foolish.

Somebody raised their voice over the gravel crunching beneath the tires to ask, "Where are you taking us?"

One of the men who picked Tamás and József up the night before turned around in his seat and stood to address the whole party, "To Villach. There is a camp there and they will take you. This morning, we were warned that the Russians were raiding all the police and patrol compounds." He sounded quite angry, nobody dared ask him any more questions.

Whispers rippled throughout the bus.

"What did he say?"

"The Russians are coming into Austria, that's what he said!"

"The Russians are here?"

"No, they're *coming*."

"Where are we going?"

"Villach, weren't you listening?"

"What's in Villach?"

"A refugee camp!"

"Should we even trust them? I mean, this is Russian territory."

"*Was* Russian territory, they pulled out last year, Austrians hate the Russians just as much as we do."

"I knew this would happen; I just knew it!"

The voices blended with the sound of the road and engine and soon it all began to sound like white noise. József and Tamás stayed quiet; the droning was calming, peaceful almost. They didn't have to think, they could just get lost in the noise.

The drive was long, and the passengers mostly gazed out the window, absentmindedly looking for anything interesting in the distance. They'd driven through a great deal of farmland with rolling green hills in the distance, occasionally, they'd drive through a small village; and each desolate village they passed seemed to be covered in more dirt and dust than the last. They were able to get on the autobahn for a good portion of the drive, but they had to make a brief stop in Graz, about two hours into their trip. Some of the refugees started to stand up when they thought they were getting off, but it turned out that they only needed fuel and had several more hours to drive.

The refugees were getting hungry and thirsty, most of them didn't have any money to spend when they stopped for fuel so after using the restroom sat back on the bus, but the elderly man bought everyone a bottle of Coca-Cola from the store. He told one of the young kids to pass the bottles out to everybody on the bus, which they greatly appreciated.

They drove the rest of the way to Villach; it was late morning when they finally arrived and anybody who was asleep was violently jerked awake when the bus made a sharp turn at too high of a speed going into the refugee camp. The driver shifted to park and swiveled around in his seat almost in one motion, "We are here," he announced, "Everybody gather your things and get off the bus. There is a man inside with papers for you to complete."

The policemen were the first to disembark so they could speak to the other Austrians about the arrangements for the refugees. People rose wearily from their seats and wiped the sleep from their eyes, they yawned as they staggered off the bus and stood nervously on the gravel outside until everyone disembarked. A gruff man came out of the building in front of them with a clipboard and a cup of coffee.

"Hello, follow me," he ordered and just as soon he turned on his heels and headed back inside.

As the refugees entered the cafeteria, another Austrian handed each person a stack of papers and an ink pen, directing them to fill it out. József looked around the gray mess hall, it was boring and a little dirty, but it was at least warm. They started whispering as they took seats.

"Hello," the man with the clipboard said, "Please sit and fill these forms out as best as you can. If you have your identification or any documentation, please let us know, it will speed up the process. When you are done, we will show you where your barracks are."

Everybody was required to complete dozens of intake forms to claim asylum and become a refugee, and each new camp required more paperwork. They were hungry but they were too anxious to ask when they'd be served lunch, so they tried to ignore their growling stomachs. The first page of the forms instructed them on how to complete the rest of the pages, it was the vetting process the United Nations High Commissioner for Refugees created to determine eligibility and document the asylum seekers. It became more tedious each time they had to fill out the same or similar questionnaires, and some of the questions were superfluous, they'd be asked to confirm the same information repeatedly so that those who reviewed the paperwork could see if they'd stick to their story or if their answers changed.

The fluorescent lights flickered above with that annoying noise they have, which made it extraordinarily hard for József to concentrate on his papers. Everybody else seemed to be making good progress on their forms, which made him feel more nervous about completing them quicker.

There were several pages that asked tremendous amounts of basic information; name, parents' names, birthdate, addresses, school, occupation, and military affiliation. József struggled with the questions about criminal history. On record, he was not a criminal, but in his heart, he held astounding guilt. As he tapped his pen on the table he wondered if that secret would resurface there, if they might find out somehow.

Fleeing the country turned out to be more complicated than just walking across the border and starting over. Young refugees thought that the most difficult part of leaving would be the actual leaving, but the paperwork alone was proving to be very laborious, and they worried that they wouldn't be accepted.

József watched Tamás, who was making more progress than him, from the corner of his eye. Some other refugees completed their papers rather quickly, one young man in his twenties started helping the young kids fill out their papers, typically a representative from the relief agencies or the hosting country would help refugees fill out their papers, but nobody was around to do that. The mother with two young children was the only one who took longer than József because she had to fill out three sets of paperwork. His legs shook as he hurried to read and answer the remaining questions.

A rather large man came into the room and cleared his throat, "Hello, is everyone done with their forms?"

Almost affirmed that they were, but József was still scribbling his final answers down. They all got up to turn in their paperwork to the camp director at the front of the room; József was the last to rise and he stumbled as he moved through the aisle between the seats.

"Good, thank you, thank you," he said as he collected the papers. "My name is Bernard Schuster, I'm the director here, and I will be showing you to your barracks. Follow me." He left the building quickly, expecting the refugees to follow.

He was already halfway down the walking path with great speed, even with a slight limp, by the time the refugees got to the door. Outside, the sun was shining but the wind was still fierce, making it miserable. They tried to catch up to Herr Schuster who was speaking as he walked.

"To the right is the recreation room, it's connected to the mess hall where you just were, it's not much to look at but you'll find something to do to entertain yourselves." The building was so bleak and unassuming, it was hard to believe that they'd find anything fun to do inside.

"Hurry up everyone, come on," he huffed even though nobody was lagging behind him. "Right up here are the barracks where you'll be sleeping. Women and young children are in this building," he pointed to the left up ahead, "And men are in that building down the path. You will all share a bathroom with the others in your barracks. Each person gets their own bed, but you will have to put in a request for some extra blankets or pillows, you can get more only if we have extras. The doors can be locked from the inside at night. The guards' barracks is the next one over, right there," he pointed towards the concrete and brick buildings which all looked identical.

"Women and young children come this way please, unaccompanied boys ten and older will be in the men's barracks," he stopped and turned around, looking at the two young boys who'd come alone. "How old are you two?"

They were small, they could have been eight or nine, but they asserted, "We're ten!"

Herr Schuster scrutinized them for a moment, then shuffled the papers he was holding to find their intake forms. They had in fact indicated that they were ten years old on their papers. "Okay," Herr Schuster conceded. "This way ma'am," he waved for the mother and her children to follow him down the footpath. He briefly showed them the inside of the barracks and returned to the others outside.

"Okay, your turn," he announced.

They hurried to get inside the barracks, glad to be out of the cold. The large room was narrow, boring, and dark, and the beds were just thin cots lined up in crowded rows; the Hungarians didn't know what to expect but they were expecting at least a little more than that. There were already many refugees in the barracks, they looked bored to death.

Herr Schuster began giving the rules and expectations while the new arrivals chose beds for themselves and stashed their belongings—if they had any—underneath. "You each have a bed and some linens to use, and you must keep your items neatly under your bed. Don't leave your beds a mess, make them up every morning. If you need extra blankets or towels you must request extras from myself or one of the other staff, your request may be accepted if more linens are available. You aren't allowed to leave the barracks at night unless you have permission, which you won't get. Under no circumstances do we tolerate thievery. Theft is a punishable crime, you are not a citizen of Austria, and we can send you back to Hungary, is that clear? Yes?" he demanded.

Everybody nodded, the younger ones looked a little frightened.

"You will be assigned a daily chore; you are required to pitch in here. You will get your assignment at lunch today. Assignments are kitchen duty for all meals, and janitorial duties around camp, including your restrooms. If you need any of our donation items, you can come by and get some after lunch. We have backpacks, clothing, shoes, hats and gloves, and an assortment of toiletries. Take only what you need to get through the winter." He nodded when he finished his statement, then he asked, "Do you have any questions?"

They looked at each other quizzically, one was brave enough to ask, "When is lunch?"

"Soon," he answered as he turned to leave.

Their barracks weren't comfortable or homey, but it was better than running from the Soviets in the winter. József looked at Tamás and shrugged; they went and chose the first available beds they saw and sat down, not having any belongings to tuck away underneath. Reality was sinking in; it was grim and terrifying. They were officially refugees with nothing at all, alone in a foreign country, József had no clue what had happened to his brother and Tamás knew that his parents must be worried sick. Not knowing what else to do, they sat quietly and tried to absorb everything around them.

Some of the men sat at a small plastic table in the corner, a pair of seniors sat in tattered sofa chairs, everybody else laid on their beds. Bruised and weary faces, both young and old, leered at the newcomers. A few said hellos or welcomed them, some even introduced themselves, but for the most part everybody tried to mind their own business.

József excused himself to the communal bathroom, eager to relieve himself after a long bus ride. In the bathroom, finally alone, József saw himself in the mirror. There was much better lighting than at the abandoned house, he got a better look at the bruises, blood, and bags under his eyes. He felt like he'd already changed, but he couldn't define what that meant yet. He splashed lukewarm water on his face, trying to clean up a bit. He still felt completely horrible but at least he'd gotten some of the dried blood off.

CHAPTER 38
"IF YOU GO TO AMERICA, YOU WILL BE SAFE"

After the second war, Austria was divided into the English zone and the Russian zone, so where we were was in the Russian zone. When the Russians finally left Austria, it was about 1955, a year before the revolution, everybody was still scared they would come back. The patrolmen that picked us up were only free from the Russians for about a year, so if the rumor was true, that the Russians were coming, they really took it to heart. So, to help us out, they put all the refugees on a bus down to Villach which was near the border of Yugoslavia and Italy. It was a small town then. We stayed a few weeks and from there we were sent up to Salzburg to a refugee camp. You know, I don't remember much from there, just a couple of things here and there, but the days were all pretty boring.

Each time we got to a new camp there was paperwork to be filled out, the same questions but asked a different way. It was our vetting process, I filled up a truckload of paperwork from Hungary to the States, I mean, just paperwork everywhere we went. You know, I never think about it until this Presidential election[39] with all the talk about it but what they were having us fill out was the background check. It was to make sure that we would say the same thing over and over, so we didn't change our story.

Rather than stay in Austria like many others, I wanted to go to America. My father said we have relatives in America, maybe they could help you. America was the land of opportunity, there was no other way to say it. If you go to America, you will be safe. I wanted to get as far away from Russia as possible. My father gave me the last known address of our relatives, but I never did try to contact them.

---

[39] The 2016 United States Presidential election between Hilary Clinton and Donald Trump.

CHAPTER 39
THE FIRST REFUGEE CAMP

Lunch was a simple yet delicious meal of stew and bread, and for many it was the first hot meal in days. Some said it was the best meal they'd ever had, some ate too quickly, and others savored each bite.

An Austrian with a clipboard went around assigning everybody to their duties, he explained that the duties they were assigned to could change at any given time when refugees came and went so, they could still cover all of the responsibilities. József and Tamás were both put on breakfast duty, they were glad that they could still stick together. They'd have to wake up earlier than everybody else to prepare the kitchen, but that also meant that they had easy access to food, which was a benefit.

The refugees were able to get some toothpaste and a brush, a bar of soap, and a change of clothes, and after lunch they were able to take a shower and get cleaned up; it was wonderfully rejuvenating. They used some of their soap to wash their dirty clothes as well, right there in the shower with them. Afterwards, they had to find enough places all over the barracks to hang the clothes up to dry so they'd be out of the way.

They spent the rest of the day chatting with some of the other young Hungarians, they talked about everything and anything, but the conversations usually began with, "Where are you from?"

And then somebody would inevitably say, "Oh yeah? I know a guy from there. When did you leave?"

They'd ask, "Did anybody come with you, or are you alone?"

And of course, they were always curious, so they'd ask, "Have you heard any news from back home yet? Do you know what the Russians are doing?"

After dinner, József flopped onto his cot, completely exhausted.

YOUNG MEN GO WEST 185

Tamás was busy organizing his few items under the bed, he wasn't thrilled about putting his bar of soap directly on the ground, but he figured he'd try to find something to put it in tomorrow. He fluffed his pillow and tried to get comfortable, but that was hard to do on an old military cot.

He caught József off guard when he said, "I'm sorry about your brother. I know you're worried, but I'm sure he's alright."

József couldn't find the right words, he didn't think that Károly was okay, but he said, "Thanks." He could feel Tamás' eyes on him, but he was busy pretending that the ceiling was very interesting so he didn't have to look.

Their beds were only a foot apart so he couldn't just pretend he didn't see Tamás who had propped himself up on his elbow to look at József. Tamás took a sharp breath in as if he were about to continue, but he stopped short, thinking better of it.

That irritated József for some reason, he sat up to look his friend in the face to say, "He's not okay, he's alone. I left him there, I should have waited for him or tried to get him or something! The Russians probably shipped him off to Siberia if they didn't just kill him!" He was talking loudly, everybody around them surely heard but they pretended not to notice.

"You just don't get it," he continued, "You didn't leave your brother behind; you didn't have anybody, you were alone." As soon as the words left his mouth he knew he shouldn't have said them, he couldn't go back in time and stop himself.

Nobody said anything for a while and everyone else in the barracks pretended like they weren't eavesdropping. József was afraid that he'd ruined their friendship, he didn't know what to say to make the situation better.

Tamás whispered, "You're right. I don't have anybody." He wasn't angry, in fact he was exceptionally calm which made József feel more guilty for what he'd said. Tamás' eyes watered and his voice broke when he said, "I don't have anybody."

After several minutes of uncomfortable silence József made an attempt at an apology. "Tamás, I—um—I'm sorry. I didn't mean it like that, you just didn't come with anybody, that's all I meant, I wasn't trying to be mean."

Tamás' voice was soft, "No, it's true, you're right, I don't have anybody. My parents are dead, I didn't have siblings or a girlfriend, or even any friends. I've never been good at making friends. . . I left because I was afraid to be alone. Or because I didn't want to die alone. I don't really know." He stopped to take a breath, the tension was thick, but the silence felt worse.

"I thought if I could escape then I could make a new life, but when we got caught, I wanted to go home because I was afraid, like a coward." Tears welled up in his eyes as he spoke.

"You're not a coward, I didn't mean it like that."

"I am, I'm not brave like you. I wanted to turn back and go home."

József was ashamed that he'd upset Tamás so much, he tried to console him, "We're in this together, and I'm your friend now."

There was a heavy pause before Tamás asked, "You mean that?"

It felt weird to József to comfort Tamás while he was just as lonely and afraid, and because Tamás was much older than him, but he confirmed, "Yes, we're friends. And we will go to America together, it will be better there, I just know it."

Tamás nodded in agreement. They didn't know what else to say so they just closed their eyes and eventually fell asleep.

József didn't sleep well, though, he kept tossing and turning, trying to get comfortable. He tried too hard to sleep which, para-doxically, prevented him from getting any. He was wide awake when the bell sounded outside the barracks.

They rang the bell at dawn, at mealtimes, and for emergencies. The bell sounds were all the same except for emergencies, that bell was long and eerie. The morning bell woke everybody up, but only the people who had breakfast duty were required to get out of bed at that time and make it to the kitchen as soon as possible. About forty-five minutes later, the second morning bell rang, which signaled to everybody else that they could go to the mess hall for breakfast.

"Sleep alright?" Tamás asked, he was surprisingly chipper.

József mumbled, "Sure," as he hunched over to put on his boots. Tamás said that he felt refreshed and went about getting himself dressed, paying little mind to József.

József felt miserable, his mouth was parched, his eyes were crusty, and he felt more tired than he had before bed. He made up his bed quickly, then stumbled to the bathroom where he lazily ran his hands through his hair and splashed water on his face. He didn't feel refreshed, or like his hair was fixed, but he had to at least try to compose himself.

Tamás went to the toilet very quickly and gave József a pat on the shoulder as he left, József was still looking in the mirror at himself. He asked himself, "What was that about?"

One of the ten-year-old boys from the day before was also assigned to breakfast duty, he waited with Tamás at the door. He was quite anxious, he was fidgeting with his hands and avoiding eye contact with everybody. József tried nodding politely at him, but the boy wouldn't look up. All three of them were new, they didn't know what exactly they were supposed to do, but just as Tamás said that he hoped that somebody would come to fetch them, there was a knock at the door.

Tamás unlocked the door to find two older gentlemen outside, they stayed in the family barracks where they had small individual rooms to themselves. They introduced themselves as Sámuel and Artúr, they'd been doing breakfast duty for several days already.

"Are you kids ready? Let's go," Artúr waved them out of the barracks. He was in a hurry to get to the kitchen and out of the cold.

They followed the older men to the mess hall, it was well below zero outside and the poor ten-year-old only had a thin sweater, nothing warmer. József hunched his shoulders up to shield his neck from the wind and the ten-year-old tried to huddle between the other guys to stay warm. The mess hall wasn't far away, but every second in the cold was unbearable.

Sámuel tried the door but it was still locked, "Hey! Hey, is anybody in there?" he yelled. "Usually it's already unlocked," he explained to the new guys on duty.

They banged on the door a few times, hoping a camp employee would hear them. A short and rather robust man came bounding up from behind them.

"Sorry! Sorry! I'm coming," he said as he rifled through his keychain to find the correct one.

Once he finally had the door unlocked, they all hurried inside, Sámuel turned on the lights and went straight to the kitchen to turn on the ovens.

"Ah, we have some new kids!" the Austrian said, "Good morning, I'm Herr Weber, you can ask me anything as long as I'm around, I'm one of the volunteers here." His Hungarian wasn't perfect, and he had a thick German accent, but they could at least understand him.

Tamás chimed, "Good morning, Herr Weber, thank you!"

Herr Weber nodded to Artúr, "Well then, you can show them what to do, can't you?"

"Yes, of course," Artúr confirmed.

"Great! Then I will leave you to it!"

Artúr explained their responsibilities, the new guys looked overwhelmed to say the least. "It's a lot to remember but it's easy work. And, the best part, you can eat as much breakfast as you want," Artúr smiled. "Folks start coming in for breakfast around 7:00, it's 6:15 now, let's get to work!"

Sámuel had already started up the appliances and pulled the food they needed to prepare from the fridge and freezer; the new guys went to work setting up the dining room.

József asked, "Can we really eat as much breakfast as we want?"

Sámuel replied, "You can have your plate of breakfast when everybody else eats, then you can eat whatever is left over when everybody is done," he leaned over the counter to get closer to József and said mischievously, "But we usually eat some of the food as it cooks before anybody else gets in."

Everyone smiled and laughed, kitchen duty didn't seem so bad after all.

CHAPTER 40
"I COULDN'T WAIT UNTIL I HAD A DAUGHTER"

It was kind of tough for us kids, we had to get up early to do chores at very young ages. Charles and myself went to the grocery store and stood in line to get milk and other things. You know, in Europe during that time refrigerators were pretty much nonexistent. You were buying what you needed for that day and used it up, and if you didn't, then the milk spoils and whatnot. That was us kids' job, Charles and me. Well, I was only three or four years old, just big enough to stand in line and put money on the counter to pay for it, but not much else.

My younger brother Laci was born in 1943, he was three years younger than me while Charles was three years older than me, all of us three years apart except my sister, Edit, who was born in 1952. I was 12 years old when my sister was born, my oldest brother was 15, he was too old to help with the baby, and my younger brother was 9 so he was too young to help with our sister.

My father and my mother both worked, so I was the babysitter. My mother worked in the theater at the ticket counter and my father worked as the usher, so I took care of my sister, and make sure she ate and went to bed. On Sundays, I made her hair and took her to church when my mother worked, and sometimes afterwards I would buy her some ice cream cones. I loved having Sundays with my sister. And I got very good at braiding hair, making ponytails and all different types of things. You know, in the summer, us boys got very short buzz cuts on our hair, to keep us cool, but girls didn't have to get a haircut, so it grew longer, and longer, and you have to keep fixing it.

I didn't choose to be Babysitter, but you do whatever you had to do for the family. That was from 12 years old until I left, she was 4 when I left. Until then, I was the one who took care of her. I loved her very much. I couldn't wait until I had a daughter.

When I came to the states, in Portland I lived with the Stillwell family, they had a little girl and I took care of her because I missed my sister. And when I met Linda's family in '58, '59, well she had a little sister called Dee, and Dee was taking the place of my sister too. She was just about the same age as my sister was when I left. You know, when you miss somebody and you meet somebody with the same age and whatever of the person that you miss, that other person helps you not to miss them.

Linda and me never did have any girls, just four boys. When the boys were young, we met a foster girl in the neighborhood, and we adopted her. But Barbara was too old to braid her hair like Edit. She was about 15, 16 when we adopted her, she already had a life you know, dating boys and going out and all that stuff.

He really wanted a girl, and he was jealous of the fact that his brother had two girls. They adopted a teenage girl when their four boys were still young, she was sixteen, and she passed away in her twenties. He didn't get the chance to raise a girl, though, so he was overjoyed when I was born. He had one other granddaughter born before I was, but her mother left, and nobody ever saw her two kids again. I was his "only" granddaughter surrounded by half a dozen boys, so I was the golden child. I could do absolutely nothing wrong in his eyes. I could take a sharpie to his leather chair, rip up all the flowers in the garden, sneak off without telling anybody where I was going (usually just to great-grandma's house on the property, but sometimes I'd take my five-year-old self to the blackberry field *across the highway*), stay up way too late, and beg for him to make me cinnamon-sugar toast in the middle of the night and eat it in their bed, but he still doted on me.

CHAPTER 41
REUNITED

Right before lunch another dozen refugees arrived on a bus, they got off right in front of the mess hall and were directed to go inside immediately to eat before getting the paperwork to fill out. József happened to be outside waiting to go in and eat when he saw the new people get off the bus when he thought he saw somebody he knew.

"Pál?" he called out.

He wasn't sure who called his name, the sun was shining right in his eyes, and he was a little disoriented from the bus, he turned his head in every direction trying to find who called him.

"Pál?" József yelled again, waving his hands, "Oh, my God, it is you! I can't believe it!"

"József? What the hell? You're here, you made it out!" Pál exclaimed, he couldn't believe his eyes.

They started running and nearly tackled each other in a big embrace. Young men were used to holding up a male bravado around their friends, and they didn't often let their guard down or show affection, but they were just so happy to see a familiar face they didn't care if anybody looked at them sideways.

"I barely made it, I'll have to tell you all about it! But when did you leave? I didn't know you wanted to!"

"I left two days ago, walked right across the border!" he said with confidence.

He and József began walking towards the mess hall for lunch, chatting happily away, but they walked right past Tamás without even a glance, which hurt his feelings more than he expected. József was so caught up with the excitement of seeing an old friend that he snubbed his new friend, but he wasn't trying to be malicious. They got their lunch trays and sat next to each other, Tamás didn't think he was welcome to sit by them, so he sat alone. They talked throughout their meal, while they put their trays away, and up until Herr Schuster came in to hand out the intake forms to the new refugees.

The rest of the room quieted down but József kept whispering to Pál, "What do you mean you don't want to go to America?"

Herr Schuster shushed him, his face turned red, and he closed his mouth. Pál cracked a smile and held in his laughter while Herr Schuster proceeded to explain the rules at camp and how to fill out the paperwork. His job was tedious, and each time he had to explain the same thing he was visibly less enthusiastic about it.

Everybody who wasn't new to the camp went back to their barracks, they didn't need to stay while the new refugees completed paperwork, but József stayed with Pál. They continued whispering, trying to keep as quiet as possible while the others concentrated on their papers.

"Where are you planning to go?" József asked.

"I want to stay close to home, maybe I'll go to Switzerland, or Sweden, I can't remember which is which," he shrugged, "It doesn't really matter though as long as I'm not in Hungary, right?"

"But you could come to America with me!"

"Nah," he said dismissively, but the way he said it was almost playful.

"That's where the land of dreams is! Just think about it!"

"I don't know, I might want to go back one day."

"But you just escaped! Don't be stupid," József was raising his voice by then.

Pál made a noise indicating that he didn't know what to say next, so he didn't say anything. József sat back in his chair and huffed, he was quiet until Pál was finished. They'd obviously been irritated with each other, but they weren't going to fight about it. Pál handed over his paperwork and Herr Schuster asked József if he'd finished his paperwork, not realizing that he wasn't new. József explained that he'd just stayed with his friend, but Herr Schuster couldn't understand why József would want to sit in the mess hall doing nothing that entire time, so he just waved him off. When everyone had finished, Herr Schuster told them to follow him out so he could show them around. He showed them to the barracks and dropped the women and children off first, then took the men in. There weren't enough beds, the camp directors didn't realize that, so they had to scramble to set up a few more cots to accommodate everyone.

Tamás was sitting on his bed with a book when József bounded up to him, "Hey Tamás, this is Pál! He's a friend from school, we used to work together!" He turned to tell Pál, "This is Tamás, I met him when we escaped."

They said hello, but they all felt the tension, so Tamás excused himself for the restroom.

"Odd guy, isn't he?" Pál asked.

"He's just shy," József explained, but he felt like Tamás seemed stranger than user.

In fact, Tamás felt hurt, he felt like he'd been ditched for Pál and he knew that it seemed petty to be jealous of József's old friend, but it reminded him that he didn't have anybody else.

Later that afternoon, several of the refugees met with an immigration counselor, his name was Hans Maier, who came to the camp. Herr Maier worked with the UNHCR and other aid organizations to help refugees get all their paperwork completed in order to immigrate. It was terribly boring for all of them, and even more confusing. Each person had to wait their turn to speak with the counselor so that they could be given the correct application forms to fill out, depending on where they were going. They filled out their forms, it was tedious and long, and when they handed their completed forms back to the staff, they were told they would have to wait to talk to the counselor again in a week or two. It was irritating, but they were at the mercy of the immigration system. Several young men and women were applying for refugee status in America or Canada, which they knew could take a while for approval. Very few wanted to go elsewhere, and still fewer wanted to stay in Austria with hopes of returning to Hungary one day soon.

The counselor said their applications would be reviewed and that he, or another counselor, would be back within a few weeks to talk to everybody again, but that the applications might not be approved at that time.

Someone asked, "Why would you come back to talk to us if the applications won't be approved?"

"I, or somebody else, will be coming back to talk to you in case there's any information missing in your paperwork after we review it, some people may need to fill out additional forms, that sort of thing. I'll come back to touch base with everyone and have any new arrivals fill out their forms. Just know that it could take months for your visa applications to be approved, there are a lot of applicants right now, have patience."

Some of the refugees muttered, they were disgruntled, but there wasn't anything they could do about it.

PART FOUR:

THE REFUGEES

"No one leaves home unless home is the mouth of a shark."

—*Warsan Shire, Somali refugee*

CHAPTER 42
EUROPE'S RESPONSE TO THE REFUGEES

Officials in Austria, Yugoslavia, and the UNHCR moved extremely fast to help the Hungarian refugees. In fact, within 48 hours of the first refugees entering Austria, a handful of countries had already sent in aid and volunteers and began funneling the refugees out. It was the first major immigration crisis that was being witnessed, in real time, all over the world. Dramatic photos and footage of refugees tramping through the snow in the middle of winter and of shabby refugee camps were displayed through newspapers, radios, TV, and even on cinema reels; but the refugees couldn't have known how significant those events were at the time.

When the refugees began flooding into Austria, neither Austria nor the United Nations High Commissioner for Refugees was equipped to handle the crisis, so it was quite chaotic in the beginning. The UNHCR was established in 1950 as a direct result of World War II to assist millions of displaced persons, but it was only supposed to be a temporary organization set to expire in 1958. In July 1956, the High Commissioner, Gerrit van Heuven Goedhart, died from a heart attack, and the position wasn't filled until December when Auguste Lindt was elected. Luckily, the senior staff at the UNHCR were capable of managing the Hungarian refugee crisis effectively.

The other agencies and NGOs handling the situation also performed exceptionally well under the circumstances, and consequently shaped the way that refugee crises were handled thereafter and secured the UNHCR as a permanent branch of the United Nations.

Unfortunately, if we look at the world today, we wouldn't see the same type of efficiency and intensity in handling today's refugee crises. People have unfortunately grown more indifferent the more that their aid is needed. It was truly a unique mass migration; almost 200,000 refugees were resettled within a year, the vast majority of whom were resettled within three months of leaving Hungary. No other refugee crisis of that magnitude has been handled as quickly, neither before nor since.

Several thousand refugees left between October 23 and November 3, but the crisis began in earnest on November 4 when the Soviets invaded Budapest again. Roughly 10,000 people made a snap decision to escape that morning and crossed the border into Austria. Several more days would also see upwards of ten thousand people cross in one day, but everyday more and more people came to the conclusion that escaping was safer than staying. On days when thousands of refugees walked across the border, it was easy for others to navigate the forest or swampy no-man's-land between Hungary and Austria because they could see the direction everybody else was going, but sometimes people would walk around in circles, lost for days, sometimes crossing in and out of the country.

The Soviets moved to guard the borders early on, but they didn't do much to thwart the escapees; they seemed unconcerned with it for several weeks before they finally cracked down on the border in the third week of November, which led to some deadly shootings and many captured Hungarians. Thousands of people left Hungary every single day of November and December, and refugees continued trickling out throughout January, and people left as a result of the revolution all the way until the end of 1957.

On November 7, the French Red Cross sent a plane full of supplies to Vienna to help with the onslaught of refugees, and they took a handful of refugees back to France on the return flight.

On November 8, 1956, just four days after the influx of refugees poured out of Hungary, President Eisenhower of the United States granted 5,000 Hungarians a visa for America. Four hundred refugees were relocated to Switzerland by train on November 8, as well.

By November 9, several hundred refugees had already been transported out of Austria and into France, Switzerland, Belgium, the Netherlands and Sweden—Sweden began resettling Hungarians almost immediately after the revolution began in October, and Swedish politicians tried urging other countries to do the same.

By the end of November, nine European countries had already taken in 21,669 refugees. And by the end of December, 92,950 refugees had been relocated to 37 countries, including the UK, Canada, and America.

By January 1957, 170,000 refugees were already registered in Austria at the time the Soviets sealed the borders, and throughout the beginning of 1957 refugees continued sneaking out in much smaller numbers. Altogether, nearly 175,000 Hungarians had fled into Austria, and another almost 20,000 into Yugoslavia.

In Europe, the League of Red Cross Societies financially and physically supported over 35,000 refugees throughout 44 camps at one time with the help of only 350 social workers and health care workers, and in order to operate they had to employ nearly 700 Austrian citizens and still relied on volunteer labor. Over 100,000 refugees passed through the camps that the League of Red Cross Societies operated.

About 20% of all Hungarians who had a post-secondary education left after the revolution, including about 5,000 current university students. Many brilliant engineers, doctors, professors, lawyers, writers, artists, and intellectuals left for the west and that isn't by coincidence. In many of the countries that the refugees ultimately immigrated to, they were offered college scholarships to continue their education or given jobs that aligned with their previous work experience and education level.

Some of the freedom fighters who were interviewed for James Michener's book *The Bridge at Andau* were outspoken about how they viewed anybody who left before the fourth as a coward. They asserted that none of the actual freedom fighters would have left while they thought they still had a chance, and that anybody who left in October or the first few days of November was cowardly. While it is true that there seemed to be a chance that they'd be successful until the fourth, it's not fair to judge everybody as cowardly for leaving when they had the chance.

People of all walks of life desperately wanted out and were ready to do what it took to leave. Michener was there in the village of Andau during and after the revolution where he witnessed the events at the bridge. As a reminder, the bridge at Andau was neither a real bridge, nor in Andau. It was basically a raised footpath over the canal, which was entirely in Hungary, a few hundred yards away from the Austrian border, and even still several kilometers away from the village of Andau. Regardless, that was the name everybody knew the bridge by, and it served as the passageway to freedom for tens of thousands of refugees.

Michener recalled meeting a woman who crossed the marsh to get into Austria, she said that she'd been imprisoned by the Russians for a few days in a bunker but that she'd escaped; she appeared wealthy by the way she was dressed, and she'd been walking for three days in high heeled shoes. A man without legs caught a bus from Budapest to the last stop before the border and pulled his body about 25 kilometers through the mud and ice with his hands. A woman who had given birth on the journey crossed with her newborn child. Several mothers and their babies traveled without their husbands because the husbands insisted that they leave the babies behind because they didn't want the babies to cry and give them away, so instead of leaving their babies behind, mothers left their husbands and escaped with their babies. There was even a guard who was stationed in the guard tower near the bridge at Andau who'd helped refugees cross into Austria, he'd grown tired of serving the communists so did what he could to deceive the other guards, like pretending like he would "take care" of the refugees they caught but then guided them across the bridge and fired his gun into the sky as if he shot them.

He saw some of the most incredible acts of kindness and bravery at the bridge, even after the Soviets used dynamite to destroy the bridge. When the canal was frozen over it was easier for the refugees to cross, but one day a young father with his wife and child came to the flowing river and had no other choice but to cross through the water. He took off his clothes, held his child above his head, and waded through the ice-cold water, he left the child on the bank where the Austrians and Michener were waiting to welcome refugees and went back for his wife, whom he also carried across above his head. Those who didn't take their clothes off to cross the water were likely to get frostbite, hypothermia, and even die. After the bridge was blown up, three young Austrian college students took logs into the canal in the middle of the night to repair the bridge as much as possible—it wasn't perfect, and it was quite precarious, but it was enough for people to cross.

Then he met Mrs. Georgette Meyer Chapelle, a brilliant photographer who captured scenes of refugees that winter for the world to see. She stayed at the border with him for several nights, monitoring the banks for refugees who needed guidance into Austria in the moonlight. One night, the two of them witnessed the watchtower guards ripping the temporary bridge down and burning it. The guards saw a large group of refugees, perhaps thirty, walk right into the guards burning the bridge, they were caught and carted away.

Shelley Rohde of the British *Daily Express* was on night-duty with Michener one day when they heard a baby wailing loudly, it wouldn't stop crying so they investigated and found more than twenty refugees who'd been wandering around aimlessly in the swamp for two days. They'd tried to navigate the border without a guide, they were starving and half frozen to death, and by that point they didn't care if the baby would give them away to the guards, they just wanted out of the swamp.

Michener watched tens of thousands of Hungarians cross the border, he was amazed by their fortitude and the kindness of the Austrians. As one could imagine, Austria was unable to accommodate thousands of new refugees each day with the displaced persons camps they already had since the end of WWII. They used police and military barracks, abandoned buildings, schools, of course hospitals for the injured, and they even had to erect tents to house people. Without the help of foreign aid Austria wouldn't have been able to pull it off. Despite the enormous pressure that Austria was under, they acted quickly and often enthusiastically. Villages near the border, such as Andau, would send a scout out at night to try guiding refugees across the border or to pick them up as they wandered around. On the busiest days they took the women and children into the villages by car, bus, or truck, and told the men where they could meet them in the village.

CHAPTER 43
AMERICA'S RESPONSE TO THE REFUGEES

Tracey Voorhees, Chairman of the President's Committee for Hungarian Refugee Relief noted that up until then, "no comparable mass movement into America had ever occurred in so short a time—of persons all penniless and few of whom could speak our language," (Markowitz).

Contradictory and vacillating opinions existed in America during the crisis, since the U.S was in the midst of the Cold War and the era of McCarthyism, they were wary of the communists. While many Americans wanted to help the Hungarian underdogs fleeing from the communist Russians, there were also people who feared them because the Hungarians *could* have been communists themselves who would pose a threat if they were admitted into America. Ever since the colonial period, Americans have been nationalistic and deeply suspicious of immigrants, a mindset that contradicts the "melting pot" ideal of America.

A man named Francis Walter, a Pennsylvania Democrat in the House of Representatives, co-wrote the Immigration and Nationality Act of 1952 with Pat McCarran of Nevada. The law banned "subversives" from entering the United States, a broad term that included communists and leftists alike. Historically, the United States has always favored immigration from western and northern European countries, but during the Cold War Americans were especially opposed to immigrants that *could* have been communists because of the countries they came from.

Walter was also chair of the House Un-American Activities Committee, the committee that went on witch-hunts for communists during the McCarthy era. He had such an immense decision-making power in immigration policy that he was nicknamed "Mr.

Immigration." At the beginning of the Hungarian refugee crisis, Walter was an advocate for relief programs and even visited Austria in mid-November. He proposed that the United States allow 17,000 Hungarian refugees to fill the empty "slots" from the Refugee Relief Act of 1953, a bill that he himself had proposed; and Eisenhower approved for 15,000 Hungarians to receive visas, after already declaring on November 8 that 5,000 would be awarded visas. Walter continued to assure the public that they'd vet the refugees well, and at minimum only a few "undesirables" would slip through the cracks and get admitted. The public was ardently anti-communist, but as Walter put it, "what better evidence of anti-communism can you have than bullet holes in a man's body?" (Bentz).

On November 26, the White House announced that they would allow 21,500 displaced Hungarians to enter the United States. Of those admitted, 6,500 would receive visas from the Refugee Relief Act, but the rest would be allowed in as "parolees" under section 212 of the Immigration and Nationality Act. President Eisenhower explained that it was necessary, as the visas were almost exhausted under the Refugee Relief Act.

However, by the end of 1956, Walter had changed his tone. At first, he supported the idea of bringing refugees to America, but then he changed to a more modest and restrictive approach to handling the crisis that would "protect" America's interests. During TV interviews, Walter said that the administration couldn't vet the refugees effectively because they were going "too fast," therefore allowing "undesirables" to get in. He argued that to preserve national security they had to slow down their efforts to admit the refugees. Walter's motivation for his dramatic shift in support may have been to preserve the Refugee Relief Act of 1953. After his appeals to influence the United States to help the Hungarian refugees, people were worried that the Refugee Relief Act had major issues and suggested it be scrapped or considerably liberalized, neither of which Walter wanted to happen.

During 1957, Walter began to oppose relief for the refugees and even argued that the United States should've instead helped prepare the Hungarian refugees for their next revolution against the Soviets "rather than sapping the strength of the resistance by letting them come to the United States," (Bentz).

Even though Walter flip-flopped, he still held popularity among

Hungarians both in America and abroad. He showed exquisite skill in being able to manipulate public opinion and other politicians, and his wavering rhetoric was mostly a political strategy to maintain and garner more support. In 1957, with the allyship of Senator John. F. Kennedy, Walter ended the quota system, and in 1958, he back-pedaled on his earlier sentiment that Hungarians only be allowed in under parole and allowed Hungarian refugees to apply to be a permanent resident in the United States.

A month after saying that the US should admit as many refugees as possible, Walter began warning that many of the refugees were communists and spies disguising themselves as persecuted people seeking refuge, and it was not just Walter who became reluctant to admit refugees. After the initial sympathy for the refugees, many people within and outside of the government feared that the Hungarians would pose a danger to American citizens.

Representative George Long of Louisiana said it was "hard to generate much enthusiasm for people who had deserted their homeland in [a] time of crises. . . [and] had migrated. . . to the promised land—America," (Markowitz). He was worried about what would happen to the native-born American citizens (no, he did not mean indigenous people, he meant the white immigrants' descendants) if the US kept letting foreigners in who sought "greener pastures." People were afraid that the immigrants—whom they thought might disguise themselves as refugees, but really wouldn't qualify—would take away jobs from Americans.

It was Vice President Nixon who was able to sway President Eisenhower and the United States Congress to allow more refugees visas. A week before Christmas, Nixon visited Austria and Camp Kilmer in New Jersey, where most of the refugees were processed upon arrival, and he was able to convince Eisenhower that the refugees were not "communist spies or undesirables" and that the screening process to accept refugees would make certain that they would present "no significant risk of internal subversion" in America (Markowitz). He also voiced his opinions that the refugees were good people and that there would be plenty of jobs for them that wouldn't take away from American workers.

Nixon went as far as to ask Congress to do away with the idea that the US should only take in a fixed amount of refugees, instead, they should allow their "full share of escapees from communist tyranny." He argued that "we should not place a ceiling on what we will do in fulfilling our traditional natural mission of providing a haven of refuge for victims of oppression," (Markowitz). Which in itself is an ironic statement to make about the "traditional natural mission" of the United States of America, the country that was a refuge for Puritans from Great Britain but only at the expense of killing and oppressing the indigenous populations, the country that not two decades prior had put a ceiling on Jewish refugees fleeing from Nazism and denied them entry because of inherent antisemitism and self-preservation.

Nevertheless, Nixon was persuasive, and when Congress reconvened after the Christmas holiday, they overwhelmingly wished to support Hungarian refugees, but the House and Senate were more hesitant. In January 1957, Eisenhower argued to Congress that the US, as a world leader, should accept more refugees and asked for "permanent legislation granting him discretionary power" to allow refugees visas. Then he asked for Congress to pass legislation that would "permit aliens paroled into the United States who intended to stay here to remain as permanent residents," (Markowitz). Before this, refugees who were considered parolees were, by law, only temporary aliens in the country.

By March 1957, only 1,600 of the 27,000 refugees who'd entered the United States remained at Camp Kilmer awaiting resettlement. The Commissioner of Immigration and Naturalization thought the program was "without comparison in our history. . . and yet without sacrifice of our national standards," (Markowitz). The swiftness with which the program was carried out was one measure of its massive success, but that statement begs the question: if they could pull off the Hungarian refugee crisis without sacrificing national standards, then why hasn't there been a similar response to another international crisis?

By August 1, 1957, more than 33,000 Hungarian refugees were admitted to the United States. In May 1957, the President's Committee for Hungarian Refugee Relief was dismantled, Camp Kilmer closed, and refugees would not be welcomed as easily, or warmly, thereafter. In the end, though, more than 38,000 refugees resettled in the United States, nearly double what the President initially wanted to allow.

The demographics of the refugees are interesting and atypical of a post-war European country. About 83% of those who entered the US were under the age of 40, 64% were male, and less than 1% had a background in agriculture. Hungary was primarily rural, but most people who fled were from large cities rather than the countryside because of the push to collectivization. People who had once owned farms were forced out of the profession or left willingly because they refused to join the collective, and many moved to the cities after the Soviet invasion; József's own family had a farm but then moved to the city after 1945. People who owned their own land were less likely to immigrate, but those who rented in the city and didn't see much prospect for their future career (because of limitations put in place by the communists) had more reason to escape.

Refugees from Hungary (October 28, 1956 - August 3, 1957)

Arrivals & departures	Austria	Yugoslavia	Number	%
Arrived	174,285	19,688	193,973	100
Left	148,496	11,242	159,738	82.4
Emigrated	143,400	8,082	151,482	78.1
Repatriated	5,096	2,564	7,660	4.0
Integrated	-	596	596	0.3
Remained	25,789 (13,000 in camps)	8,446 (all in camps)	34,235	17.6

**Emigration of Hungarian refugees from Austria and Yugoslavia
(figures as of August 3, 1957)**

Destination	Austria	Yugoslavia	Number	%
All Countries	143,400	8,082	151,482	100
Europe	71,112	6,603	77,715	51.3
Americas	59,899	1,310	61,209	40.4
United States	33,656	135	33,791	
Canada	23,123	1,073	24,201	
Latin America	3,115	102	3,217	
Oceania	9,202	9	9,211	6.1
Australia	8,247	2	8,249	
New Zealand	955	7	962	
Israel	1,869	160	2,029	1.3
South Africa & Rhodesia*	1,318	-	1,318	0.9

*6 refugees went to Rhodesia, now Zimbabwe.[40]

---

[40] Table transcribed and simplified from *The American Jewish Year Book.*

Chapter 44
Patience

A week went by before the immigration counselor returned; he didn't have any news for them about their application statuses. Herr Maier greeted everyone cordially and asked for a few people to come speak with him, evidently, they needed to revise or fill out more papers. There were a few new refugees who arrived during the week, and they were given the application packets to fill out. All of the waiting and wondering kept Tamás awake at night, he was obviously anxious, but József kept his composure so that he wouldn't let Tamás know that he was also worried that their visas would be denied.

Another week passed and more people became restless and irritable, wondering about their fate. Even the most composed were starting to show signs of distress, unaware that they would actually be among the first few thousand able to get a visa. Herr Maier returned every few days and sometimes he gave a few people the good news that their applications had been approved and they were getting out of there, but the waiting was unbearable for the rest of them. Many were jealous and some took it personally when somebody else's visa was approved while they still waited. Each time he arrived they would all wait around outside the cafeteria, hoping that they'd be called in.

Life in the refugee camps became monotonous and sometimes the refugees developed what was coined as "camp psychosis" which exhibited as being passive, depressive, and/or aggressive. It was mostly the Hungarians who had defected from the Hungarian military who developed "camp psychosis," though. There were about 700 defectors interned at the Wals-Siezenheim camp near Salzburg, they didn't have the same rights as a civilian refugee, and many tried escaping the camp in order to sneak into a regular refugee camp for the chance at getting a visa elsewhere.

The people in charge of the camps worked with the humanitarian organizations to help relocate the refugees efficiently, though they couldn't move at the speed that the French Red Cross moved when they flew in supplies to Austria on November 7 and brought refugees back on the return flight. Sometimes, countries accepted Hungarians without first assessing their ability to sustain them, but that wasn't feasible to continue doing so they had to be strategic.

Aid organizations created refugee camps wherever they could, in police and fire departments, military bases, schools, and abandoned buildings. Some of the camps, particularly in abandoned buildings, weren't suitable to live in, and the temporary camps constructed out of tarps and tents were less than ideal to live in during the winter.

They began moving refugees around to different camps to accommodate new people, so if somebody was in the process of getting their visa to Germany approved, then they could be moved to a camp closer to the German border to make transportation easier later.

József's friend Pál was transferred to another camp, closer to Switzerland because that's where he wanted to get a visa to, so he could be closer to home. When he found out that he was being relocated, he was excited to tell József because it meant he was one step closer to immigrating. Even though József knew it was good for Pál, he was saddened by the news because he would lose his friend again. They spent one more day hanging out together, talking about all their hopes for what life would be like after camp. Pál left the next morning, they promised they'd write to each other and see each other again one day.

On the fourth visit from Herr Maier, he brought a few volunteers from aid organizations to help make travel arrangements for the refugees; they arrived just after breakfast and immediately went into an office to prepare and collect paperwork. József and Tamás no longer had kitchen duty, but they waited around in the cafeteria after breakfast for Herr Maier anyways. They were hopeful, but Tamás was nervously tapping his feet and picking at loose strings on his jacket. They chatted about mundane things for a while, just to pass the time, but they anxiously watched as Herr Maier opened the door each time. Sometimes the refugees came out of the room disappointed, evidently, they did not get a visa yet, but more often than not they came out in high spirits. József looked on as several of his new friends raced happily out of the cafeteria while he waited.

After a few excruciating hours their names were called out together and they thought that must be good news. They were jittery and stumbled slightly as they stood up and pushed their chairs in, walked into the office, politely waved to the volunteer inside, and sat down slowly. Herr Maier closed the door behind himself, he didn't want to waste any time getting to the point. He was actually rather unenthusiastic when he told József and Tamás that they had both been approved for visas to go to America, and that they'd be allowed to go together, but he couldn't make any promises that they'd stay together once they got to America, they could be split up.

They sat on the edge of their seats and started laughing, they were nervous and excited at the same time. Herr Maier put his fatigued hand in the air to halt their excitement and said they still had more forms to fill out before moving on, and that spots had to open at other camps first before they could be transferred.

The kind, young volunteer smiled at the two young men, she nodded her head to acknowledge their excitement and handed over another packet of papers to both of them. Herr Maier motioned towards the documents and said they had to fill them out, and to ensure that they were completed correctly and by the right person, they must do it within that office. They each took a pen and a clipboard and began filling out their papers. Tamás couldn't keep his hand from shaking, it was making his handwriting illegible, so he had to calm himself with a few deep breaths for a moment.

Herr Maier said, "Let me know if you have any questions," as he busied himself shuffling papers on his desk around.

The volunteer began translating some of the documents that were in English, evidently there wasn't enough time to get them transcribed into Hungarian for the refugees to read, or perhaps they ran out of Hungarian copies. The paperwork took the boys at least twenty minutes to get through, most of the papers were signed consent and confirmation that they were in fact who they said they were.

Soon enough they had finished the papers, shook Herr Maier's hand, and jaunted out of the office. They were ecstatic and told everyone that they'd been approved for visas, their happiness was so infectious that even the most bitter old men cracked a smile when they saw how happy József and Tamás were.

Later that night after the buzz wore off, József sat in the recreation room, holding a book but not reading it. He was busy daydreaming about America, about what he might tell his parents when he wrote home. Some of the men in the barracks played card games to pass the time, others read newspapers or books from the scant collection of paperbacks, most of them sat talking to one another, but nobody spoke to József, he was in his own world.

A pair of gentlemen sat across the coffee table from József, quietly talking to each other, whispering about how happy all the young kids looked, wondering when they would get their visas. Both of them were unmarried and in their 30s, perhaps 40s, they didn't have priority over the young kids and women.

One of the gentlemen, Milán, was generally a quiet man. He'd been at that refugee camp since before József arrived, which was in the middle of November. Then one day about a week later, another bus came with some new arrivals and on it was a man named Alexi, whom Milán had known in Hungary. Milán was leaving the mess hall at the same time, but he wasn't paying attention to the new refugees because it wasn't out of the ordinary to see more arrive but when Alexi got off the bus, he saw Milán almost immediately.

József watched the whole reunion happen. Alexi cracked a huge smile and took off for Milán, calling out his name. It took a second before he recognized Alexi's voice, so by the time he turned around, Alexi was already going in for an embrace that nearly knocked Milán off his feet. They held each other for a long time, gave careful kisses on the cheeks, cried tears of joy, and promised never to leave each other again. It was a pure, wonderful moment that gave hope to others that they'd see their loved ones again. They were never separated again, and a young fellow in the barracks even agreed to switch beds so that they could sleep next to each other. It was a coincidence, maybe a miracle, that they ended up at the same camp together at the same time. There were dozens, perhaps more than one hundred camps all over Austria that the refugees moved through, and the volunteers were able to relocate many refugees extremely quickly.

At first, József felt a little uneasy about the apparent relationship between the two men, he had been told that it was unnatural for men to be so intimate with each other, but he began to see them as human, no different than he, and he was happy to see them so happy. The two men didn't flaunt their relationship in anybody's face, which made most people more comfortable to be around them, and the more time people spent together in the camp, the more human everybody seemed. This crisis was happening to everybody, from all walks of life.

"Hey, kid, you okay?" Milán asked József.

He snapped out of his daydream. "Huh? Oh, yeah, I'm fine, just thinking. I just got my visa approved for America today, you know."

"Yeah? No kidding? That's great, kid! We're happy for you!" Alexi said enthusiastically. Both he and Milán smiled and József's cheeks flushed.

"Have you gotten your visas yet?"

They shook their heads, "No, not yet."

"Well, I hope you get them soon," he said.

"Yeah, we hope so, too, kid," Alexi smiled.

József nodded and again stared at the book in his lap, Milán and Alexi went back to their conversation. Not long after it was lights out and everybody began settling into bed.

After breakfast the next day József was walking back to his barracks when some young kids ran past him out onto the barren field within the compound.

One yelled as they passed by, "Hey, József! Do you want to play football with us?"

It was Csaba, a little boy about twelve years old, the same age as József's little brother László, with light skin and dark stringy hair. He had taken a liking to József, who made an effort never to ignore Csaba and to make him feel included, which went a long way for the little boy.

He agreed to join their football game and jogged to the middle of the field where all the little boys were happy to see him. They were already split into two teams, one had four players and the other five, so the team of four got to recruit József. They cheered as the other team whined, "We're gonna lose now!"

"OK, we're first! You kick the ball, József, you're the tallest!" Csaba instructed József.

The teams stood facing each other, and after József kicked the ball the little boys fell into chaos, they squealed and laughed, not really caring that they weren't playing by the rules. They didn't have clear boundaries on the grass, and the goals were just some jackets left on the ground on either side of the field. They ran this way and that, they yelled instructions at each other, but nobody followed them, and some boys kicked at absolutely nothing. The ball was old and needed more air, and the ground was muddy and hard to run in, but no one seemed to mind. Even József had to admit that it was fun just running around, acting like a kid. They even giggled when they fell, and nobody counted penalties, they were just kids trying to be kids. They played for the best two out of three, and József's team ended up winning but it didn't really matter because they were having fun.

Someone screamed "Goal!" and the littlest boys tackled József to celebrate. He hit the ground and all the boys began piling up on top of him, they were so excited.

The kids at the refugee camps did their best to play games with each other, even in the dead of winter, just to keep some semblance of normalcy. The adults around camp tried to put on a brave face for the kids, but sometimes it was the kids who put on the bravest faces. Especially the ones who'd left without their parents, they were completely alone and terrified.

Chapter 45
The Christmas Bazaar

One day at breakfast, Herr Schuster gave each refugee a little spending money because they had some monetary donations from relief organizations that exceeded the demands at the time. It was an unexpected and exciting treat for them. Herr Schuster told them all that they could take the train up to Villach, a nearby city, to visit the Christmas bazaar if they wanted. He gave them directions to walk to the train station, about a twenty-minute walk away, and reminded them that they had to pay attention to the time because the passenger trains stop running at a certain time and they'd be stranded.

Several of the young men planned to go to Villach together and decided that they would meet at the courtyard at 9 o'clock to leave. While they waited for everybody to arrive, a young man named Rudolf doled out cigarettes to his friends, who accepted graciously. Aid organizations had donated cigarettes to the refugee camps, and some young people, including József, took up smoking while at camp because there simply weren't many other things to do.

"Smoke?" he offered, holding his open pack to Tamás and József.

József took a cigarette, he'd had them a few times before, but he didn't consider himself a smoker until then. He wanted to fit in with the other guys.

Shaking his head Tamás said, "I don't smoke, I don't think it's good for you," he always felt like he needed to defend himself.

Rudolf shrugged, he thought Tamás was a little bit prudish. Somebody struck a match and everyone lit up their cigarettes. Ádám, who acted like a hooligan, rudely exhaled his smoke into Tamás' face. He was a short and dense bloke who hung around Rudolf often. Alexander, another one of Rudolf's friends, tried to socialize with everybody; he was a fairly decent kid, as opposed to his mates.

Alexander extended his hand towards József first, his cigarette hanging limply from his mouth, "Hey, Alexander," he introduced himself, "But most people call me Alex."

József and Tamás shook his hand in turn and introduced themselves. Tamás was relieved that at least somebody who was friends with Rudolf was a nice person, but he couldn't help but think that if they were in the real world, Alex wouldn't be his friend. However, at camp everybody had to stick together. Life at camp didn't feel like they were in the "real world" anyways, so friendships that would have never happened in real life blossomed at camp.

"We need to make it to the train station by 9:30 so we can catch the next train to town," Rudolf explained as he flicked ash onto the ground.

It was one long road and one right turn to get to the train station. *You can't miss it,* Mr. Schuster had told them. The station was a major landmark on the outskirts of the sleepy village.

They walked down the gravel driveway through the main gate of the camp for the first time since arriving a few weeks prior. Rudolf walked backwards for a moment, watching the camp shrink in the distance. The camp was so bleak and depressing from afar, it was only a few brick buildings surrounded by some dead trees and ugly stumps.

They didn't talk for the most part, listening to the sound of ice crunching under their boots and the wind that ripped past their ears. Silence was a pleasant break from the constant conversations about the resistance, immigration, and the Soviets that were had back at camp. Occasionally, somebody would point to something in the distance or complain about the cold, but they mostly just smoked their cigarettes in silence. After 20 minutes or so, they arrived at the train station and everybody bought a ticket for Villach and waited for the train.

When they were told that they could go to the market, the market itself didn't really seem all that thrilling, but they were happy just to be out of that camp for the day. When the train arrived in Villach and they stepped onto the platform, they felt like normal people again.

Villach was much bigger than most of the refugees were used to, with shops and restaurants that dazzled with lights, and holiday decorations on the main street. The outdoor Christmas bazaar could be seen from the train platform, it spanned many city blocks, and it was filled with people shopping in every direction, this far exceeded their expectations; they were impressed and excited.

It was an open-air market, a festively decorated collection of tents and tables where vendors and farmers came to sell their handmade goods and foods. With the holidays coming up, the citizens of Villach were running around town to collect everything on their list. Up until then, it hadn't even occurred to József that Christmas was approaching, and most people were still going about their regular lives.

They looked at each other and chuckled gleefully before they headed across the street to the market. They chatted aimlessly as they walked and marveled at everything they saw. There were Christmas wreaths and garland hung around buildings and on lampposts, string lights on trees, and red ribbons and bows decorating the vendors tables. The vendors offered samples to people who passed by, they shouted that they had a deal and bargained to make a sale. Their tables were full of goodies like candy, cakes, spirits, little dolls and wooden toys, and even household items like glassware.

Tamás told the group that they needed a plan to meet up together right outside of the market at 14:00 at the latest, just in case they got separated. They agreed, even though Rudolf thought that a 14:00 call time was too soon. Alex reminded him that it wasn't even 10:00 yet, they had plenty of time and the market wasn't so big that they'd get lost.

Rudolf agreed, he saw something in the bazaar that caught his eye and beckoned the others to follow him. They all had to weave in and out of people, cutting right through the flow of traffic to follow Rudolf to a wine and liquor vendor. Rudolf knew a little bit of German, so he spoke with the old clerk and exchanged a few shillings for an amber bottle of liquor while the rest of them looked on at the variety of bottles in awe. The others were exhilarated, they watched and stifled their laughs, it felt rebellious, even if a little stupid, to buy liquor when they could have spent that money on something else.

"I don't think you can have alcohol at camp," Tamás said, always the worrier.

"Don't worry, nobody will tell. Right?" He gave a menacing look to Tamás. Then he smiled wide and winked at his friends. "Don't be such a downer," he clapped Tamás on the shoulder.

He and his friends chuckled and walked off, leaving József and Tamás behind. They followed for a few minutes but then drifted apart, they would catch up to the guys later or meet outside the market at the designated meeting spot in the afternoon.

They walked on, browsing all of the tables and popping their heads into stores in the town center, gazing at the decorations around the city, and looking at the gifts for sale with no intention of buying anything. They contemplated going to the cinema, but they figured that they'd rather spend their money on food that wasn't prepared at camp.

There were plenty of things to choose from in the food section of the Christmas market: freshly fried pastries, breads, hot meats, produce from local farmers, even imported meats, cheeses, and fruits. Some of it was packaged nicely, obviously meant to be bought as a gift.

Tamás pulled József towards a bright display of fruits and vegetables with a sign that read *Aus Italien Importiert*, he figured that it meant "Imported from Italy." The old man minding the table nodded and smiled and they nodded back politely. They were amazed at all of the fruits, typically they didn't have a large selection of fruit in Hungary, especially not during the winter, so that really excited them.

There were citrus fruits in hues of oranges and yellows, figs, persimmons, chestnuts, and of course there were apples and various root vegetables which were commonplace in rural Hungary, but the new fruits enticed them more. Eventually Tamás plucked up an orange and a purple fig, József felt pressured to make a choice so he picked up the same fruits, and an apple for good measure. The vendor told them how much they owed, and they pulled a few coins from their pockets, counted the right amount of money out and handed it over. The vendor double checked the money they gave him and nodded his head, wishing them a good day. They thanked the man and left happily with their fruits.

"Do you know what these are?" József asked Tamás as they wandered towards the nearby picnic tables.

"They're called oranges, but I don't know what these are," he held up the fig. "I've had grapes from Italy before and they were really good, and this is also purple so it should be good too," Tamás explained.

József laughed at Tamás' logic but it was good enough for him. They saw Rudolf, Ádám, and Alex slinking off to a remote area of the park to indulge on the liquor and apple strudels they bought.

"Shall we join them?" Jozsef asked.

Tamás shrugged indifferently, he wasn't keen on Rudolf.

Their little posse was too deep in conversation to notice Tamás and József approaching. When they sat down at the table, Alex greeted them and offered the bottle of liquor for them to take a swig, which they declined. Rudolf, Alex and Ádám passed the dark liquor between them rhythmically, each taking small swigs.

József watched as Tamás took a bite of his fig before he would take a bite of his own. It was smooth and heavy in his hands, he waited for Tamás' reaction. Tamás' eyes widened in surprise as he tasted its sweet inside, but when he pulled the fruit away from his mouth, József saw the strange seed-like flesh inside and was slightly put off by it. Tamás reassured József that the fruit was delicious and encouraged him to try it, so he bit into his fig and was pleasantly surprised with its taste. He finished it in no time, sparing only the stem, and he grabbed the orange next. Before Tamás could stop him, József bit down into the thick, sour skin of his orange. Tamás laughed as József spat out the chunk of skin and winced from the sour taste.

"What?" he shouted at the others who all laughed at him.

Rudolf howled, "You don't eat the skin!"

Even Tamás snickered when he told József, "He's right, you have to peel this fruit. Here," Tamás reached for József's orange and showed him how to peel it. He stuck his thumb under the skin where the chunk was missing and peeled some more away before giving it back, "Like that."

József was embarrassed at his ignorance and angry that they all laughed, his cheeks flushed red. The others finally stopped laughing at him and he peeled his orange, putting the skins in a pile on the ground next to him. He saw that the fruit came in little sections, so he smartly pulled one off and finally ate the sweet, edible part of his orange. József thoroughly enjoyed the orange once he peeled it, he thought it was even better than the fig. He wanted to save the apple for later, back at camp for when he tired of having the same plain foods day in and day out.

József remembered as a young boy how much he liked apples because they were considered a special treat like cakes and candies, they weren't as readily available in Hungary after the Soviet takeover and the introduction of the farming collective. He remembered reading picture books that featured exotic fruits and vegetables from Mediterranean countries, József did not remember when imports were cut off and those foods became inaccessible, but Tamás did. The Soviets controlled where the food was sent after harvest, rather than giving that control to the farmers themselves, and they exported the majority of the produce and saved the best for the high-ranking communists.

The apple strudels the others ate smelled delicious, Tamás decided he wanted one after all; he asked József if he wanted one, which he did, and he went to buy apple strudels for both of them. József tried to pay him back for the pastry, but he wouldn't take the money, after all, it wasn't their money to begin with, so he didn't think of it as a loss at all.

They sat and talked mindlessly for a few hours until they needed to go back, happy to have something to distract themselves with.

CHAPTER 46
"THAT TRAIN IS FROM RUSSIA!"

Hungary was self-sufficient for a long time, we grew enough of our own food, the soil was exceptionally good for farming, the climate was nice and moderate, and life was relatively good. The first nomads who settled in Hungary thought it was a great place to start a civilization. The land was lush and green, the soil was rich and full of nutrients for the crops, and the rivers brought plenty of water. In Hungary, there are three major rivers: one from the Black Forest, Duna (Danube)*; one from the northeast, Tisza; and one from the west, Drava. They all meet down where the border of Yugoslavia is. They provided ideal growing conditions.*[41]

I remember one of my cousins was working on a railroad, loading carts with food and supplies from Hungary and transporting them elsewhere. One day he was working and it got hot in the afternoon, it was not uncommon in the winter for the afternoons to be hot. He says he took off his winter coat and left it in the cart he was loading. It was potatoes, potatoes grown in Hungary, and they were going to Austria, maybe Italy.

Well, my cousin goes off to lunch and comes back and the train is gone, with his coat inside it. And your winter coat is very important, and you could not just go buy another, he needed to get it back. So, he goes to his boss and his boss says, "You can catch the next train and get your coat, then come back to work."

So, he gets on the train, gets to the station the first train had stopped at, and asked to see the manager of the site, he says, "Look, I

---

[41] There are more than a dozen major rivers in Hungary. The Tisza is the longest river, the Duna (Danube) is the second longest, and the Drava is the seventh longest.

left my coat on the cart, it was such and such train with such and such
name on it, it came from Hungary, it was carrying potatoes."

The man says, "No, no trains came from Hungary, that train is
from Russia!"

That man showed him the documents and sure enough they said
the train was from Russia. So, what does my cousin do, he goes to the
cart and finds his coat and brings it back and he says "See, this is my
coat, I loaded this cart in Hungary."

In between Hungary and the next train stop the documents were
changed to say the carts were from Russia, but those potatoes were
grown in Hungarian soil.

The standard of living in Hungary decreased when the Soviets took
over and forced collectivized farming onto them. Farmers were strong-
armed into the collective and whatever they produced would be sent
out of Hungary, usually to the USSR, leaving Hungarians with very
little of their own crops.[42] Some of the farmers, rather than joining the
collective, destroyed their farms and killed their own livestock which
was highly illegal and could have meant death for them, too.

After WWII, hyperinflation made Hungarian currency almost
worthless, and the prices of food skyrocketed as the availability
decreased. Taxes often increased and at the same time wages were
docked or decreased; then the production demand of industrial jobs was
raised but the wage didn't rise in accordance. The citizens, excluding
the wealthy and elite ruling class, suffered from food insecurities,
though not as much as citizens in the USSR during the two intentional
famines.

My grandpa's family secretly raised pigeons and rabbits in their
attic to supplement their diets with more meat than was allowed with

---

[42] On a related note, the first great Soviet famine was from 1932-1933, in which
5.7 to 8.7 million people died, was in the major grain-producing regions of the
USSR including Russia, Ukraine, Kazakhstan, the Caucasus, the Volga, the
Urals, and the Kuban region. Author and professor Michael Ellman states that
between 1932 to 1933 the grain exports from those regions amounted to 1.8
million tons of grain, enough to feed about 5 million Soviet citizens for a year,
but the USSR continued to export grain during a widespread famine.

their rations. Raising your own livestock or growing your own food outside of the collective farming system was illegal.

CHAPTER 47

SALZBURG

The days blurred together for the refugees in the camps; days were spent waiting around hoping to speak with an immigration counselor, and nights were spent wondering and worrying. Life at camp was terribly boring, but they were treated well, housed (even if the housing was sometimes less than ideal) and fed by hundreds of volunteers who worked around the clock to help refugees. Compared to other mass immigration emergencies, the Hungarians were relocated very quickly, but while it was happening the waiting felt never ending.

A few days after they went to the Christmas bazaar in Villach, Herr Schuster announced during breakfast that a bus was coming to pick up several of the refugees after breakfast to transfer them to Salzburg, Austria. It was a last-minute plan to transfer the refugees that day, so they were excited, they shifted in their seats as he made an announcement.

"This afternoon many of you are going to get on a bus to Salzburg, and from there you'll move on to Germany later. Most of you have already gotten your visas to the United States of America or Canada, but some of you are still waiting on it, if it can't happen then you'll stay in Germany for a while longer. If I call your name, it means you're going on the bus, so make sure you pack all of your belongings and clean up your bed before you leave." He called out a list of names and those who were on the list rejoiced.

"Now, if your name wasn't called there is no way I can get you on the bus, your turn is coming, just be patient." When he finished, he left immediately, avoiding any questions or complaints that might arise.

Energy in the cafeteria was high, people were talking, laughing, and patting each other on the back. Most of the refugees who had to stay were happy for the ones who were called to leave rather than jealous, but a few younger kids were obviously envious. Older men and women knew that if people were frequently being relocated when their visas were approved, that meant the process was moving quickly and it wouldn't be long before it was their turn.

Two of the refugees from the list were on breakfast duty in the cafeteria, but the others on their shift kindly told them, "Go pack up and get ready to leave, we'll take care of the cleanup, don't worry about it!"

Everyone poured out of the cafeteria to go pack up their belongings, they were in a hurry just to sit around and wait for the bus. Most didn't escape with much, some had a backpack or a suitcase, but others didn't have anything except a spare outfit or two that they'd acquired through the donations. József didn't have a bag so he needed to find something to pack his few pieces of clothes in. He rummaged through the donations box with no luck finding a backpack, so he left the barracks in search of camp staff.

He walked all the way back to the cafeteria where he found Herr Schuster in one of the offices in the back organizing the paperwork for all the refugees to leave later that afternoon. "Hi, sorry to bother you, Herr Schuster, but do you know if there are any backpacks or suitcases I can take with me? I didn't see any more in the donations bin. I didn't bring one. I—I would have had one, but it was taken by the Soviets you see, then I came into Austria without it and now I have some things, some clothes you know, and I don't have anything to carry—" he was rambling.

Herr Schuster cut him off, "I get it, I don't have any suitcases, but I can give you a paper bag." He went to the kitchen, came back with a bag, handed it over and told József to leave and pack his things so that he could get back to what he was doing. József thanked him and left quickly, feeling a little embarrassed.

Back in the men's barracks, everybody was sitting around chatting with each other one last time, but József went straight to his bed to pack up the clothes he wasn't wearing, a few personal hygiene products, and the small Hungarian Bible he'd been given. He was ecstatic when he got it since he'd lost the Bible he left home with, he needed something to remind him of home and his faith. He read the Bible from time to time, but he started questioning some of the verses that he'd never thought much about until then. He still treasured the Bible, and he would keep that copy for the rest of his life.

Then he stripped his bed of the sheets and went to throw them in the dirty linen basket. Without anything else to do, he sat on the floor beside everybody in the barracks who were sitting around, chatting, just killing time. They waited anxiously until a white bus arrived to collect them just as lunch began, and thankfully the camp director let them eat quickly before they had to leave. Everybody was in high spirits, even the ones who had to stay—they knew that their turn would come soon.

Herr Schuster instructed them to get on the bus as soon as they finished their lunch, they would be taking off once everybody was onboard. The bus driver had a clipboard with the necessary paperwork and a list of names, he checked people off as they entered.

People were crying both happy and sad tears as they said their goodbyes. Everybody carried their meager belongings onto the bus, checked in with the bus driver, and took their seats. As always, József and Tamás sat together. A young mother with her two children sat in the row across the aisle from József, the kids looked sad and scared. József leaned into the aisle to talk to the little boy, they'd played football together a few times and he really took to József. Nobody ever talked about what happened to their dad though.

"Hey, Mátyás, aren't you happy? We got our visas!" József said joyfully, trying to coax the young kids into smiling.

Their mother, Hanna, gave József a faint smile, she appreciated that he was always so kind with her children. "Yes, this is a very happy day," she said, "Isn't it, my dears?" She sat between them and gave them each a little hug, the little girl buried her head in Hanna's side.

József squeezed Mátyás' arm kindly and said, "It's going to be okay."

They were all anxious and elated at the same time. It wasn't long before the bus took off and they watched as the camp disappeared in the distance, they were grateful to be moving on.

The bus ride was boring, and people stopped chatting with each other shortly into the ride, so they were left alone with their own thoughts. József couldn't help but think that he might not see his family again since he was going so far away. He missed his whole family, but he missed his little sister the most.

Occasionally, someone would point to something interesting out the window, after all, they had never been outside of their country, so everything was new to them even if it looked relatively similar to Hungary. There was beautiful, old-world architecture in Salzburg mixed with the remnants of the United States occupation, like English signs and American restaurants; all kinds of capitalistic western influence that was forbidden in Hungary.

The bus arrived at the refugee camp outside of Salzburg in the late afternoon, and they noticed how much bigger it was than their previous camp. Everyone got off of the bus, clutching everything that they owned in the world, and stood outside awaiting further instruction. A few staff members went to collect them, they were ushered inside of a large and lifeless building used as their mess hall and given more paperwork to fill out. This time they were given a small identification card to sign and carry on themselves at all times, it made József feel like an official refugee. The staff told them that they were able to help themselves to the water dispenser or the restroom, and that they'd be able to put their things down and claim a bed in the barracks before returning to the mess hall and completing the paperwork.

The paperwork had all been translated into Hungarian so they didn't have any trouble completing it, and it didn't take long. Eventually, someone came in to collect the paperwork from the refugees, he told them that they were working hard to get all of them resettled as quickly as possible. The Austrian, a representative who was supposed to help people immigrate, asked the crowd, "Is anybody thinking about moving back to Hungary one day?"

A few people raised their hands.

"If you want to go back, then you might as well stay close instead of going all the way to England or America," he said, it sounded reasonable enough, but he lost his audience when he said, "The Hungarian government has offered to let you return now, if you wish, without punishment."

The Hungarians laughed out loud at that. "Do you think we are stupid?" one asked.

Only a small percentage of people who escaped actually wished to go back one day, but they weren't keen on the idea of returning immediately. If any of them returned, even with the promise that they wouldn't be punished, they knew they would still be jailed, or even killed. The Soviets lied, the Hungarian government lied, they turned on people all the time and accused people who'd been to outside countries of being western spies and jailed them for it. It also wasn't unreasonable to assume that the Soviets would prevent Hungarians from ever leaving again after their attempted escape. Even if they promised the refugees that they'd be allowed to return safely, there wasn't a single reason to believe they'd stay true to their word.

The Austrian government agreed to try to repatriate Hungarians, but they hesitated to send thousands of unaccompanied minors back to Hungary because they couldn't be certain that the parents would have wished for their children to return. Some of the children were 10 years old or younger, and their parents had told them to walk across the border alone. *That* was safer than staying in Hungary. Sometimes, like in József's case, the unaccompanied minors were 16 or 17, therefore closer to adulthood and treated as such.

The stay in the Salzburg camp was quick for József and the others since they already had their visa applications approved and were on their way to other countries, Salzburg was merely a layover. József didn't have time to settle in before they were moved again to the next location to prepare for their long journey.

He didn't remember the camp's name, but I have narrowed down the possibilities to two camps: Roeder, which was actually a US Military base in Salzburg, or a displaced person's camp called Hellbrunn. Unfortunately, there isn't a lot of published information about either camp during 1956 or 1957, but there are photographs of former first lady Eleanor Roosevelt at the US Military Base Roeder with Hungarian freedom fighters from May 1957.

The displaced persons camp, Hellbrunn, was used after WWII ended for Jewish people who had lived through the concentration camps and couldn't, or didn't want to, return home so they were housed in camps until they could immigrate elsewhere. Many concentration camps were repurposed as displaced persons camps in former Riech territories, but Hellbrunn had not been a concentration camp. Most of the refugees that were in Austria were resettled by 1952, so all but three of the camps had been dissolved, and Hellbrunn was one of those three.

I can rule out another known camp in Salzburg called Siezenheim, because that was used as an internment camp for about 700 Hungarians who had deserted the military, and as an internment camp it was more akin to a prison camp than a regular refugee camp. The Hungarians weren't happy with the conditions there, they weren't horrible in comparison to other prison camps, but they didn't have the freedom to leave camp freely or to get visas, some tried escaping and sneaking into a "regular" refugee camp, and many went on a hunger strike.

CHAPTER 48

BREMERHAVEN

"Are you excited?" József asked Tamás the night before they were to leave as they laid on their beds and stared at the ceiling.

He shrugged, "Yeah, but I'm also nervous. Aren't you?"

József thought about it. "I guess I am a little nervous, but what do you really think is going to go wrong?"

"Well, assuming they didn't make a mistake and we *are* leaving tomorrow, you know they could have made a mistake, but if we *do* leave tomorrow, the bus could break down, or it could catch on fire, or the train could derail, or the Russians could invade or bomb us, or Germany could lose our papers, or even reject us when we get there. There's a lot that could go wrong, actually!" Tamás was working himself up.

"Yeah, that all *could* happen, but I think we'll be fine, Tamás."

"I hope you're right," he said, but it was very clear that he didn't believe it.

"I know I'm right. Goodnight, get some sleep," József chuckled and rolled over.

After breakfast, they were given a sack lunch and put on buses bound for the Bremerhaven Army Airfield in northern Germany. There were so many people going that they needed two of the city buses that they requisitioned to transport the refugees to the train station where they'd be put on a train and taken about 1,000 kilometers, it would take more than 10 hours and when they arrived, they would be put on another bus to get to the actual army base. They traveled nearly the entire length of Germany, and everybody was bored to tears by the end of it.

József and Tamás sat near some of the guys from their previous camp, they talked about unimportant things and pointed out their windows at the landscapes and cityscapes. Most of them had never been far from their city, let alone outside of the country, and they watched in amazement as they passed through Germany. It was beautiful, and even though the landscape was similar to Austria and even parts of Hungary, it felt very foreign. They passed by barren farmland, deserted and bombed-out buildings that hadn't yet been repaired since the end of WWII, and even brand new developments in cities that sometimes clashed with the beauty of the old architecture around.

Upon arriving at the Bremerhaven military base, the bus had to pull over at the gate and some American officers checked the outside of the bus. They were eager to get off, but they had to wait through an inspection first and sit still as one of the officers walked down the aisle of the bus and scrutinized the refugees, it greatly intimidated them. Nobody spoke or moved, they just waited until the Americans gave the bus driver the clear to keep driving onto base to drop them off. They looked at everything as the bus crept forward, most of them were excited, but others were unnerved to be on a foreign base with so many uniformed men.

They groaned and yawned as they exited the bus, stiff from the long day of travel; they stood around apprehensively as enlisted men and officers moved around the base in a hurry. The smell of salt water washed over them as the breeze picked up, it was invigorating. Some looked around for the sea, a port, or even a ship in the distance, but from their location they couldn't see the harbor on which the base sat. Most of the refugees had never seen the sea before, they hadn't seen much of anything beyond the curtain of occupation, let alone been to the sea or on a ship.

Men in military uniform and UNHCR volunteers gathered the refugees and escorted them into a mess hall, they spoke, and a volunteer translated for the refugees. They were asked to sit, given some paperwork including an identification card to fill in, and then advised repeatedly to always keep that ID on them. Most of them had an ID card from the refugee camp in Salzburg that identified them as a displaced person with a temporary address, but they had to carry a new one that identified them as a refugee with permission to be on the

Bremerhaven Army Airfield, and listed the country they were destined to go to.

They filled out their IDs and the medical history and the long examination consent form, which confused and overwhelmed some of the younger men and women. Since it was late at night, they were guided to the barracks they'd be living in for the next few days, on the way an American officer gave them a brief tour of the compound as a translator interpreted for them. The officer pointed to the mess hall where breakfast would be held, and to an administration building they could access for help during working hours, and towards the harbor where their ships docked. They were able to catch a glimpse of the dock and the rolling black waves behind, they stopped in their tracks to stare. It was a wonderful sight; the sea was their path to freedom.

Their guides urged them to continue moving, the translator promised that they'd get to look at the sea again later on. They were in such high spirits and talked amongst themselves while following the guides to the barracks; some of the teenaged boys cheered and shook their friends by the shoulders, and some cried joyous tears.

Despite their jubilance they settled quickly in the barracks where others were already getting into bed. They secured their little belongings on the cot provided for them and talked, musing about what their future might hold.

Chapter 49
Operation Safe Haven

József couldn't have known the significance of the refugee crisis at the time, he felt lucky to be granted a visa for America, but he didn't realize how lucky he truly was.

First of all, in November, the Eisenhower administration only agreed to allow 5,000 refugees a visa, but they would actually end up allowing over 33,000 Hungarian refugees a visa by August 1957. Secondly, the United States only admitted 1,000 unaccompanied minors through the Hungarian Refugee Program, and József was one of them. He was among the first few thousand refugees whose visa applications were approved, and he was on the second naval transport of refugees sent to the United States in late December.

Operation Safe Haven was underway and by May 1, 1957, the US Military Air Transport Service had relocated 13,120 Hungarian refugees to the United States in 214 flights, and the US Military Sea Transport Service had moved 8,925 refugees on five ocean voyages from December 18, 1956, through February 14, 1957. An average of 61 people were on each flight and an average of 1,785 on each of the 5 voyages, which all left from Bremerhaven.

The International Committee for European Migration, which worked with the UNHCR, worked extremely hard to convince other countries to support their efforts in granting asylum for Hungarian refugees. The ICEM transported 9,664 refugees on 133 flights to America as well, an average of 72 people per flight.

In November of 1956, Camp Kilmer in New Jersey became the main location to house Hungarian immigrants. Camp Kilmer was a former US Army camp during WWII, serving the Army Service Forces Transportation Corps and became the largest center for troops preparing to deploy to Europe, and later for troops who returned from war. From November 1956 to May 1957 Camp Kilmer processed over 30,000 of the 31,709 refugees who had arrived thus far, the ones not processed there were Jewish, and they were housed elsewhere in New York because Camp Kilmer was not kept Kosher.

There were already several hundred Hungarian refugees being housed at Bremerhaven when József arrived, and more would arrive each day afterwards. Several people were able to reunite with somebody that they knew in Hungary at Bremerhaven because so many of the refugees had gone through Bremerhaven. They were housed in the barracks near the soldiers and always had a soldier nearby to help them and monitor them. Usually, a soldier or two was assigned to escort groups of the refugees back and forth from mealtimes and wherever else they were summoned in large groups, just to ensure that nobody was lost and everybody arrived on time. Everything was very regimented.

The refugees were usually given medical examinations at Bremerhaven the day of arrival, or the morning after. It was necessary with thousands of new arrivals to a base every few weeks because illness spread so rapidly in close quarters. There were also several untreated wounds from the revolution that had to be treated on base, such as gunshot wounds, shrapnel wounds, hearing or sight loss, and broken bones. There was also a doctor onboard the ship for continued care of the wounded.

Men and boys were separated from the women and told to dress down to their underwear for the physical exam. The physician and his assistant reassured them that it was a routine part of the process, they were making sure that everybody was healthy and physically fit enough for the sea voyage.

Young men like József stood awkwardly, sheltering themselves with their arms, but the older men were more composed. The physician poked and prodded each man and boy, he examined everybody's skin, eyes, ears, noses and throats for signs of infection or disease. He tested reflexes and muscles for any weakness that could indicate an unseen infection or disease. The translator explained everything as he went along, from one man to the next, occasionally writing things down. He asked each one if they had a physical disability or an allergy, it might be important information for the crew of the ship to know in case of an emergency.

Most people passed their health examination, they were both physically fit and without disease or infection, but the whole process was nerve-wracking. The few who showed obvious signs of illness were asked to stay behind for further testing; they worried that they'd be barred from leaving the base, but in most cases, it was just a common cold or the flu and it didn't disqualify them from seeking asylum.

They were allowed to explore the base for the few days they were there, but there wasn't much to do besides look at the sea and sit in their bunks, which they were quite happy to do since the barracks were much cleaner than the ones at the refugee camps in Austria. The experience was thrilling, they felt incredibly lucky to stay on an American military base because they admired the Americans, and they were grateful for it all; going to America was literally a dream come true. The food was good and plentiful, everybody was kind, and there was often a translator nearby to help them communicate. Refugees watched the waves crash on the pier and pinched themselves to wake up because everything felt so surreal. After the excitement of gazing at the sea and watching the ships come in wore off, they mostly stayed within the barracks until embarkation day.

There were five naval voyages on a US Navy Ship named after decorated army officer and war veteran Brigadier General LeRoy Eltinge. The USS General LeRoy Eltinge was launched in 1944 as a transport ship during WWII and was recommissioned to transport troops and refugees as part of the International Refugee Program. The ship had a capacity of more than 4,000 and carried 1,747 refugees on the second voyage across the Atlantic, the one that József was on.[43]

It was December 20, 1956, not even two months after József left home when he boarded the USS General LeRoy Eltinge in Bremerhaven, Germany. Many of the refugees on that trip proudly wore a button on their coat that identified them as a freedom fighter, and some even wore their Hungarian Army uniforms and carried Hungarian flags. One man carried a Hungarian flag on a pole, he'd tied a black

[43] An artist named Edward Hilbert and his wife Judy were on the second, possibly the third, naval passage from Bremerhaven to the US on the USS General LeRoy Eltinge. He chronicled his escape and four-month ordeal through his drawings and in 2007 a cartoon documentary titled *Freedom Dance* was produced based on his account and his drawings.

band around the top to signify mourning; they mourned people they lost, the loss of the revolution, and the fact that they'd had to leave their homeland. Eighty-eight children onboard were younger than ten, there were nearly 200 adult women, and almost 1,500 adult males. Most of the men were single men in their 20s, they were all given single bunks meant for troops, while the families with children were given cabin spaces where they could be together.

It may have taken more than a day to board all the refugees and crew members and prepare to depart, and refugees remembered they set sail through a thick fog. They gathered on the deck, not wanting to miss a moment of that life-changing moment and cheered as they left. Spirits were high and they were on board during Christmas, the crew even set up festive decorations and Christmas trees in the mess halls to bring the holiday cheer to all the refugees who'd had a rough few months to say the least. On Christmas Eve they were gathered in the dining hall for a Christmas celebration with food, music, dancing, and a crewmember even visited them dressed in a St. Nicholas costume bearing treats and small toys for the children. On December 31, the last night of their voyage, the refugees threw a party in the recreation hall with live music and dancing.

Chapter 50
"I Guess That's How Life Goes"

Between the four of us who left Hungary—me, my brother, and our two friends—I thought I was the only one who made it.

I never knew what happened to my brother until I had been in the United States for three years. I got a letter from my father that Charles was in Germany. He was in a refugee camp in Italy after the Russians caught us, Charles snuck across the border when he was let go. The Russians let some people go with the understanding that everyone is going to go back home and register with the police. He was 19 and he says, "Oh yeah, sure, I'm gonna promise."

Father gave me Charles' address and we started writing back and forth. I didn't see him again until 1988. The only way he could have gotten to the United States was by signing up for the United States Army. So, he signed up, came to the states for basic training, and then they stationed him in Germany and he was sent right back to Europe for the next few years.

You know, it's horrible, I don't even remember my friend's name.[44] And we were great friends at home. He had this bike—a motorbike—and he'd let me borrow it to drive out to my grandparents' house in the country. All I had to do was put gas in it, and since we worked at the shop we could take a little gas from there. It was kind of an unwritten rule that you can take gas from your own shop, but not from other shops, that would be stealing. Well, he ended up in Sweden after he left the refugee camps. Somehow, we found each other and wrote back and forth for a while, but time went by and letters stopped coming as often, then pretty soon you don't get a letter at all, you don't know what

---

[44] I named him Gellért.

happened, so you write to them but you don't get a reply. And then it's all lost. I guess that's how life goes, and you just move on.

————

By the time I had asked my grandpa to tell me his story he was in his late 70s and developing Alzheimer's. He'd already forgotten a lot and details were getting mixed up, so I had to confirm some of the details of how Charles came to America with his daughter. It turns out that he hadn't actually told the complete story and all of the gruesome details to his family, so we knew just about the same vague information.

Charles had most likely entered Austria first since he was closest to Austria, but perhaps he went more south to Yugoslavia. From there, he was relocated to a refugee camp in Italy where he lived until 1958 or early 1959, and then was given the opportunity to sign up for the United States Army to be able to come to America. Shortly thereafter he met his future wife, Dolores (Dee), at a military dance, and in traditional military fashion, he married her very quickly.

Charles was stationed in Germany where he was a cook on a military base. After Charles' military service, he became a naturalized citizen of the United States in January 1963, and he settled in Framingham, Massachusetts with his family. They were able to make frequent trips to Hungary, even with their young children.

CHAPTER 51
USS GENERAL LEROY ELTINGE

At breakfast the morning after the ship set sail, the refugees were astonished at the sight of all of the food in the dining hall. Most of the Hungarians had lived a life of scarcity and hunger, made to rely on ration coupons that were never enough, they'd been forced into collectivized farms and saw most of the food that they had grown be sent out of the country.

József and Tamás met before breakfast, they'd been separated into different sleeping quarters but by then they'd grown more secure in separation because they knew they were finally on their way to safety. They chatted as they walked through the passageways and up stairways to the deck, everything on the ship seemed so impressive. But seeing the life rafts that hung above the decks in case of an emergency was not exciting.

"Do you think we could all fit on those lifeboats?" Tamás wondered.

"I don't know, probably, but we won't need those, everything will be fine. I mean, how many ships actually wreck in the ocean?" József was nonchalant about it, he didn't know much about the ocean or shipwrecks.

"Thousands!"

That made József's eyes widen. "But American made ships are better, they must not crash and sink," he tried to reason, but he wasn't too sure.

"They still get in shipwrecks on the ocean, some of the best built ships have sunk."

József looked at the boats overhead and out at the vast and choppy sea. He hadn't thought about the possibility that they'd make it that far just to drown in the ocean. "It'll be fine, we're going to make it to freedom."

Still, they were both a little sick to their stomachs, they walked quietly the rest of the way to breakfast. It was freezing on deck, and the wind sometimes blew so hard they'd stumble or fall against a wall when the ship rocked.

They made it to the dining hall just as it started to drizzle. As they waited in line for breakfast, their mouths watered at the sight of all the food, they'd never in their lives seen so many options at one meal. The cooks had laid out a buffet of sausages, ham, eggs, hashed potatoes, biscuits with gravy, toast, coffee, juices, and fresh fruits, some of which the Hungarians had never seen.

József served himself a small portion of the meat and eggs, there was a sailor in front of him filling up his plate, he smiled over at József and said, "Go on, take more than that, you can eat as much as you want."

He smiled awkwardly, not knowing what the sailor said. The sailor figured that the Hungarians didn't speak English, even if he was a little late in figuring it out, so he mimed dishing up more food and eating to indicate that they were allowed to have more food.

They understood the pantomime and nodded their heads, the sailor moved on, and József happily took a little more eggs and meat. Tamás felt a little guilty taking so much food, he thought that there might not be enough for the people who hadn't eaten yet, so he only took modest portions. Everyone moved through the line slowly and watched, awe-stricken, as the cooks came out with more trays of food to replenish the buffet.

József was delighted to see a bowl of fresh fruits at the end of the buffet, including oranges, which he recently discovered he liked. He happily grabbed what he thought was an orange and he and Tamás sat at a large table with a few sailors and refugees mixed together. Everybody was in a pleasant mood and the United States military servicemen did their best to communicate and make the refugees feel welcomed.

Eager to eat the orange, and remembering his mistake from Villach, he cut the fruit up with a dull butter knife. He took a bite only to taste the bitter flesh of a grapefruit; he choked, not expecting such a sour taste, and forced himself to swallow the citrus so he didn't appear rude by spitting it out. The sailors nearby chortled, realizing that József must not have known it was a grapefruit. He smiled self-consciously and wiped his hands, he thought he'd just picked up a really sour orange.

A sailor handed him a few packets of sugar, "Here, use this, it makes the grapefruit taste better," and pretended to pour the sugar onto the fruit to show him.

He took the sugar and nodded; the sailor smiled reassuringly. All the refugees around looked at the sugar packet with bewilderment, they'd never seen one before and were amazed at how many packets were just sitting on the tables. Hungary had to reintroduce the ration system in 1951 because of chronic shortages and public supplies crises; sugar, bread, flour, butter, and meat was rationed to ensure that everybody could get at least some of the necessities. People queued outside stores in order to get their rations and sometimes every family wasn't able to buy the ration that they were entitled to because the state-run stores would run out after being resupplied.

"I think you're supposed to put the sugar on the fruit. They have enough sugar to put on whatever they want!" Tamás was in disbelief.

"I suppose so," József said.

He tore the packet and poured the sugar carefully onto the slices of grapefruit he'd cut. It was definitely better, he still didn't love it, but he ate the whole fruit so that he didn't seem wasteful. They finished their breakfast quickly and by the time they left it was raining hard out on the deck.

Everybody walked as fast as they could to get inside, they were getting drenched, and they didn't have many clothes to change into. They went to Tamás' quarters to hang out until the next meal—there wasn't much else to do. They took off their wet coats and sat back on a bunk as József pulled out a pack of cigarettes he'd saved from the refugee camp; he'd taken up the habit at camp as a way to ease stress and boredom.

The ship's crew told the refugees that smoking wasn't allowed in the bunks, the warning was translated into Hungarian as well, but most of them didn't pay any mind to it, nor to the "no smoking" signs in the bunks. József took a long drag, savoring it, and blew it out towards the ceiling as he memorized words on the warning sign.

"'No smoking in bed,'" he read out slowly.

Tamás chided, "Somebody is going to catch you."

The other refugees snickered and said they hadn't been caught yet.

"I'm not smoking, see the sign? It says not to," József quipped with his infectious grin.

They all cracked up as József read the sign out again, "'No smoking in bed!'"

József didn't know how to read a single word in English until that voyage, "no smoking in bed" was in fact the first English phrase he memorized. He was quite proud of himself for that, and for sneaking the cigarettes in the cabin without getting caught.

For the most part, the refugees spent their time in the bunks if they weren't in the dining hall because a fierce winter storm raged in the Atlantic Ocean for several days. It was too cold and miserable outside and the boat rocked ferociously. Most of the refugees had never been on a boat, let alone a ship of that magnitude, they turned green with seasickness. The doctor on board distributed Dramamine like it was candy to the refugees who wobbled to him on unsteady legs while the ship knocked them about. The children were the most afraid of the open sea and the parents tried their best to explain to the young ones that they were perfectly safe, but they didn't even believe it themselves. The religiously inclined refugees prayed repeatedly that they'd make it safely through the storm, and at night people regularly fell off their bunks when a particularly powerful wave crashed into the boat.

The storm was relentless and caused the journey to take several days longer than it should have, for a while the ship hardly made any progress in the ocean, it couldn't fight against the waves and wind. The Hungarians thought they'd made it all that way just to die at sea.

Chapter 52

The Dream

József had a nightmare, one that had haunted him many times before. It was difficult to fall asleep with the sway and queasiness, and when he finally did, he tossed and turned uncomfortably, nearly falling to the floor. In the dream he relived a memory from several years before, it was always the same dream.

He had gone home early to an almost empty house, only his mother and baby sister Edit were supposed to be home, everybody else was gone at work or school. The Soviet soldiers who forced home-owners and renters alike to let soldiers board in their homes were also supposed to be gone.

József smelled something delicious in the kitchen and went to investigate, his mother was his favorite chef, but he heard an odd noise upstairs that stopped him in his tracks. He called out for his mother, he didn't hear an answer, only loud thumping. He ran up the stairs and as he got closer to his parents' bedroom, he could hear small whimpers and ugly grunts. József was barely a teenager but he knew what was happening. He slammed the door open and saw him, a grotesque Russian beast, on top of her.

His mother screamed, "Go! Get out of here!"

József couldn't move, he was paralyzed with fear and anger.

The beast turned and they locked eyes, he smirked before leaning back over Ilona, unbothered by the little boy's presence. József saw his mother's tear-stained cheeks and wondered why she wasn't fighting back, then he ran for the closet. He took his father's rifle, he'd only used it a few times before, but he'd never aimed to kill because his father always told him that you never point a gun at something you don't intend to kill.

József loaded a bullet into the chamber and aimed at the Russian's back. Hearing the metal clink, the beast turned his head and started to get up. József didn't have time to think so he pulled the trigger. A bullet went through his upper abdomen and exited through his ribcage; blood splattered all over Ilona and the bed, and the beast hit the floor.

Ilona pulled her dress back down where it belonged, she was trembling, she couldn't catch her breath. Baby Edit woke and began crying loudly. József dropped the rifle and stared at the body, knowing that the others would have him killed and perhaps his whole family for the crime. Ilona stood, embraced her son, and wiped her tears. Seconds felt like minutes as they held each other quietly, listening to the baby's cries, watching the Russian shake and choke on his blood.

Ilona stepped back and took a hold of her son's face and spoke with a conviction he'd never heard from her, "We have to hide the body. Clean the blood. No one can ever know, or they will kill us for it."

József nodded solemnly, he stared at the growing pool of blood that poured from the Russian's back and mouth. Ilona wiped the blood from hands on her dress before she picked Edit up from the bassinet in the corner, shushing and rocking her back and forth.

József didn't have time to process what had happened, he rushed downstairs for a mop, bucket, rags and bleach to clean the mess. Edit calmed down quickly enough and went back into her bassinet while József began soaking up the blood from the floor. Luckily, they had wooden floors so as long as he worked quickly there wouldn't be a visible stain. The blood seemed to spill out faster than he could mop it up. Ilona ripped the covers and sheets from the bed and rushed to soak them so they wouldn't stain but left one sheet to use on the dead Russian.

She was calmer than one might expect in that situation, in order to keep her son calm, too. She coached him through everything, "We need to take him outside, and bury him, quickly."

They laid a sheet on the ground and rolled the heavy body onto it, wrapping it up like a cocoon. It became soaked with blood quickly, they had to work together to carry it down the stairs and to the garden, dripping blood the whole way.

"Dig a hole behind the barn, you bury him. I'll clean the blood. Dig the hole deep," Ilona told József before she hurried back inside to clean.

He stared at the house for a split second, he was in shock, then he began digging. He was shaking, it was making him weak, but he continued as quickly as he could.

When he pushed the body into the hole the sheet unraveled and revealed the Russian's face, his eyes were wide open, and blood trickled out of his mouth. It looked like he was watching József. He shoveled dirt onto the Russian's face first, he couldn't stand to feel watched. With each shovelful he held back his tears, fear was setting in. When he was finished, he smoothed the dirt out and spread dirt over the bloodied earth to help hide the evidence. He was young, but he was clever; he knew he had to spread the dirt he'd dug out evenly so that there wouldn't be a large mound where the body was and wet the ground so the blood would wash away. He took his clothes off, rinsed his feet, and went inside.

His mother had hastily cleaned the floors and furniture in the bedroom, but it was good enough until she had more time. She was already at work scrubbing and washing the clothing and linens, she took József's clothes and told him, "Go back over the stairs and floors and make sure there's no blood spots left."

He nodded but didn't move.

"We're going to be okay," she assured him, even though she didn't believe it herself. He nodded again and left.

Details would change in the dream from time to time, and that's how he could distinguish that he was in the nightmare and not real life. Sometimes the Russian would look up and smile after he'd been shot, or he'd speak as József buried him, other times his baby sister was missing, or they'd be interrupted while they cleaned up the crime scene.

They buried the soldier, cleaned the evidence, and never spoke about it again. The other Soviets didn't look too hard for their missing comrade. József was so afraid of being punished, especially when he returned to visit his parents in the late 80s when the Soviets were still occupying Hungary, that he didn't tell anybody, not even his wife, until the 90s after the Soviet Union was disbanded.

CHAPTER 53
NEW YEAR'S EVE

József woke, sweating and shivering, the blanket had fallen off while he tossed and turned, the cabin was freezing, the ship still heaved back and forth in the storm. His heart beat so fast and he felt too sick to sleep again, so he lit a cigarette to calm his nerves and stared at the ceiling for several hours. The memory always seemed so fresh, even several years later.

He often thought about that day, about that soldier, and about what would happen to him and his family if the Soviets ever found out. And he'd worried that the immigration counselors would somehow investigate his past and find out about the crime and bar him from getting a visa, then send him back to Hungary for trial.

In the morning, he looked worn and weary, and his bunkmates graciously pointed it out.

"I just couldn't sleep last night, seasickness," he told a half-truth.

"Let's get to breakfast, they have information for us about arriving in America tomorrow!" another teenager cried out.

They proceeded to the dining hall, it was still windy and bitterly cold outside, but at least it wasn't raining so they didn't get soaked as usual. The lines for breakfast moved quicker each day that the refugees got used to the food, they knew what they liked so they could dish up their plates quicker without wondering what all of the food was. Everybody sat, eagerly awaiting the announcement from the crew. A career translator didn't accompany them on the voyage, but there were at least a few Hungarians who spoke enough English to translate for the rest, like the college professor who got up to translate the announcement at breakfast.

A clean-cut, attractive captain walked to the forefront of the dining hall and addressed everybody, "Good morning."

Most of the Hungarians had picked up a few English terms or phrases already, they collectively said, "Good morning," back in their thick accents.

The women smiled at the captain adoringly, he had good looks and charm. He told them, "Late tonight, perhaps after midnight, we will arrive in the New York Harbor and tomorrow we'll transfer you to Camp Kilmer, in New Jersey, where you'll be processed. Tomorrow is New Year's Day, January 1, 1957, it's the start of your new lives!"[45]

After the translation there was a round of cheers and some applause, while it pleased the captain to be revered as the bearer of good news, he held his hands out in a gesture to settle the crowd. They had little concept of what New York or New Jersey were, all they cared about was the fact that they were so close to America.

"When we dock at the harbor you'll be transferred to Camp Kilmer on buses, your safety is very important to us, we will be there to guide you every step of the way," he paused for the translator.

"When we get to Camp, first your luggage will be inspected by customs, then you will have a brief health examination, then Immigration will check your visas, take your fingerprints and photograph, and issue you an alien registration card and a camp identification card."

The college professor translated everything and answered a few questions. They didn't even complain about having to complete more paperwork at that point, they were just happy to be so close to freedom. The immigration process for the Hungarians was, for the most part, completed at Camp Kilmer, and it was done in as little time as an hour for each refugee. The camp was staffed with many volunteers that helped process immigration paperwork, arranged transportation to resettle the refugees, and placed them with employment, shared housing with other refugees, or with sponsor families.

"Have all of your belongings gathered and packed in the morning,

---

[45] The refugees arrived in the New York Harbor, but immigration records aren't complete, and many haven't been recorded physically or digitized, so I was unable to find the exact physical location of their arrival. Passenger lists for the ships of Hungarian refugees only list people's names and the date of arrival, but not the port of entry. However, the refugees were at least processed at Camp Kilmer, for the most part, since the immigration processing center on Ellis Island closed its doors in 1954, two years prior.

eat a quick breakfast, and be ready to disembark."

When the captain was done speaking people cheered and whistled, spirits were higher than they'd ever been. They were grateful, relieved, and scared all at the same time. Everybody chatted happily as they finished breakfast, and young boys whooped and slapped each other's backs as they left the dining hall.

The refugees spent their last day onboard the ship the same way they spent every other day: bored, excited, and seasick. Some of the refugees thought they'd go up and wait on deck for as long as it took to be the first to see America when their ship finally rolled in. It was freezing, and the weather in New England, especially at night, was poor, but they didn't mind. Late that night, after they should have gone to their quarters, they finally saw the glow of New York City.

One young man ran through the hallways, knocking on the doors of the quarters where the other Hungarian men slept, shouting, "We're here! We're here!"

Hungarians left their rooms in such a hurry that some had forgotten their coats and shoes, and others dressed themselves while they ran upstairs to the deck. The sailors didn't bother to stop them, in fact it was heart-warming, and their excitement was the reason the sailors felt so proud to be helping refugees come to America. A few sailors even joined and pointed out the different buildings they saw on the horizon to the Hungarians. When the refugees saw the Statue of Liberty they whistled, cheered, and yelled into the darkness.

Jubilations rang out around the ship as more people left their rooms to see. It was New Year's Eve, and New York City held a huge celebration in which they set off fireworks that could be seen from the ship. The skyline was engulfed in a hazy cloud that lit up with bright colors each time a firework went off.

In Hungary, they celebrate New Year's Eve in similar ways as many do, with festive gatherings, food (pork and lentils are the traditional essentials), cakes with a lucky medallion that someone will find in their piece, and later on fireworks became part of the festivities. They called it Szilveszter, named after the Pope Sylvester I, from the 3rd century.

Arriving in the land of dreams on December 31st was wonderful kismet, and they got to share that joy on the deck of a decommissioned war transporter in frigid temperatures.

CHAPTER 54

A NEW LIFE

In Germany, 1,747 Hungarian refugees boarded the USS General LeRoy Eltinge, but 1,748 disembarked in America. While docked in the New York Harbor, waiting to transport the refugees to the camp on January 1, 1957, a baby was born.

A young woman named Gabriella Matusek gave birth to her first child, a 6.5 pound boy they named Heinrich Tibor Matusek, but they nicknamed him LeRoy, after the ship. It was not only a joyous celebration for Gabriella and her husband Harry, but that happiness spread throughout the entire ship. Several newspapers throughout the United States picked up the sensational story of the Hungarian baby born on a ship on New Year's Day.

They were all taken to Camp Kilmer that morning, accompanied by dozens of sailors and soldiers of the United States military. Since the military oversaw transporting refugees, and the camp was a military compound, security was a high priority, and the refugees were never left unattended. The crew of the USS General LeRoy Eltinge waved all of the refugees off as they descended from the ship; they waved, cheered, whistled, patted the Hungarians on the back and hugged some whom they'd been friendly with as they left. Other soldiers took charge of moving the refugees onto buses to transport them to camp. The Hungarians watched out the windows in utter amazement, pointing to everything they saw with enormous smiles plastered on their faces.

Camp Kilmer was a former military staging area for troops and ships to assemble before shipping off to the European theater of WWII. There were over 1,100 buildings, many rows of barracks, a 1,000-bed hospital, 9 post exchanges, 7 chapels, 5 theaters, 4 telephone centers, 3 libraries, and a post office. The camp was originally 1,500 acres, situated in between the Piscataway and Edison townships, with New Brunswick, New Jersey, to the south across the Raritan River. In the mid-1960s, the majority of the acreage was sold to Rutgers University and local governments, and now Camp Kilmer no longer exists.

The refugees were hustled through the entire process in as little as an hour, the incoming refugees arrived either via ship or plane and from the port of entry were transferred to Camp Kilmer and processed in the following manner. First, a routine check performed by US Customs, then a routine check performed by the US Public Health Service, then the US Immigration and Naturalization service would check each passenger's visa, take their photographs and fingerprints, and issue an alien registration card, they would also get a basic data card and a civilian identification card to keep on them at all times.

The health exam was quick, but it was more awkward than at Bremerhaven with more than a thousand men stripping to their undergarments to be examined and prodded at the same time. Several had fallen ill on the ship, and a few were still recovering from injuries and needed a more urgent and thorough exam, so they were taken to individual patient rooms; and of course, the new mother and her new baby were taken to a recovery room immediately.

Camp Kilmer was busy, there were thousands of Hungarian refugees already there and more arriving all the time and they were resettled in the US almost as quickly as they came. Refugees would sometimes only spend a few hours or a day at Camp Kilmer before being sent off somewhere else. Soldiers ferried refugees from the airports and docks to the camp almost nonstop, the immigration officers worked long hours each day to process everybody, many employees' spouses volunteered and jumped into the action because all hands were needed on deck to pull off Operation Safe Haven. Relocating more than 30,000 people across the ocean and processing them almost entirely at one camp in just six months was a Herculean task, but they pulled it off. The Catholic Hungarians believed the Lord worked quickly, but the volunteers worked quicker.

It cannot be stressed enough how *fast* the entire process was for those refugees who left in the fall of 1957. The ones who were among the first 100,000 to leave were sometimes resettled in as little as a week, and the rest were transported out of Austria within the first twelve weeks of becoming stateless. Generally, people wait many months, years even, for their paperwork to be completed to become a refugee. Refugee crises like this were unheard of before WWII, after which the UNHCR was created to aid refugees. Even prisoners of Nazi concentration camps were sometimes stuck in a displaced persons camp for several years, waiting to be relocated. And ever since 1956, progressively worsening humanitarian crises have been handled at a snail's pace comparatively.

József was resettled with the foster family in Oregon in January not even three months after leaving Hungary. He didn't realize how significant those events were at the time, he was just a sixteen-year-old boy, and to him, America was legendary; he assumed refugees were always helped that quickly by countries willing to take them in.

People with businesses and farms all over America offered jobs and housing to refugees, some of whom were Hungarian themselves, so they felt a connection and duty to help. American Hungarians would sponsor their own relatives as well, which reduced the burden on the state to find them housing. Catholic priests offered young Catholic Hungarians jobs or internships, families with room to spare offered to take in unaccompanied minors, landlords offered shared housing for groups of young adults, and universities and hospitals offered jobs for highly skilled and educated refugees who'd been doctors or professors in Hungary.

The volunteers at Camp Kilmer did their best to place refugees in jobs that were appropriate for their level of education and experience, and for the most part it was a success and very few Hungarians were left unemployed. However, there were some refugees who were placed in jobs that didn't befit them, such as a lawyer placed as a farmhand, an architect as a secretary, or a doctor as a butcher.

Life at the camp was similar to Bremerhaven or the Austrian refugee camps; they woke up, ate in a mess hall, sometimes went to church, hung around in between mealtimes, and went to sleep in a barracks full of people.

One morning, József heard from somebody in the camp that there was a plane taking off that day and there were unfilled seats on it. It was organized by the Catholic church, and it worked similar to a lottery system; for example, a flight would be scheduled with 30 seats available and refugees without a plan yet were offered tickets to wherever the next plane was headed. The young single refugees often took whatever opportunity came to them first.

József ran across the camp to find Tamás in the barracks, he knew it was their chance. "There's a plane leaving today, there's seats open, we can get on the plane, but we have to leave *now*!" he yelled in delight.

"When is it leaving?" Tamás asked.

"I don't know, later today, we have to go to the Catholic organization first to find out if we can get on it, but I think we can!"

They'd been living a hectic life for months; this was no different. They ran like mad to the Catholic church on base, some officers outside told them to slow down, but they weren't stopping for anything. Inside, a volunteer Hungarian translator was waiting to assist.

She greeted József and Tamás, "Hello, why are you running? What can I help you with?"

They were out of breath, and they didn't even know how to begin, they took turns stumbling through a litany of ways to start a sentence.

"Hello-"

"Hi-"

"How are you?"

"Sorry, we ran here!"

"We heard, well, he heard-"

"There's open spots on a plane later-"

"It doesn't matter where it's going!"

"Can we get on the plane?"

"If it's possible! Please!"

"Please?"

"Catch your breath, take a seat, we'll have a look, okay?" she reassured them.

They thanked her and apologized for barging in like that as they sat down on chairs against the wall. She went down the hall and through a door where she stayed for several minutes. They tried listening as they waited, but she was speaking in English, and they couldn't understand. Soon, she popped her head out of the door and waved them back, and they walked down the hall trying to be as quiet as possible. She stepped aside so they could enter the office.

"Hello," they practically whispered to the volunteer coordinator inside.

He greeted them cordially, "Hello, boys, I'm Mr. Bailey, how are you?"

By then they'd picked up a few phrases in English, but they were embarrassed, they only nodded back at him and handed over their identification cards so he could verify their names, they'd become used to doing that at camp. He kept the cards on his desk while he checked their names against the refugee lists.

"So, Miss Georgia tells me you're lookin' to get on the plane headed to Portland today, is that right?" he asked, but it was more of a statement.

They nodded and he rummaged through a messy pile of faxes and letters on his desk for several moments, humming to himself.

József, Tamás, and Miss Georgia all watched him quietly until he exclaimed, "Ah ha! It looks like we can make it work. There's a family in Portland that can take *you* in," he nodded to József, "and there's a farmer out east who can take another employee on!"

Miss Georgia translated, but before she could finish, they jumped up in excitement, shouting, "Thank you! Thank you!"

"Yes, yes, we've got to get your paperwork filled out before you can get on the plane though, just to make sure we have all our ducks in a row."

Again, Miss Georgia translated, but she didn't know an equivalent phrase for "ducks in a row," and they looked extremely confused about why they needed ducks, but they nodded anyway.

Mr. Bailey started shuffling his papers again, explaining what documents he was filling out and why they were needed to transfer refugees across the country, but neither József nor Tamás really cared *why* he needed to fill out more forms. They were told to pack their belongings and meet at the church in an hour in order to be bussed to the airport. It didn't really matter where they were going, but they asked Miss Georgia anyways, who asked Mr. Bailey.

He happily declared, "Portland, Oregon, you'll love it there!"

It was clear from their faces that those words didn't mean much to them; certainly, if he had said a city like Los Angeles or New York, they may have recognized it. He took them to a map posted on a bulletin board. He pointed to where they were in New Jersey, "Here's where we're at right now, New Jersey," and he slid his finger all the way across the United States and said, "And that's where you're going, to Oregon!"

They looked a little taken aback, Miss Georgia asked, "What's wrong?"

"I can't go there!" József worried.

Miss Georgia translated for Mr. Bailey, they both looked confused.

"Wait—" He walked past them, signaling for them to follow, and pulled down a map of the world that hung on another wall. He pointed to Hungary, barely visible within Europe, "Here's where you were, and now you're over here," his index finger dragged all the way across the Atlantic Ocean, "And you're over here now, see? So, Portland is not that far! You've already come much farther than just going across the United States."

They were taken aback; they hadn't realized exactly how far they'd come. Everything in Europe was much closer together, America seemed so large in comparison, but they hadn't known how wide the ocean really was; the distance across the Atlantic was much wider than the distance between the American coasts.

The wide-eyed József looked at Tamás, who said, "I guess it depends on how you look at it! We're already here, what more is a few hundred miles?"

That made Miss Georgia snicker, "It's more than a few hundred miles, it's a few thousand!"

Both of their jaws dropped.

Chapter 55

The Plane

Their first ever plane ride was bound for Portland, Oregon. Tamás would be working as a farmhand in Eastern Oregon, he'd get room and board until he could earn enough to live on his own, and József would stay with a Catholic family in Portland until he was old enough to live on his own at 18. They assumed they'd be close enough to hang out, since they'd be in the same state, rather than hundreds of miles away from each other. Reality was beginning to set in; they'd be on their own in a completely foreign land where they didn't speak the language, separated from their families and everyone they once knew.

A few dozen refugees were on that flight, some were going to live with an employer, some were getting communal housing with other refugees, and some were going to live with a foster family. The flight attendant welcomed them aboard warmly and introduced herself as Barb, it was a joyous occasion in the land of dreams. She asked the officer who escorted the refugees to the plane if there was anybody who could translate for her so that she could give the safety briefing.

The officer didn't know the refugees that well, so he asked the passengers, "Does anybody speak English?"

A man stood up, "Yes, sir." With his accent it sounded like *Yesshur*. Most of them would always pronounce the 's' in English as they would in Hungarian, as 'sh.' "I speak English, not well, but some."

She smiled and said, "Thank you, darlin'," with a drawl."

He blushed, which his friends teased him about. She gave the instructions for how to use the seatbelt and the emergency life vest and pointed to the exits. The refugees put their seatbelts on as they watched her, they inspected the life vest and looked at the doors she pointed at while she spoke. He translated most of what she said, but he didn't know some of the words she said so he just skipped over them or said them in English as if they were the same words in Hungarian. The Americans were none the wiser, and the refugees got the gist. The flight crew prepared for takeoff and the officer said goodbye to the refugees.

Everybody cheered, "Thank you, goodbye!" as they settled into their seats. He smiled and waved while backing out of the door to the rolling staircase.

Tamás leaned over to ask József, "Can you believe we're flying?" He was practically yelling to get over the roar of the engine as the plane began taxiing on the tarmac.

"No!" József laughed nervously.

They grinned ear to ear at each other. The whole cabin erupted in cheers and clapped as the plane lifted off. That takeoff felt as momentous as when the ship left Bremerhaven, but that was much louder because there were several thousand people on the ship.

Most of the Hungarians had never been on a plane before so being airborne felt extremely odd and many had motion sickness just as they had on the ship. Barb noticed their faces and quickly passed around the handy little vomit bags—several were used. The queasiness was the downfall of traveling they couldn't escape.

Once the plane was cruising at altitude they felt better, except when there was turbulence, and they chatted jovially and pointed out the windows to the landscape below. It was a spectacular experience, even with the sickness.

The trip had a scheduled stop at Stapleton airport in Denver, Colorado, to refuel in the late afternoon; it was supposed to be a routine stop. They marveled at the snow-covered mountains in awe as they descended and tried not to vomit. Refueling stops don't usually take long, but the technicians noticed something was wrong with the plane and needed to inspect it further.

"It's going to take longer than expected," Barb explained, "The technicians need to make a quick repair but it's nothing to worry about, we'll be back in the air in no time."

"What'd she say?" they asked the young man who'd translated for her before.

"I think they have to repair the plane," he shrugged.

Their worries grew the longer that the repairs took. After an hour they were all asked to get off the plane so the technicians could work on it, the refugees didn't really understand what was happening, but they deboarded and Barb escorted them into the airport. They were supposed to be in Portland by then and it was past dinner time, they were starving and the little packages of snacks on the plane weren't going to cut it. Barb arranged for them to have a meal in the airport while they waited.

Eventually, they were called to board the plane again. Assuming that they would take off shortly, they buckled themselves in and waited patiently. Their nerves got worse the longer they sat on the tarmac while the technicians continued to work on the plane. Barb apologized profusely to them, trying to explain that everything would be alright.

An hour after getting back on the plane, they were asked to get off a second time. It was already pitch black and they assumed they were spending the night in the airport somehow, but the pilot explained that a different plane was on its way because the technicians couldn't fix the repairs on the original plane in time. A simple pitstop became a long nerve-wracking ordeal, but they were finally able to board a new plane several hours later. Too tired and afraid to jinx it, they didn't really speak until they were sure they were taking off. They held their breath and gripped the arm rests as they lifted off once more.

CHAPTER 56
"AT THAT TIME, PHONEBOOKS WERE BIG"

After my father passed away, we were notified that he passed so Linda and myself went back for the funeral, by the time we got over there we discovered that Charles and Laci had went through the apartment and got rid of everything. We thought they would at least keep the pictures, but no, we only got one picture out of the whole thing. You know, my mother was already gone by that time, and my sister was already gone, and we don't have many pictures of them.

A gal in Los Angeles found us in the phonebook when we lived there in the sixties, she called and we talked on the phone for quite a while. She says her last name was Kutnyak also, says she was about to move back east and was always looking in the phonebooks to find relatives in there. And you know, at that time phonebooks were big. Our name got in there for the first time, "Linda and Joseph Kutnyak" it says with our phone number next to it.

Well, we talked for quite a while, I told her how I left Hungary after the revolution, and she told me of her parents and grandparents that she could remember. What I was told from my father was we do have relatives in Milwaukee, Wisconsin; they were a brother and sister that come to the United States. The sister married a man named Smith, but the lady from LA was descended from that brother.

––––––––––

When I spoke to Charles' daughter, my second cousin, I mentioned that my grandfather held a grudge against both Charles and László (but especially László) because he assumed that they had thrown everything out of their parents' apartment after they had both died. Their mother, Ilona, died in the late 80s, and then their sister Edit died the next year, and all three brothers were living in the United States when their father Károly died. They all flew back for the funeral and when Joseph got to their father's empty apartment, he discovered that everything had been cleaned out, including the family photos. Joseph assumed that his brothers had thrown everything away, so he was angry at them, and he hardly ever spoke to his younger brother László again.

My cousin thinks that thieves broke into the empty apartment and robbed the place because when Charles and László got to the apartment after their father's death, it was already emptied out, they apparently didn't throw away anything. Joseph assumed they had and he resented them for it, and his brothers had a falling out of their own—perhaps over money. After the falling out, Charles said, "I only have one brother and he lives in Oregon," meaning Joseph. I bet that my grandfather held the same sentiment about László.

My grandfather didn't talk about László at all during my child-hood, and he didn't mention that László had come to the US. I assumed that László still lived in Hungary, it was my cousin who told me that he'd immigrated here. I asked my grandmother about it and apparently, my grandparents had sponsored László so that he could immigrate to the US after he'd escaped into Yugoslavia. He moved in with them in Los Angeles for a while, but it wasn't long before he stopped attending his English classes and only wanted to communicate in Hungarian, he purposefully avoided making friends with people who weren't Hung-arian, and he stopped taking care of his personal hygiene. Allegedly, he also ate raw onions and garlic as a snack, which is just dreadful.

She said that László's grift was filing lawsuits in order to get money, and the many legal cases, lawsuits, and personal injury cases I found in which László was the plaintiff confirm this. After my grand-parents moved back to Oregon in the 70s, László stayed in Los Angeles alone. He isolated himself, he had his small circle of Hungarian friends and never wanted to stay in touch with his family unless he was going to get money out of it. Charles helped him out with money often, and flew him to Massachusetts for visits, and eventually they had a falling out over money after their father's death in 2001. László didn't even visit with his parents when they flew to America for an extended visit in 1976, and he didn't go back to Hungary when his mother got sick, nor for her funeral, but he did go back for their father's funeral.

When I was diving into our family tree, I was quite amused to find out that the three brothers' names were (from eldest to youngest) Károly József, József László, and László—I didn't find a middle name for him. It's quite common for men to name their eldest son after themselves, so Károly made sense, but then giving the oldest child's middle name to the next child, and then again for the third just made me think, "But there were *other* names to choose from!" I'm just glad they went with something else for their only daughter, then she named her daughter after herself as well. Károly II went by Charles for most of his adult life, it's the English equivalent, although he never formally changed his name.

Charles may have realized how sick he was getting before he was diagnosed with B-cell lymphoma in 2023, or he may have known about the diagnosis for a while before telling his family. At one point, before the diagnosis, he told his daughters that he needed to take a drive from Massachusetts to Oregon so he could see his brother once more, "in case anything happens," but he wasn't able to do that before passing away on June 9, 2023.

Chapter 57
The End of Their Journey

The plane ride over the Rocky Mountains was turbulent, and the trust the refugees had in American aeronautical engineering dwindled after the issues with the previous plane. What if the new plane also had a problem? What if they crashed? They worried that they'd escaped Hungary just to die on a plane before their new life could begin.

It was very late when they finally landed in Portland. The landing was violent and felt like they were crashing, but when they finally slowed down on the tarmac the refugees broke out in uproarious cheers, and some cried happy tears.

"Ladies and gentlemen, welcome to Portland, Oregon," Barb said, clearly exhausted.

"I hope I never have to ride a plane again!" one said.

Everyone agreed and laughed, only the very young child said the plane ride was exciting.

"I'm so glad that's over," József groaned, holding his stomach.

"I think I'm going to vomit again," Tamás mumbled, his face green.

József dramatically moved over in his seat to get away from Tamás, which made them both chuckle. They watched the technicians on the ground roll the staircase up to the door, the flight crew turned lights on, and everybody unbuckled themselves. It had been a long day, and a long winter, they were ready to get off the plane. As they gathered their suitcases, several United States military officers and exhausted looking social workers gathered outside on the runway to collect them. The flight crew stood at the door and shook hands with the refugees as they got off the plane, welcoming them to their new home. The Hungarians thanked them profusely, some even hugged the crew. The officers greeted each refugee as they reached the ground, many still unsteady from the flight.

A list of the passengers had been faxed to the National Guard in Portland, since the military oversaw coordinating transportation, officers had to be at the airport to hand them over to the social workers who would finish getting them all resettled. The officers checked the IDs everyone got from Camp Kilmer to ensure that everybody who was supposed to be there was in fact there.

The officers, who were no longer needed, said their goodbyes as the social workers walked the refugees into the airport and to the gate they were meant to meet the sponsors at. One of the social workers gathered a handful of people whose sponsors wouldn't be able to collect them until the morning to take them to a hotel for the night, yet another first for many of them. They said goodbye to their fellow Hungarians and promised to stay in touch, and they parted ways.

József and Tamás were quiet, not really knowing what to say but assuming they'd get to see each other later, anyways. They saw a few people rise from their seats up ahead, they'd clearly been waiting for the Hungarians to arrive.

"Well, folks, your journey ends here," a congenial social worker said. She stuttered through their names and introduced them to the sponsors who were picking them up. Most of them didn't speak enough English to know exactly what was being said, but they understood their names and hand gestures. The sponsors, mostly older Catholics, smiled and waved for the refugees to come forward.

József's sponsors, the Stillwells, stood up to collect him. They were about his parents' age but were dressed far more modernly, and the father carried their sleepy little girl in his arms. They'd heard about the refugee crisis at their congregation, and they put their names down on a list of people who'd be willing to help, they had some spare room in their house and several children already so taking in another child wasn't a problem. When József signed up to take the flight to Portland that morning they got a last-minute call asking if they could take him that day, and they were happy to. The Stillwells introduced themselves, József nodded politely.

The social workers were trying to hurry everyone, one of them announced who he would be taking in his car to drive out to eastern Oregon where they'd be staying. Tamás was among the young men whom he was taking, he didn't want to wait until the morning and didn't mind driving so late, but he didn't see any reason to dawdle at the airport. He checked his watch impatiently and shuffled notes in his binder as they said their goodbyes.

"We'll write to each other," Tamás assured József.

"Of course we will," he promised.

They didn't know what else to say and time was running out, so they hugged tightly and parted ways; it was bittersweet, they'd been through so much together in just a few short months. Tamás walked away with the others toward an exit, he looked back one more time to wave goodbye, and with a sad smile József waved back. The Stillwells watched him patiently, but the social worker was checking her watch.

"Well, József, we'd better get going then," Mr. Stillwell declared.

The social worker told the Stillwells that she would check in with them in the morning and bid her goodbyes.

"Let's go now, son," Mr. Stillwell said. József would eventually get used to the way Americans called everyone "son."

The little girl in his arms rubbed her tired eyes and looked at József curiously.

"This is Jane," Mrs. Stillwell said as she rubbed her daughter's back.

"Hello," József said in his best American accent with a huge smile.

She buried her head in Mr. Stillwell's neck, peeking out at József shyly, her parents laughed.

"Come on then, let's go home. The other children will be so happy you're here."

He nodded. József had gone such a long way, he had no idea what to expect but he was shocked at the generosity of the Americans he'd met thus far.

CHAPTER 58
"I WORKED SO HARD TO BE AMERICAN"

When we got to Portland, a few of the guys, they got jobs with some ranchers out in Eastern Oregon, cause they want help and they had room, so they offer to help out the refugees by giving them jobs and places to stay. And then they had a new group of friends, but so did I. I was going to school, and I learned English quicker than some of the other guys. Then I got a job at the newspaper and hey, I was American, then! I worked at the Oregon Journal, then the Oregonian, then the Los Angeles paper. Then by the time I left that paper I was the department head. So, you learn the language, you can get ahead.

My boss told me, "You speak, you eat. You don't speak, you don't eat." Meaning, you better learn your English language, boy!

All the Hungarians were staying in the same apartment and speaking Hungarian with each other at home and at work, they don't want to learn English. I was going to school in the daytime, learning English in the nighttime. Then I kind of outgrew them. You know, for a lot of Hungarians I translated for them at first. I helped them with their banking because they didn't know how to write their checks so I would do that, write the dollars and the cents and stuff.

And some of them wanted me to help them write letters to their gals. And oh, I was a bad boy. . . They wanted me to write things like, "I like you," and, "I think you're great," and instead I wrote, "I love you," and, "I'm thinking about marriage with you," and that was all fine and funny until the letters came back and I had to do some translating. Uh oh! They were saying like, "I love you, too!" and, "Do you really love me?" and I had to make up some stuff like, "Oh yeah, she says you're a really handsome guy and she likes you, too."

One of the things they ask you is, "Hey, how many times you been back to Hungary?"

"Well," I says, "I haven't been back."

They says they been back two, three times, and they gonna go back and live there. I didn't want to. I wanted to be American! I worked so hard to be American. But they didn't want to be American, so I kind of outgrew them. We didn't stay in touch cause everybody was working and trying to make a life for themselves, and then I met a girl. . .

So, I met one Hungarian, George, he was living in West Portland just by the college. Linda lived over there with another gal. I was over there one Sunday with my friend, and he says, "Hey, there's a couple gals living over there, and I never met them yet!"

So, we started throwing bottle caps against the bedroom window, trying to get their attention. They heard the noise and they went to the window to see what it was all about, and there was these two Hungarian boys, I was this 18-year-old boy, sitting over there throwing bottle caps at them. And that was it, that's how we met. We went together for a couple of years until 1960 when we got married, and from then on, it's history.

AFTERWORD

It's appalling and ironic to see Hungary's responses to refugees seeking asylum in their country. Refugees from the Middle East have been seeking protection from political and religious persecution for decades, and the Hungarian government spins xenophobic, anti-immigrant rhetoric to turn the citizens against the refugees. They reject most applicants even when they are literally begging at the border, the police have assaulted the refugees, they've physically pushed them back over the Serbian border, and kept them in deplorable conditions behind barbed wire. Government officials call refugees "poison," and "potential terrorists," and have rejected European Union agreements to take responsibility for refugees. But when Ukrainian refugees started flooding into eastern European countries in 2022, Hungary changed its reception of refugees to welcome them more readily than they had before.

Also ironic is that Viktor Orbán, the Prime Minister (1998-2002 and 2010-), is very comfortable with Putin and Russia. Orbán has been described as a Putinist, fascist, a right-wing ideologue, an authoritarian, and even a dictator. Putin can be described similarly. Hungary has a tumultuous past and the government doesn't make great decisions, but you must remember that the government doesn't represent the people.

When I began talking about my grandfather's escape and the revolution on social media, I received a lot of comments along the lines of, "Why should I care about Hungarian refugees if they don't care about refugees now?" and, "Hungary doesn't treat their own people right, why should the rest of the world have to?" and, "The Soviets were the ones who liberated them from the Nazis, you know," and, "You know they're fascist now, right? So, the revolution didn't really matter." I've literally been called a fascist by the communists, and a communist by the fascists. They know they have no logical argument and they're an indoctrinated extremist, so they resort to calling you the enemy. After all, slinging false accusations is how the Nazis, communists, and Americans (during the Red Scare, especially) got rid of their political opponents.

Somebody recently said to me, and I quote, "There's absolutely no genocide with communism. Even with Stalinism there wasn't, that's literally fascist propaganda," and after I was done laughing, I explained that he was, in fact, extremely incorrect—he hadn't insulted me or my intelligence yet so I was even nice to him, I explained as if he were just sorely misinformed instead of a genocide-denying tankie (a person who worships the Soviets). He stuck to his story, telling me, "You're just promoting Fascist Nazi propaganda, those genocides never happened." Not only was he denying genocides committed in the Soviet Union, but he denied *all* the other genocides at the hands of communist governments in Asia! The wild part was that he indicated that he believes in the Palestinian genocide, which is still unfolding as I write this, but he doesn't believe in other documented, historical genocides!

Once, I posted a video about the brutal and relentless sexual assaults committed by the Soviets and someone commented, "That's what Hitler's friends get." As in, the innocent women and children of Hungary deserved to be raped for the next 45 years because the fascist leader of their government decided to join forces with the Nazis. That's not "an eye for an eye," that's not justice or fairness, that's despicable, and morally uncorrupted people understand that.

People often forget that two things can be true at the same time. The Soviets were victorious in WWII; the Soviet Union was also an antisemitic, genocidal, dictatorship. The Nazis were evil; but the innocent people of Germany didn't deserve to be brutalized by the Soviets. The Hungarian government was a fascist dictatorship before and during the war; but again, the innocent citizens didn't deserve to be brutalized by the Soviets for it. The Hungarian government is now a right-wing autocracy and has treated refugees horribly in recent years; but the refugees from the 1956/57 crisis deserved help.

The way that society has generally ignored the evils of the Soviet Union while simultaneously demonizing Nazi Germany is hypocritical, and it gives the Soviet-sympathizers more confidence to say what they want, and it generally flies under the radar and usually isn't removed for hate speech like promoting Nazism is.

But that begs the question, *why* is it more accepted to be a fanatic for communism than to be a fanatic for fascism? People ignore the similarities between the two and the crimes of the Soviet Union for several reasons, whether they realize it or not. They ignore it partly because communist theory sounds nice so they defend a country that claimed to practice it, because the Soviets were the "good guys" who helped defeat the Nazis, therefore they must not be evil, and because they're thinking in logical fallacies. They use the either-or fallacy people still fall for, "Either you're a communist, or you're a fascist!" which ignores any other option, and a fallacious deduction of approval of one thing just because you disapprove of another: "So if you hate fascism then you must love communism!"

Whether or not the Soviets were worse or better than the Nazis is subjective, but what is objectively clear is the Soviet Union committed their own genocides, ethnic cleansings, colonization, and mass atrocities before, during, and long after the Nazis, using many of the same techniques.

It's fine to be a communist or Marxist, there is nothing inherently wrong with communist theory. Marx didn't say, "Kill all your rivals, imprison anyone you want, starve millions to death, relocate millions more into concentration camps, and reign terror on everyone," but that's how communist countries tend to operate. Communists aren't inherently bad people either, nor are Russians; however, the problem lies with those who ignore, or even praise, the crimes of the Soviet Union.

The strangest part is I've spoken with people who idolize the Soviet Union and at the same time vilify the Communist Party of China or of North Korea for their crimes; the irony is completely lost on them. The USSR had imposed communism on both of those countries, then they followed the same playbook that the USSR had laid out.

Even I think that communism, in its true theoretical form, looks appealing on paper compared to the alternatives. Abolishing classism and inequality, dismantling capitalism and the oligarchs, striving to put control of production in the hands of the workers, and giving each person the resources they need all sound good, but communism was never achieved. What the USSR had was an authoritarian dictatorship with a fascist aroma and a dash of socialism.

Personally, I'm not convinced that communism would ever be successful in a large society. The peaceful idea of a commune, an intentional community of shared resources, works with a small number of people, let's say 400 people. However, when everybody is supposed to be equal in a large society, it leaves room for a dictator to rise and consolidate power, land, and wealth, which is exactly what happened in the Soviet Union. To be fair, Lenin, the premier of the USSR before Stalin, was much more moderate, but when Stalin began accumulating power it turned into a totalitarian regime which operated in many of the same ways as Hitler's Nazi party.

Honestly, I may write another book that dives deeper into the comparisons between Hitler and Stalin as leaders and of their regimes, I might give it a Dickens-esque title like *A Tale of Two Mustaches*.

APPENDIX

The Sixteen Points

1. We demand the immediate evacuation of all Soviet troops, in conformity with the provisions of the Peace Treaty.

2. We demand the election by secret ballot of all Party members from top to bottom, and of new officers for the lower, middle and upper echelons of the Hungarian Workers Party. These officers shall convene a Party Congress as early as possible in order to elect a Central Committee.

3. A new Government must be constituted under the direction of Imre Nagy: all criminal leaders of the Stalin-Rákosi era must be immediately dismissed.

4. We demand public enquiry into the criminal activities of Mihály Farkas and his accomplices. Mátyás Rákosi, who is the person most responsible for crimes of the recent past as well as for our country's ruin, must be returned to Hungary for trial before a people's tribunal.

5. We demand general elections by universal, secret ballot are held throughout the country to elect a new National Assembly, with all political parties participating. We demand that the right of workers to strike be recognised.

6. We demand revision and re-adjustment of Hungarian-Soviet and Hungarian-Yugoslav relations in the fields of politics, economics and cultural affairs, on a basis of complete political and economic equality, and of non-interference in the internal affairs of one by the other.

7. We demand the complete reorganization of Hungary's economic life under the direction of specialists. The entire economic system, based on a system of planning, must be re-examined in the light of conditions in Hungary and in the vital interest of the Hungarian people.

8. Our foreign trade agreements and the exact total of reparations that can

never be paid must be made public. We demand to be precisely informed of the uranium deposits in our country, on their exploitation and on the concessions to the Russians in this area. We demand that Hungary have the right to sell her uranium freely at world market prices to obtain hard currency.

9. We demand complete revision of the norms operating in industry and an immediate and radical adjustment of salaries in accordance with the just requirements of workers and intellectuals. We demand a minimum living wage for workers.

10. We demand that the system of distribution be organized on a new basis and that agricultural products be utilized in a rational manner. We demand equality of treatment for individual farms.

11. We demand reviews by independent tribunals of all political and economic trials as well as the release and rehabilitation of the innocent. We demand the immediate repatriation of prisoners of war (World War II) and of civilian deportees to the Soviet Union, including prisoners sentenced outside Hungary.

12. We demand complete recognition of freedom of opinion and of expression, of freedom of the press and of radio, as well as the creation of a daily newspaper for the MEFESZ Organisation (Hungarian Federation of University and College Students' Associations)

13. We demand that the statue of Stalin, symbol of Stalinist tyranny and political oppression, be removed as quickly as possible and be replaced by a monument in memory of the martyred freedom fighters of 1848-49.

14. We demand the replacement of emblems foreign to the Hungarian people by the old Hungarian arms of Kossuth. We demand new uniforms for the Army which conform to our national traditions. We demand that March 15th be declared a national holiday and that October 6th be a day of national mourning on which schools will be closed.

15. The students of the Technological University of Budapest unanimously declare their solidarity with the workers and students of Warsaw and Poland in their movement towards national independence.

16. The students of the Technological University of Budapest will organize as rapidly as possible local branches of MEFESZ, and they have decided to convene at Budapest, on Saturday, October 27, a Youth Parliament at which all the nation's youth shall be represented by their delegates.

ACKNOWLEDGEMENTS

I'd like to thank my second-cousins, Péter and Robin, for answering questions I had about their parents, Edit and Károly (respectively). Thank you, grandma, for sending me the photos from grandpa's youth. Thank you to my new friend Péter, whom I met through social media, for answering my many random questions about Hungary, including how to pronounce certain Hungarian words. And thank you to the random people on social media who had a small piece of information which helped direct me in my research, such as that one man who knew the names of two of the refugee camps in Salzburg which I had no luck finding myself, but from his two little comments I could narrow down my search with specific search terms.

About the Author

Dawn-Eve Mertz has a BA in Classical Civilization and an MA in Teaching Secondary English. She has a taste for the macabre, so in her spare time she reads and researches genocides and mass atrocities. As a teacher, she designed and piloted a course about World War II, her area of expertise, which was highly successful and is still used in the school district. After 6 years in education, a pandemic, a baby, and several health conditions, she's taken a step back from teaching to pursue other goals.

She began writing *Young Men Go West* in 2017 after recording her grandpa's stories and finally set out to finish it after his death in 2023. She researched the Hungarian Revolution and the Soviet Union for years to write her debut nonfiction.

SELECTED BIBLIOGRAPHY

Aczel, Tamas. "Hungary's Revolt by Rebel Leaders." *Life*, 18 Feb 1957, 105-129.

Anarchist Workers Association. "Anarchist Worker." *Internet Archive,* 1976.

Cellini, Amanda. "The Resettlement of Hungarian Refugees in 1956." *Forced Migration Review,* Feb 2017.

Colville, Rupert. *"Fiftieth Anniversary of the Hungarian Uprising and Refugee Crisis."* UNHCR: The UN Refugee Agency. 23 October 2006.

Coriden, Guy, E. *"Report on Hungarian Refugees."* Central Intelligence Agency, 2 July 1996.

"Deconstruction of a Myth? Austria and the Hungarian Refugees of 1956-57." *Institut füf die Wissenschaften vom Menschen.*

Erdős, Kristóf. "Neue Heimat Salzburg. Die Geschichte Der Ungarischen Emigration in Salzburg Nach Dem Zweiten Weltkrieg." *Mitteilungen Der Gesellschaft Für Salzburger Landeskunde,* vol. 151, 1 Jan. 2011.

Gati, Charles. *Failed Illusions: Moscow, Washington, Budapest, and the 1956 Hungarian Revolt.* Stanford University Press, 2006.

Hochschild, Adam. *The Unquiet Ghost: Russians Remember Stalin.* Mariner Books, 2003.

Iszak, Frank. *Free For All To Freedom.* Create Space, 2011.

Korda, Michael. *Journey to a Revolution: A Personal Memoir and History of the Hungarian Revolution of 1956.* HarperCollins, New York, 2006.

Kővágó, József. *You Are All Alone.* Praeger, 1959.

Markowitz, Arthur. "Humanitarianism versus Restrictionism: The United States and the Hungarian Refugees." *The International Migration Review,* vol. 7, no. 1, 1973, pp. 46–59. JSTOR.

Medish, Vadim. *The Soviet Union Second Revised Edition.* Prentice-Hall, 1985.

Michener, James. *The Bridge At Andau.* Random House, Inc, 1957.

Molnár, Miklós. *A Concise History of Hungary.* Cambridge University Press,

2001.

Pál, Viktor. "The Case of the "Bee" Waste Collection Trust in Hungary." *Discard Studies,* 12 April 2021.

Pongracz, Gergely. "Interview with Gergely Pongracz 17/6/96." *The National Security Archive,* 1996.

Rayfield, Donald. *Stalin and his Hangmen.* Random House, 2004.

Sapir, Boris. "Hungarian Refugees." *The American Jewish Year Book,* vol. 59, 1958, pp. 307–12. JSTOR.

Sebag Montefiore, Simon. *Stalin: The Court of the Red Tzar.* Alfred A. Knopf, 2003.

Sebestyen, Victor. *Twelve Days: The Story of the 1956 Hungarian Revolution.* Pantheon Books, 2006.

Sodaro, Amy. "The House of Terror: 'The Only One of Its Kind.'" *Exhibiting Atrocity: Memorial Museums and the Politics of Past Violence,* Rutgers University Press, 2018, JSTOR.

"Special Message to the Congress on Immigration Matters." *The American Presidency Project.*

Steinbock, Daniel J. "The Admission of Unaccompanied Children into the United States." *Yale Law & Policy Review,* vol. 7, no. 1, 1989, pp. 137–200. JSTOR.

United States Citizenship and Immigration Services. *"Operation Safe Haven: The Hungarian Refugee Crisis of 1956."* United States Citizen and Immigration Services, 14 Dec. 2022.

United Nations, General Assembly. *Report of the Special Committee on the Problem of Hungary.* Report No. 18 (A/3592), United Nations, General Assembly, 1957.

United Nations, General Assembly. *The Situation in Hungary.* Report No. (A/RES/1312), United Nations General Assembly, 12 December 1958.

United States, National Security Council. *Document NO. 2 Minutes of 290th NSC meeting, July 12, 1956.* United States, National Security Council, 13 July 1956.

United States, National Security Council. *Document NO. 4 National Security Council Report NCS 5608/1, U.S. Policy toward the Soviet Satellites in Eastern Europe.* United States, National Security Council, 18 July 1956.

Made in United States
Troutdale, OR
08/04/2024

21763545R10188